NO LONGER PROPERTY OF
SEATTLE PUBLIC LIBRARY

Biking Uphill in the Rain

TOM FUCOLORO

Biking Uphill

in the Rain

THE STORY OF SEATTLE FROM BEHIND THE HANDLEBARS

UNIVERSITY OF WASHINGTON PRESS *Seattle*

Copyright © 2023 by the University of Washington Press

Design by Thomas Eykemans
Composed in Crimson Pro and Josefin Sans

27 26 25 24 23   5 4 3 2 1

Printed and bound in the United States of America

All rights reserved. No part of this publication may be reproduced
or transmitted in any form or by any means, electronic or mechanical, including photocopy, recording, or any information storage or
retrieval system, without permission in writing from the publisher.

UNIVERSITY OF WASHINGTON PRESS
uwapress.uw.edu

LIBRARY OF CONGRESS CATALOGING-IN-PUBLICATION DATA
Names: Fucoloro, Tom, author.
Title: Biking uphill in the rain : the story of Seattle from behind the
handlebars / Tom Fucoloro.
Description: Seattle : University of Washington, [2023] | Includes
bibliographical references and index.
Identifiers: LCCN 2022062224 | ISBN 9780295751580 (hardcover) |
ISBN 9780295751597 (ebook)
Subjects: LCSH: Cycling—Washington (State)—Seattle—History. |
Urban transportation—Washington (State)—Seattle—History.
Classification: LCC GV1045.5.W2 F84 2023 | DDC 796.609797/772—
dc23/eng/20230210
LC record available at https://lccn.loc.gov/2022062224

♾ This paper meets the requirements of ANSI/NISO Z39.48-1992
(Permanence of Paper).

Dedicated to the more than 5,100 people
who have died in Seattle traffic collisions
since the arrival of the automobile

Contents

Preface

It was a chilly morning in late January when my spouse, Kelli, and I took one of the best bike rides in our more than a dozen years together. Kelli held onto the wooden side panels of the payload area in the front of our large new cargo bike as we coasted down the hill leading from our house to the hospital where our daughter, Fiona, was living. Kelli's legs were tucked up toward her puffy winter coat, her feet pressed against the front panel of the cargo box extending out in front of the handlebars. We had bought this bike to carry a child, not an adult. But despite Kelli's contortions, her healing C-section wound was comfortable.

As we rolled down the hill, letting gravity carry us closer to yet another long day inside the neonatal intensive care unit, we giggled and laughed. Despite the confused looks from bystanders, something finally felt right again. "For the first time in weeks, I felt more like myself," Kelli said later, remembering the ride. "It was a literal breath of fresh air while we were spending ten to eleven hours a day in the hospital." We had been living in the hospital after severe preeclampsia threatened Kelli's life and forced our child into the world three months early. I doubt that any of those bystanders watching us zip down Brooklyn Avenue Northeast in Seattle could have guessed that our two-pound six-ounce daughter was intubated and on life support a few blocks away. Those few minutes on our bike were pure, defiant joy. Our family was going to make it through this, and we were going to do it our way. "It reminds me of survival," Kelli said. "I was so happy to be here after having moments that I wasn't sure I would make it."

A few months later, we were riding in a bikeway along the west side of Lake Union toward downtown Seattle, Kelli on her own bike and little Fiona secured in her infant car seat in the front of the cargo bike along with her feeding tube and oxygen tank. It was one of the happiest bike rides of my life. Fiona had gone through terrible things in her first couple of months of life, and we'd sat helplessly by her side the entire time. On that bike path, our family moved together under our own power. No beeping machines. No schedule other than our own. It was pure freedom. A seaplane took off from the lake, and the downtown skyline grew larger as we traveled closer. We were among a constant stream of people biking.

The Westlake Bikeway was an instant success the day it opened in 2016.[1] Many people had worked for years to organize in support of the project, including Kelli through her previous job at Cascade Bicycle Club. I had reported about every step of the frustrating and difficult process as editor of *Seattle Bike Blog*. Another former Cascade staffer, our friend Brock, was among those on the path. We stopped to talk, and he was happy to take a photo of us on our first-ever family bike ride. Most of our ride to the Space Needle and back followed comfortable trails and bikeways separated from car traffic, and most had been constructed since I'd started writing *Seattle Bike Blog* in 2010. A citywide wave of advocacy for safe streets had pushed the city to focus on building bike routes that were safe and welcoming for people of all ages and abilities, and Fiona snoozing away in the front of our bike showed me what that really means. If I felt safe biking with her on routes like these, then most people could feel comfortable biking there too.

Of all the cities in the United States, Seattle hardly seems like a place for bike culture to flourish. How can anyone think that a bicycle is a good way to get around a city that has hamstring-straining 19 percent inclines in the heart of downtown? Biking from the downtown waterfront to the Seattle University campus just one mile east requires climbing as high as the tallest point in the entire state of Florida.[2] And rain falls on that hill 152 days a year.[3] Yet bicycling is a major part of Seattle's past, present, and future.

This book explores how each generation since the 1890s has redefined the role of the bicycle in Seattle. Early on, this far-flung city was often out of step with the bicycling trends in Europe and the East Coast, adapting the technology at its own leisurely pace. Once Seattle was finally ready to embrace bicycling, a ship of gold from the Klondike River came ashore and launched a period of rapid growth for the young city, and many of those growth plans formed around bicycling. Then cars arrived, and bicycling fell out of favor in Seattle as it did in most US cities. But in the 1960s and 1970s, Seattle was on the forefront of rediscovering the potential of the bicycle. Bicycling was a bipartisan darling, with Democrats building bike lanes while Republicans led large group rides through downtown. Meanwhile, some community leaders also saw potential in the humble bicycle to subvert car culture, challenging the dominance of automobiles and the roadway infrastructure that supports them.

I was twenty-five years old when I started *Seattle Bike Blog* in 2010. I had initially planned on becoming a newspaper reporter back in the Midwest where I had grown up, but that door slammed shut when the 2008 recession hit. I had landed a great internship at the storied *Kansas City Star* fresh out of college, but I walked into a newsroom that summer in the midst of a series of major layoffs. I wanted to be a journalist, but the main bridge leading to that career had collapsed. Instead, I sold the car I had worked almost every day after high school to buy, and Kelli and I used that car money to move to Seattle.

Biking from odd job to odd job around this beautiful city, I wondered why there were so few good bike lanes. Seattle had all these amazing places to ride, like the Burke-Gilman Trail, and we filled our free time with bike adventures around town. But most of the regular busy commercial streets to and through neighborhoods were just as stressful as the ones I had biked on in Saint Louis, Kansas City, and Denver. Seattle had a reputation for being bike-friendly, yet the on-street bike lanes always seemed to end abruptly or were too skinny to be comfortable. What was the holdup? I decided to put my journalism skills to use and find out. I bought the domain SeattleBikeBlog.com, taught myself how to design and host a blog, and started asking people questions.

I practice independent advocacy journalism, meaning I follow the ethical standards of journalism while reporting with an openly stated assumption: more people biking safely is a good thing. My funding comes from a mix of advertisements and a monthly reader support program, so I am neither part of the city government nor part of an established advocacy organization. In the process of reporting *Seattle Bike Blog* daily, I watched the city's bike movement go through a renaissance. I covered inspiring acts of creativity and heartbreaking tragedies, saw the city's politics morph to embrace biking, and witnessed the city's transportation culture change.

Writing daily news for a decade, I learned a lot about Seattle's bike history. But there was so much more I wanted to know so I could better understand how the city I love to pedal around came to be this way. Researching for this book was an opportunity to dive deep into the archives to uncover lost stories and answer questions I still held even after more than ten years of daily reporting: How did Seattle's first bike paths influence the development of the city? If biking was so big at the turn of the twentieth century, why did the city's transportation culture so violently and completely restructure itself around the needs of automobiles? How did Seattle react when automobile drivers started crashing into and killing people? What was it like to live in the path of future freeways? What happened when neighbors revolted against freeway plans that threatened their communities? What role did race play in public debates about highways, which were often routed through communities of color? How did the Burke-Gilman Trail come to be? How did Seattle's bicycling movement evolve to become what it is today, and who was left out along the way?

In attempting to answer these questions, the book evolved into something bigger: a history of Seattle as seen from behind the handlebars. I dug through the archived papers of important political figures in local bicycle history like Seattle City Councilmember Myrtle Edwards and Seattle Mayors George Cotterill, James d'Orma "Dorm" Braman, Wes Uhlman, and Charles Royer. I searched for surviving records from long-gone bicycle organizations like the Seattle Cycle Club, the Queen City Cycle Club, and the Queen City Good Roads Club. I scoured every Seattle history book I could get my hands on in search of stories about bicycling and to better understand the context in which bicycle history was unfolding.

Frank B. Cameron deserves a special shout-out for his 1982 book *Bicycling in Seattle 1879–1904*, which was an excellent base from which to build my early-history chapter. I read bicycle history books from other parts of the world to better understand the global context of Seattle's bike story.[4] I befriended archival librarians, especially at the Seattle Municipal Archives, which houses official city departmental and public policy documents, the Museum of History and Industry, which houses an excellent collection of photographs, and the University of Washington's Suzzallo Library, home of the personal archives of many powerful figures and organizations in local history. I learned how to use microfilm and created my own digital archive of the weekly Cycle News column, published from 1894 to 1904 in Seattle newspaper *The Argus*. I conducted contemporary interviews, watched old city-produced videos and films, and flipped through many dusty boxes of photos.[5] I also spent countless hours digging through newspaper archives. This research is the foundation of this book's part 1, Bicycles and the Making of Seattle, a selective timeline of bicycle history leading up to when I started *Seattle Bike Blog*. Part 2, Seattle Enters a Bicycle Renaissance, shifts in perspective, focusing on the contemporary bicycle scene I witnessed as a firsthand observer. Part 2 is less of a chronological timeline than part 1, exploring how Seattle's bicycle culture grew in many different directions and became part of a larger movement for safer streets.

What I found doing historical research surprised me. The deeper I went, the more complicated and human the story became. Bicycles meant different things to different people throughout the city's history. White settlers arrived in what is now modern-day Seattle to stake their claims to the land of the Duwamish people in the 1850s, only about forty years before bicycling became the favorite pastime of Seattle residents who could afford one.[6] Many areas of the booming city developed around bicycling, and the imprints of those old bike tires can still be seen in the shape of the city today.

For a short time, city engineers and land owners used the bicycle as a tool for developing city land, at times building white-only communities, precursors to the car-centric and racially exclusive suburbs of the twentieth century. But throughout the city's history, there have also been people outside the power center who used their bicycles in ways that have reverberated throughout Seattle and beyond. Some people saw bikes as a means to organize political power while others saw them as a way to get away from it all. Some even decided to strip down, hop on their bikes, and crash the Fremont Solstice Parade in an act of naked creativity that became part of the intangible something that defines Seattle.

A recurring theme in this book is that transportation issues constantly intersect with many other major social issues, from affordability to climate change, racial justice to gender equality, public health to economics. It's usually a mistake to view any transportation debate as happening solely between the curbs on either side of the roadway. Transportation investments often demonstrate who has the true power to make major public decisions and who doesn't. Freeway construction in America demolished poor neighborhoods and displaced communities of color under the guise of "urban renewal."

Now, as many cities are seeing an influx of people moving to central neighborhoods where it's easy to get around using transit, walking, or biking, gentrification and the suburbanization of poverty are again displacing many communities of color, this time to a region's aging and lower-priced suburbs. The contemporary story of bicycling in Seattle is still being written. During the mass protests in Seattle following the 2020 murder of George Floyd in Minneapolis, some people used their bicycles and the strategies of previous bicycle protest movements as part of the renewed demands for racial justice.[7] But at the same time, a Seattle Police officer was caught on video running his patrol bicycle over the head of a protester lying in the street.[8] It has never been enough to simply advocate for bicycling. One must advocate for a better world through bicycling.

Biking Uphill in the Rain

Introduction

Ivan was picking at the protective film covering the adhesive on the bottom of a reflective four-foot-tall plastic post when he heard the first police siren approaching. The wail warbled over the droning rush of freeway traffic above him—even after midnight on a Monday morning in June 2013, the elevated stretch of Interstate 5 in downtown Seattle was plenty busy. Ivan tossed the film aside, stepped from the sidewalk into the street, and stuck the base of the post on top of the white line marking a bike lane that city workers had recently painted on a steep block of Cherry Street under I-5 between downtown and the densely residential First Hill neighborhood where Ivan lived. He had purchased a much stronger adhesive than what came preapplied to the base of the slender plastic posts, but he felt bad about using something that city workers would have difficulty removing, so he'd left the extra-strength adhesive at home. Another police siren cut through the air. Ivan leaned into the refrigerator-sized cardboard box he had dragged down the hill from his small apartment. He had overfilled the box with plastic posts, some of them jostling loose and spilling out as he made his way slowly to the freeway underpass. Each plastic post was not too heavy, but twenty of them added up. Once assembled—a tall post attached to the wider base using a weighty metal pin—they no longer fit well in the box they had arrived in. With a base much heavier than the long plastic body, they were awkward and unwieldy.

Panic started in Ivan's chest, and adrenaline rushed throughout his body as the sirens moved closer. Or at least he thought they were getting closer, the wail amplified in that intense way that adrenaline focuses your hearing when you are suddenly afraid. But he wasn't done yet. He grabbed three more plastic posts and awkwardly clutched them in his arms as he tried to peel the film off the bottom of one post and walked five paces downhill before sticking it to the painted line. He was five paces closer to Seattle City Hall, King County Jail, and the Seattle Police Department headquarters, which was now barely a hundred paces away. Ivan had paced out his plan nearly every day for weeks leading up to this night, walking under the freeway along Cherry Street to and from work. Five more paces, peel off the film, stick the post. More police sirens. He had lost count of how many police cars were approaching, but they were definitely getting louder now.

Five more paces, peel the film, stick the post.

Final post. Five paces. Peel. Stick.

Run.

Ivan sprinted up the hill past the row of posts he'd just planted, turned down another block, and jumped behind a bush to hide low on the ground, breathing big heavy breaths as the approaching police cars rushed by and onto the I-5 ramp en route to some other emergency. Somewhere else. As his adrenaline waned and his regular senses returned, he laughed. Of course the Seattle Department of Transportation had not sent a fleet of cop cars in the middle of the night to arrest him. And of course he was hearing lots of police sirens: he was a block from SPD headquarters. What he was doing was illegal, sure, but how serious was the crime? He stayed hidden behind the bush long enough to catch his breath and calm down. The usual rush of the freeway panned back into the forefront as his superfocused hearing returned to normal. There were a few people sleeping under the freeway, as usual, and the handful of people who saw him installing the posts didn't seem to think much of it. So he returned to the scene of the crime. He didn't want to litter.

Ivan pulled out his phone and snapped a couple of photos. Plastic posts separated the bike lane from the general traffic lane for the entire length of the block, reflecting in car headlights and providing a sense of protection from traffic. He walked down the block and picked up every plastic film he had peeled from the posts, then he grabbed his deformed and empty refrigerator-sized box and dragged it up the hill to his apartment building's recycling bin.

Once home, Ivan created an anonymous e-mail account. When prompted for a name, he typed the first thing that slipped into his sleep-deprived mind: the Reasonably Polite Seattleites. He then composed an e-mail to me, the editor of *Seattle Bike Blog*, explaining at length why "they" had committed this act. He pretended in the e-mail that there were multiple people involved, as though they were some kind of vigilante group. He copied SDOT Director Peter Hahn, hit send, and fell asleep.

The Reasonably Polite Seattleites

Ivan's action and e-mail coincided almost exactly with the city's reaching an inflection point in its bicycle network strategy, transitioning from bike lanes for confident bike riders to bike routes that people of all ages and abilities could find inviting and safe. Though Ivan's action alone did not cause this shift, it became an emblem for the city's new bike strategy. It didn't hurt that his letter was, intentionally or not, pretty funny. Seattle's general demeanor is much more passive-aggressive than in-your-face.[1] When the rare person honks their car horn, for example, it's not uncommon for someone on the sidewalk to shush them.[2] This is the same city that would go viral ten months later when rowdy mobs of Seattle Seahawks fans were caught on video waiting patiently for the walk signal before crossing the street while celebrating their team's Super Bowl victory.[3] Ivan had just broken the law mere feet from City Hall to make a statement about how easy it would be to build a better bike lane, but he also grew up in Seattle and had an internalized need to be polite while doing so. At 8:06 a.m. on April 1, 2013, this is what he wrote:

> I'm emailing because this morning a friend and I installed a string of plastic pylons along the Cherry Street bike lane under I-5. I've attached a couple of pictures. In New York, Washington, D.C., Chicago, San Francisco, Portland, the city transportation department usually installs these things, which slow traffic to the posted speed limit, and afford cyclists some protection. . . . This string cost about $350 in materials and required literally 10 minutes to install (admittedly, because SPD HQ is across the street, we hurried). . . . Our intention was merely to demonstrate how an incredibly modest investment and a few minutes of SDOT's time is capable of transforming a marginal, under-utilized and dangerous bike facility into one dramatically safer for cars, pedestrians and bicyclists.[4]

But not wanting to be impolite, Ivan noted that he had used an easy-to-remove adhesive so it wouldn't be too much trouble for city crews to remove them.

I published the letter and photos on *Seattle Bike Blog*. Ivan's installation was a simple and interesting act of what some might call "tactical urbanism," a bit of civil disobedience to demonstrate a different way to use public space. I also knew his letter would get some laughs from Seattle readers. But the Reasonably Polite Seattleites were not the reason this story blew up in transportation advocacy circles across the nation. So-called guerrilla bike lanes and other civilian-made street safety changes had been done before, usually to the chagrin of city leaders and local departments of transportation.

Just a couple of months after Ivan's action, retired Marine Anthony Cardenas was jailed and charged with felony vandalism in Vallejo, California, for the crime of painting a crosswalk in his community. "I got tired of seeing people get run over here all the time," Cardenas told local TV news reporters.[5] He said he tried to appeal to the city to make it safer, but nothing changed. So he did it himself. When he made bail, neighbors reportedly gave him a hero's welcome.

Around the same time, an anonymous group calling themselves the Citizens for a Safer Tacoma started painting bike markings and crosswalks in many locations across their city thirty-five miles south of Seattle.[6] They too were met with threats of prosecution and arrest for their actions, though many people in the neighborhoods were thrilled to see their new crosswalks before city crews removed them. Officials all over the country respond to acts of tactical urbanism by calling these civil protests "vandalism" and threatening prosecution.

But Seattle's relatively new traffic engineer was not a typical big-city engineer. Rather than threatening the Reasonably Polite Seattleites with arrest or admonishing them for doing something only professionals were allowed to do, he apologized. He didn't want to remove the posts, but he had to because they weren't up to code. Then he thanked them for challenging the way the department was building bike lanes, saying he would look into making the idea permanent. Finally, he kindly offered to return the posts if they wanted them back. The world was about to meet Dongho Chang:

Hello reasonably polite Seattleites,

Thank you for pointing out some easy ways to calm traffic and provide a more secure feeling bicycle lane on our streets. Your sentiment of unease and insecurity riding on painted bicycle lanes next to high speed and high volume traffic is exactly what I am hearing from our residents as we update our Bicycle Master Plan. This strong message to me and my staff that we have to be more thoughtful on facility design and implementation is being heard loud and clear. You are absolutely correct that there are low cost and simple ways to slow traffic, increase the sense of protection, and provide bicycle facilities that are more pleasant and accommodating for a larger portion of people who ride bicycles. I am truly appreciative that you care enough to take time, money, and risk to send your message to me and my staff. It is my commitment to you that I will do my best to update our existing facilities and install new bicycle facilities that will be more thoughtful. Some of these will be low cost, such as what you demonstrated on Cherry Street, while others will require more resources to implement.

The posts that you installed on Cherry Street will be removed and I am sorry about that. . . . Please let me know if you would like the posts back and I will have the crew leave the posts in a safe area for you to pick up. Thank you, again, for your thoughtful demonstration.

Sincerely,
Dongho Chang, PE, PTOE
City Traffic Engineer
Seattle Department of Transportation[7]

Three months later, while Ivan was walking home from work, he noticed markings next to the bike lane, spaced similarly to the posts he had paced out in a panic that night. Chang stayed true to his word. Seattle was making Ivan's idea permanent. US bike advocacy organization People for Bikes would name the lane one of the best new bike lanes in the nation specifically because the origin story was so unusual and, frankly, hopeful.[8] After nearly a century of top-down, cars-first transportation planning across the nation, Seattle was doing something different. The bike lane on Cherry Street was an illustration of how the city's transportation culture was changing, and even engineers working at the highest level within the Department of Transportation were willing and eager to question the old tenets of road building in America that result in thirty-five thousand or more traffic deaths across the country every year. Chang's goal was to make the city better and safer for everyone, not to chase the impossible goal of "fixing" traffic backups.

The Story of Bicycling in Seattle

Chang didn't rise out of nowhere and set this goal himself. He was acting on a political mandate from city leaders, who themselves responded to a strong community advocacy effort that was finally getting traction with its message that Seattle should focus more on improving walking, biking, and public transit than on trying to fix car traffic. In part, Seattle was riding a national wave of increased biking. Between 2000 and 2015, nearly every big city saw a steep increase in the percentage of people biking as their primary mode of getting to work, according to US Census Bureau annual survey data. Seattle had long been a leader in bike commuting among US cities. In 1990, Minneapolis was the only other big US city with a bicycle commute rate as high as Seattle's (though both cities barely reached 1.5 percent).[9] But the 2010s saw Seattle finally get some serious competition for the top spots from major peer cities like Washington, DC. The economic recession that started in 2008 sent a lot of people looking for ways to cut costs, and biking is by far the cheapest way to complete trips that are longer than an easy walk. Public awareness and understanding about global climate change increased dramatically at the same time, and biking emits next to no climate-altering greenhouse gases. Reducing one's personal impact on climate change is a strong motivating factor for a lot of people who bike.

Seattle was also experiencing an astounding population boom fueled in large part by the tech industry. In 2000, the US Census pegged the city's population at 563,000. By 2015, an additional 100,000 people were living in the city, and there was no end in sight for the influx of new residents. With more people moving to the city and car traffic already terrible, it was clear to many major employers and city leaders that there simply was not ever going to be enough room for more cars. Ironically, office buildings downtown had trouble filling their large underground parking garages because the city had seemingly reached the limit of how many cars could get in and out of the city center during rush hour. Traffic can get only so bad before people look for alternatives, such as walking, biking, and transit. Seattle had positive reasons for people to choose to bike and negative reasons for people to choose not to drive.

Combined, these forces led to a shift in the city's dominant transportation. Like all big US cities, Seattle had focused the vast majority of its transportation investments throughout the preceding century on trying to make it easier to drive cars. Car culture was hard-wired into Seattle culture, and it wasn't going away without a fight. The powerful forces defending the status quo pushed back on even the smallest perceived encroachments into space that had been reserved primarily for parking and driving. New bike lanes easily became political lightning rods, and political leaders were constantly challenged to stand up for their stated walking, biking, and transit goals.

In 2013, the same year Ivan glued those posts to Cherry Street, I reported from an angry public meeting in which people roasted the mayor for more than an hour over city plans for bike lanes through a small neighborhood business district in northeast Seattle. As the political power behind improving streets for bicycling grew, so did a powerful backlash against such changes. Many people, myself included, were caught off guard by how strong the resistance to bike lanes could be. At times, it felt futile to try to make any real changes to Seattle's streets. Despite having local political leaders and major employers on board with more walking, biking, and transit options, several multibillion-dollar freeway projects were still in the works. Seattle talked loudly about walking, biking, and transit, but the region was not putting enough money behind those words.

What was the problem? To better understand how the city got to this point, I needed to rewind to an era long before *Seattle Bike Blog* or the building of the city's freeways or even the arrival of the automobile. So I hit the archives in search of stories about a time when bicycles were the hottest new thing in town, providing people with personal mobility to places beyond the reach of the streetcars. Perhaps by starting at the beginning, I could better understand the role bicycling played in shaping this young city and how cars became the overwhelming focus for a century of transportation investments.

PART 1

Bicycles and the

Making of Seattle

The Good Roads Lunch Room on the Lake Washington Bicycle Path was located deep in the forest in what is now Interlaken Park. It opened shortly after the path was completed in 1897 and burned down sometime between autumn 1902 and 1904. Photo by Webster and Stevens, circa 1900, Seattle Public Library, Seattle Historical Photograph Collection, no. spl_shp_5204.

CHAPTER 1

A Bike Boom in a Boomtown

The bicycle in the late nineteenth century was a product by and for a modern industrialized society, and many of the core designs and manufacturing technologies came out of France and England between 1865 and 1885.[1] But white settlers first staked their claims to what would become the city of Seattle in 1851, beginning the colonial process of claiming the ancestral lands of Indigenous people both by treaty and by violence. Transportation in the small settlement was largely by water in the early years. Seattle's white settler population was barely a thousand in 1870 when the high-wheeled "penny-farthing" bicycle was turning heads in Europe and older cities on the East Coast and in the Midwest. But although far-flung Seattle was late to the bicycling game, the rapid expansion of railroads across the nation quickly changed the city's fortunes. The city's population began to swell once the first shaky railroad connections were made in the early 1880s, though it still required a lengthy trip for passengers and products to get all the way to the end of the line up in the northwest corner of the country. Even in the rare case that someone did go through the work to get a bicycle all the way to Seattle, the city's streets were in rotten shape, the hills were steep, and the town was so small that people could easily just walk to access most of it.

Seattle's Second Avenue, a central artery through downtown today, was a dirt roadway deeply rutted and pocked with large holes in 1895. Splinters of wood stuck out here and there, remnants of a failed effort to install planks across the street years earlier. During the many rainy months, the rutted road turned into deep mud. If someone wanted to ride a bicycle in downtown Seattle at that time, they would have to somehow navigate streets like these. It wasn't easy. "An occasional lonely cyclist might be seen picking out a tortuous course among such difficulties and the general public naturally and properly wondered 'where the fun came in,'" wrote George F. Cotterill in 1895, a city engineer and early bicycling promoter who would later be elected mayor and state senator.[2]

When Cotterill made that observation, Seattle was still struggling to emerge from a devastating one-two punch. A huge fire in 1889 had destroyed much of the original downtown, then the national Panic of 1893 plunged the rebuilding city into an economic depression as outside investments dried up. Many of the city's grand efforts for rebuilding and reimagining itself went bankrupt thanks to the panic. But that "lonely cyclist" trying to find a way to ride down Second Avenue in 1895 was about to witness Seattle boom, and the bicycle would be at the forefront of the city's rapid growth.

After Being Late to the Bike Trend, Seattle Builds Its First Bike Path, 1888-1896

On June 17, 1897, the steamship *Portland* pulled into Seattle with "more than a ton of solid gold" discovered along the Tr'ondëk, known in English as the Klondike River.[3] That day, hundreds of people—including Seattle Mayor William D. Wood—quit their jobs to prospect for gold in Alaska and the Yukon or to form businesses to profit off the prospectors. As word spread across the nation, tens of thousands more made the trek to Alaska, though few found any success. Though the Klondike Gold Rush was a bust for most prospectors, Seattle successfully positioned itself as the primary supply stop and taking-off point, and this proved to be an enormously profitable business. The city's population nearly doubled in the final decade of the nineteenth century, and the trains carrying both prospectors and new residents also brought a major advancement in transportation technology that would help shape the quickly growing city: the safety bicycle, a more affordable, transportable, and approachable kind of bike that would kick off something of a bike rush to match the gold rush. The city council passed an ordinance establishing a "bicycle road fund" for building the city's first bike paths just two months before the *Portland* pulled ashore.[4]

People arriving in downtown Seattle in 1897 would find streets recently paved with brick, bustling with streetcars and people walking, driving horse-drawn carriages, and riding bicycles. Many new bicycle shops opened along Second Avenue, and they had a hard time keeping up with the sudden demand for the machines. When the bicycle fad in many trendsetting European and East Coast cities was reaching its pinnacle, it was just getting started in Seattle.[5] The bicycle became mainstream in Seattle at the same time the city's economic outlook pulled a 180. Sometimes when a new delivery of bicycles arrived by train, merchant Fred Merrill would make sure everyone in town knew about it. First came the sounds of trumpets and other horns from a marching brass band approaching from the south. Behind the band was a procession of twelve horse-drawn wagons containing 293 new bicycles fresh off the train.[6]

Fred T. Merrill Cycle Company was just one of many bike shops in town, and his new Rambler bicycles would not stay on his sales floor for long. Between 1896 and 1906, more than forty different companies registered to sell bicycles in Seattle, and most of them were on Second Avenue. During this time, more than a hundred different brands of bicycle were available, including Columbia, Waverly, Majestic, Victor, Westminster, Union Crackerjack, Hartford, Cleveland Special, and Crescent. In addition to bikes arriving by train, Seattle was also home to a few bicycle manufacturers. There was the Rainier by A. J. Williams, the Queen City Bicycle, the Seattle Bicycle, the Spinning bicycle by F. M. Spinning, and custom bicycles from A. H. Christopher, Piper and Taft, and the Cyclone Cycle Company in Fremont. One of the first bicycles ever made in Seattle was purchased by Judge Thomas Burke, whose name would grace the city's greatest bicycle trail eighty years later.[7]

Though bicycles first became mainstream in the mid-1890s, there were people in Seattle who were ahead of the trend. The first known bicycle club in town started in 1888 as an effort to organize an eighteen-person bike parade for that year's Fourth of July celebration.[8] The riders wore a gray helmet with navy blue pants and rode on top of high-wheeled bikes. After the parade, they held some races at a horse track in South Seattle, including a five-mile race between someone on a bike and someone on a horse. The cyclist did not finish, and the club soon disbanded.

Several other bike clubs came and went through those early years, such as the Seattle Bicycle Club, which organized regular group rides and operated the Seattle Cycle Track in the northwest corner of Woodland Park (near Phinney Avenue North and North Fifty-Eighth Street today). It held its first race July 4, 1894. A lap was a quarter mile, and there was grandstand seating for 2,000 spectators. Admission cost twenty-five cents. However, the track failed financially in large part because the only streetcar serving the far-flung area didn't have nearly enough capacity to move 2,000 people to and from the track.[9]

The YMCA's Triangle Bicycle Club started a more successful racing track in YMCA Park at Fourteenth Avenue and East Jefferson Street, one mile east of downtown where Seattle University's Championship Field stands today. This track was much closer to most Seattle residences. The stadium also hosted baseball and football games, though it was a miserable place to play. The field partly overlapped with the cinder-covered racing track, which was not fun to fall onto. Cinders are a kind of gravel, preferably made from light volcanic rock, commonly used at the time for covering paths and running tracks. In a 1961 interview, former University of Washington football player Ed Duffy talked about playing on the field in 1901. "We used to call it The Swamp. It was always wet. And part of the playing field lapped over the cinder track. At the end of the game, our faces would be scratched from the cinders and our uniforms would be caked with tons of mud."[10]

The Renton Hill Wheel Club, which took its name from an old name for the hill that makes up much of today's Central District, held a series of bicycle parades and races at the YMCA track in August 1896, including a women's race, a bold move at that time. Just a couple of months earlier, *The Argus* in Seattle published a front-page editorial in response to reports of women in New York racing bicycles, saying that "racing among women ought to be abolished. . . . Moderate wheeling invigorates the system, strengthens the muscles, and increases physical endurance, but excessive wheeling is positively injurious and shockingly unwomanly. Girls, observe your old ways and thereby preserve the public's respectful admiration and your own beauty. If the men want to cultivate bodily ills and the bicycle face, let 'em so do without your rivalry."[11]

Despite this sexism, women were a part of Seattle's bicycle boom from the start. A group of women, mostly public schoolteachers, formed a bicycling and photography club in 1895. Women also organized women-only spaces to help other women of all ages learn to bike, meeting every evening from seven to ten at the Central School grounds to practice. In February 1896, a group of women started "a ladies wheel club" a month before the male-led Queen City Cycle Club was founded.[12] Unfortunately, I was unable to find surviving records of the women's club.

But people weren't just riding bikes on racetracks and school grounds. In 1893, the city tested the idea of paving streets by laying brick on a 20-foot-by-240-foot section of First Avenue South downtown. It went well enough that they paved a whole block of Union Street the next year. Then in 1895, the city paved seven blocks of Pike Street as well as First and Second Avenues between Pike Street and Pioneer Square. The number of people biking on Seattle's newly paved roads jumped from several hundred in 1896 to several thousand the next year.[13] "The curiosity of 1894 became the fad of 1895, a luxury in 1896 and a necessity in 1897 and 1898," wrote Cotterill in the weekly newspaper *The Argus*.[14]

The Argus was a major booster of cycling in Seattle. The paper's owner and editor, Harry A. Chadwick, was a founding organizer of the Queen City Cycle Club and recorded its news in his weekly Cycle News column, which ran in nearly every issue from the day he joined the paper in 1894 until 1904. It is a remarkable archive of Seattle's bicycle movement, though one viewed mostly through the lens of the upper-class white men in town. Chadwick himself was not initially wealthy. He had worked on newspapers back in Maine, and he was twenty-two when he moved across the country to Seattle in 1888. He was penniless when he arrived and found a job in the *Seattle Post-Intelligencer*'s printing room. A dedicated employee who could pump out a surprising volume of work every day, he quickly began reporting and editing for various publications around town.

Then in 1894, Chadwick invested forty dollars to buy one-half of *The Argus*, which was on the verge of going bankrupt. Forty dollars was about one-third the cost of a quality bicycle at the time. He was able to save the paper and build it into a Republican-leaning alternative weekly for the city, constantly criticizing the *P-I* and the *Seattle Daily Times*. He had an opinion about everything from local politics to women's fashion to the comings and goings of wealthy elites, and he wrote them in *The Argus* every week until the day he died in 1934.[15] Though he wasn't particularly wealthy when he arrived in Seattle, he loved the hobbies of the elite, such as yachting and bicycling. He was listed as chairman of the Press Committee on official letterhead for the Queen City Good Roads

Club, and his Cycle News columns often read like the digested minutes of the club's meetings.

The Queen City Cycle Club formed in 1896 in order to influence big changes in city policy and infrastructure to support cycling and expand people's access to more of the city's land.[16] The Cycle Club soon saw the benefit of inviting other transportation interests to join their effort and reorganized as the Queen City Good Roads Club in March 1897 "for the purpose of the mutual enjoyment of its members in bicycling, to bring about improvement in the public highways and roads, to construct bicycle paths and ways, to arrange and conduct club meets and excursions, to arrange and conduct bicycle races, and to further and protect the rights of wheelmen," according to the club's founding documents as printed in *The Argus*.[17]

Several women were founding members of the club, though only men held official club leadership titles. The club's rules did not restrict membership to white people like the national League of American Wheelmen did at the time, though it is not clear from club records or other surviving documents whether any people of color were members. The club included "many of the most prominent and influential business and professional men of the city," according to a 1902 *Seattle Daily Times* article.[18] The surnames of early members read like a collection of Seattle street signs: Bell, Denny, Cheasty, Burke, Gilman, Hanford, Nickerson, and so on. Many of these men were city aristocrats and landowners, often the children of the original white settlers. Others were people in powerful positions within government and society, including a particularly well-placed member as the chair of the club's Path Committee: George Cotterill.

Throughout his life, Cotterill was a Washington state senator, Seattle mayor, candidate for the US Senate, chief engineer for the state highway department, and a Seattle port commissioner. But the decade before Cotterill started running for various public offices in 1902, he was assistant to Seattle City Engineer R. H. Thomson and worked on many major projects such as laying out the city's first sewers, building the Cedar River water supply infrastructure, and filling in the tide flats to develop the industrial district now known as SoDo.[19] Cotterill was also tasked with finding a way to build out a boulevard system in the city, and the bicycle provided the perfect means for getting a head start on that work. He rode a bike, though not as enthusiastically as his brother

Frank. But George was extremely detail-oriented and strategic, and he did not believe in waiting around for things to happen.

The Good Roads Club had the power to influence city law, which included lobbying successfully for a city ordinance to levy license fees on bicycle users to pay for bicycle path construction and maintenance.[20] The club also, for all intents and purposes, directed the spending of that public bike-path money. Decisions about where to build paths and how to budget the city's bike fund were made during club meetings under the leadership of Cotterill, who served as both the chair of the club's Path Committee and the city employee tasked with engineering the paths. He could put city-collected license fees into the paths, and he could use the club to raise any extra funds needed through donations and dues. He could even call on club members to help work on path construction and maintenance as volunteers. He mixed public and private funds in addition to public and volunteer labor to make these paths happen.

"When the bicycle vogue started almost no streets were paved," a retired Cotterill said in a 1953 retrospective piece about the city's old bike paths.[21] "A great number of dealers had sprung up and they realized there had to be some place where one could use the wheels. Out of this situation someone organized the [Queen City Cycle Club]. To raise money it conducted lotteries and guessing contests. The city council was influenced to pass an ordinance licensing bicycles at $1.25 a year. Of this sum 25 cents went to the License Bureau and the rest was devoted to construction and maintenance of bicycle paths." People could be arrested if they were caught riding a bicycle without a license, and the club was able to convince the city to pass several ordinances outlawing use of the paths by livestock or horse riders. It was even illegal to push a baby carriage on the bike paths. At the club's behest, the city hired an officer to police the paths.

Cotterill engineered twenty-five miles of bicycle trails in about five years, many of which he surveyed himself and worked nights to engineer. "It was his donation to the public cause," the *Seattle Daily Times* reported in the 1953 story. These first bicycle paths were created at a time when roadway pavement ended at Eighth Avenue and Pike Street downtown. The rest of the roads were mostly dirt when it was sunny and mud when it was rainy. Streetcar tracks could sometimes stand out above the road surface, making them difficult to cross. People had a great time bicycling beyond the city, but riding on the heavily traveled roads within the city was rather miserable. So the first bicycle path was designed and constructed in 1896 to help people head north from the paved streets downtown along the hillside to the east of Lake Union. "My job was to follow the contour of the hill," Cotterill told McDonald.

The path traveled north from downtown partway up the hillside between today's Capitol Hill and Cascade neighborhoods before meeting up with Lakeview Boulevard. After a few blocks on Lakeview, riders reached the start of the forest. The route then followed a path located to the east of Boylston Avenue before reaching a fork near Roanoke Street, about twenty minutes of pedaling from downtown. This route is very familiar to people in Seattle today, though not as a bike path. It is the site of Interstate 5 between downtown Seattle and State Route 520. I-5 construction in the 1960s leveled so much of the area that it's impossible to re-create most of this old route on a bike today, but it's interesting to think that someone driving on I-5 is following an old bicycle path. A journalist in 1902 described this bike ride in a *Seattle Post-Intelligencer* story, "A Day on Seattle's Bicycle Paths":

> The favorite path in Seattle winds out along the shores of Lake
> Union through the shady forest to Lake Washington. It is known as
> the Lake Washington path, and a track more beautiful in any respect
> would be hard to imagine. . . . On the run out to the Denny-Fuhrman
> addition one has a magnificent view of Lake Union, Eldorado hill,
> the rugged Olympics. A backward glance, however, shows the smoke
> and dreariness of the city. This is in day time. At night the city with
> its thousand scintillating lights, its brilliantly illuminated street cars
> hanging on the hillsides like steamships far out at sea, seems to welcome the returning rider back to its bustling thoroughfares.[22]

From Roanoke, the path split into two choices. Riders could continue north to cross the bridge toward the University of Washington's brand-new campus or turn east toward Lake Washington. The 1897 Lake Washington Bike Path was the jewel of Seattle's early bike network. Bicycling photographers took most of their shots along this route. Writers reminiscing about biking in those days inevitably talk about memories of adventures along the way to Lake Washington. To better understand what biking was like back then as well as the political forces supporting bicycling, it's necessary to take a deep dive into the short-but-powerful history of the Lake Washington Bike Path.

The Lake Washington Bike Path Was "a Plunge into a Delicious Oblivion," 1897

The Lake Washington Bike Path was long, ambitious, and extraordinarily scenic. "Beyond Federal and Roanoke great gullies and gorges indented the northeast slope of Capitol Hill," Cotterill said in 1953, remembering the effort it took to engineer the path fifty-six years earlier. "I couldn't cross them, so I ran the path up each gorge to its turning point. There were two large canyons and three or four small ones."[23] Inspired by a trip to Switzerland, he later suggested the name Interlaken after the alpine town because the route travels between Lakes Union and Washington. "The track's scenic attractions are like the stage settings of some old romance," wrote the *Seattle P-I* in 1902.[24] "The track winds in and out along the side of the bluff, sometimes commanding a view over all the adjacent hills, mountains and lakes, at other times shut in by the green pines and shrubs and with a view confined to the cool, dark aisles of the murmuring forest."

It was seemingly impossible for writers at the time to refrain from penning poetry when trying to describe the experience of biking along the Lake Washington path. The path was among the biggest reasons people bought bicycles from all those Second Avenue shops, and it opened up a recreational experience previously attainable only by those with the means to own a horse. Bicycles certainly weren't cheap, but they were a lot more affordable to maintain and easier to store than a horse. So buying a "wheel," as people often called bicycles then, opened up the growing population's access to the forests and lakes on the outskirts of the developed city. The area was so forested and remote that even in 1901 people biking would sometimes encounter a bear.[25]

Riders traveling the rough cinder path through the woods would likely be ready for a snack before too long, and the Good Roads Lunch Room was happy to serve up sandwiches and drinks. Often referred to as the Half-way House because it was halfway between downtown and Lake Washington, the small building was constructed on stilts above a gully deep within a forest that would later become Interlaken Park on the north slope of Capitol Hill. The Lunch Room's front porch also served as a bridge spanning the gap between the bike-path sections running along the hillsides on either side of the gully. Riders were instructed to dismount and walk their bikes across the bridge, which conveniently forced them to pass by the food and drink menus hanging on the front of the building. They advertised "meals at all hours of the day." Riders could buy ham and eggs for twenty-five cents, coffee and cake for ten cents, and sandwiches for five cents. The sign also advertised "all kinds of soft drinks" and included a menu with classics like ginger ale, lemonade, and soda water.[26]

Several of the early bike boosters were part of the temperance movement and would have frowned on alcohol sales at an establishment built by the Good Roads Club. But a closer look at photos of the Lunch Room suggests some disagreement on the issue. While the menu listed only soft drinks, someone had carved "Rainier Beer" into the wooden bike rack out front. Then it appears that someone else added the word "Root" in front of Beer. I suspect someone could order off the menu if they wanted something harder than lemonade, though I have not been able to find any confirmation of this. The crude markings on this old bike rack in the middle of the forest illustrate a debate among local cyclists that would have a profound impact on the entire state.

After his Seattle engineering job, Cotterill ran for public office on a platform strongly in favor of women's suffrage and prohibition, issues that were closely connected at the time.[27] Despite the apparent friendship between Cotterill and Chadwick through the Good Roads Club, Chadwick penned a front-page editorial in *The Argus* in 1904 arguing against Cotterill's candidacy for Seattle mayor by calling him "a radical" on "the liquor question." He went on in the editorial to praise Cotterill while also suggesting he was out of touch with the city. "*The Argus* believes that Mr. Cotterill would make a model mayor for a model city. He has decided opinions and force of character to back them up. But Seattle is not a model city. This paper does not believe that a very large percentage of the population desire to make it so."[28]

Cotterill lost the election in 1904, but won a seat in the Washington State Senate in 1906, where he was the lead sponsor of the successful 1909 Local Option Law allowing any town in the state to vote on whether to ban alcohol sales in its community. It was a precursor to full Prohibition in Washington State in 1914, the thirteenth state to pass a statewide liquor ban before the national ban was ratified in 1919. Cotterill was elected mayor of Seattle in 1912 by riding a wave of prohibitionist popularity. He remained a staunch prohibitionist even after it was repealed in the 1930s.[29]

Regardless of booze sales, the Lunch Room was clearly a favorite part of the whole Lake Washington Bike Path experience, as a *Seattle Daily Times* author reminisced in 1908:

> To take that ride in the early hours of the morning was a plunge into a delicious oblivion. These solemn depths of solitude, profoundly silent but for the silvery trickle of trickling springs; the three-quarters of a circle turn around "Cape Horn," memorable for a magnificent view of the two lakes and also for the frequency of those irritating signs "go slow," "keep to the right," "ring the bell," the "crossed logs," covered with delicate ferns and thick-leaved salal, the favorite background for snapshots, the "Half-way House" in the last gorge to the east, with its wonderful spring, its rustic bowers and refreshment towers half concealed among cool branches of hemlock and fir—the memory of them seems like the experiences of a past existence to the old-timers who in an automobile on the Interlaken Boulevard follow the same course they traveled so many years ago on their silent, sliding bicycles.[30]

I became somewhat obsessed with the old Lunch Room while researching this chapter, in part because I could see it being popular even today if it still existed. Stopping midride for a drink and a snack deep in the mossy woods of Interlaken Park sounds wonderful. The Lunch Room was also shrouded in mystery. Modern history texts even had conflicting information about the location, and I could find no word about what had happened to it. So I set out to try to find it for myself.

A *Seattle Bike Blog* reader sent me a scan of an old hand-drawn engineering plot for the original bike path, which was constructed in 1896 and 1897. It was like finding a treasure map. Using that plot, I was able to trace the old path into a digital map I could follow on the ground using GPS. While tracing it, I noticed a curious hand-drawn rectangle with an X through it next to the path in the easternmost gully before Twenty-Fourth Avenue. A blue line traveled through it, noting the presence of a stream. X marks the spot: that was the Lunch Room. I marked it on my map, then headed out to find it. I documented the adventure in a video for *Seattle Bike Blog*.[31]

The basic route of the bike path is preserved to this day as Interlaken Boulevard. The city acquired the land for the park and boulevard right-of-way in 1904, preventing further private development.[32] The boulevard was constructed much wider and with a lot more engineering and land-moving than the old path, so it doesn't follow the path perfectly. But it is pretty close. Interlaken Park is still a thickly wooded, mossy, and mysterious natural space, though there are many homes nearby. The bike path hugged the hillside, following the contours of the earth to stay as flat as possible through the difficult terrain. The route winds back and forth with the hillside, and there are several long curves where the route passes through a gully with a small stream through it. Today, the boulevard crosses these gullies on man-made earthen bridges, and the streams are funneled through culverts under the road.

During construction of the old bike path, the Queen City Good Roads Club had to build wooden bridges to cross these gullies, so the path would travel along the hillside until it reached a point close enough to the adjacent hillside that they could span the gap with a bridge. Then the path continued on the other hillside until the next gully. In the easternmost gully of Interlaken Park, the Good Roads Club constructed the Lunch Room as part of the bridge crossing the stream. It was a small house built on stilts so that it was at the same level as the bridge. Next to the house was a covered area with a picnic table. Riders could also hang out down in the gully below the bridge, listening to the stream and the other sounds of the forest.

Today the stream is still there, but no evidence of the Lunch Room remains. I parked my bike at the curve in the boulevard and hiked into the thick forest farther upstream. One side of the gully has a well-used hiking trail where the old bike path once ran, but the path on the adjacent hillside has long been closed and reclaimed by the forest. None of the trees in the photos, covered with carved initials from visitors, are recognizable, which makes sense because those old trees likely fell long ago. The structure was made of wood, which is unlikely to have survived this long.

Newspaper archives show that the Lunch Room was put up for sale in March 1901 along with its 110 chickens, and it was still open at least through the 1902 season.[33] But for a while, I could find no mention of what happened to it. Then Montlake history buff Jon Dawkins, who watched my video about the search for the Lunch Room, sent me a map from 1904 that had the answer. Seattle had hired the East Coast Olmsted Brothers landscape architecture firm to plan out the city's boulevard system, and they sent James F. Dawson to examine the area in person. He had scrawled notes all over a map of the Interlaken Park area, which included the old bike path. Next to the location of the Lunch Room he wrote, "This house has been burnt down."[34]

After the Interlaken Park area, the Lake Washington Bicycle Path continued southeast through the woods before connecting to Madison Street in what would become the Madison Valley business district. From there, riders had a choice to make. They could head northeast along a path through what would become the Washington Park Arboretum and the gated community of Broadmoor to reach the Madison Park neighborhood. This was a popular destination with its beach and resort amenities, and riders could even take the streetcar from Madison Park to downtown if they didn't want to ride all the way back. Or they could continue riding southeast toward Madrona Park if they wanted more adventure or a more secluded beach. This route would later serve as the basis for Lake Washington Boulevard.

A Growing Seattle Expands along Its Bike Paths, 1897–1902

Though the Lake Washington bike route was the most popular, there were also routes to many other mostly undeveloped areas of the city. One route went to Green Lake near the north end of the city limit. Another route went along the north shore of Lake Union from the University of Washington to Fremont and the then-independent city of Ballard, which had instituted its own bicycle license scheme to pay for its part of the path. The Ballard path was quirky. At one point, the terrain was too hilly to bypass some abandoned farm structures, so the path builders took the walls off an old farm shed and ran the path straight through it.[35] Most of these paths were maintained by the Queen City Good Roads Club, though students at the University of Washington got sick of waiting for the club to connect the network to their new campus and in 1900 made their own path connecting campus to the Latona Bridge, which predated the University Bridge. It immediately became one of the most-used bicycle paths in the city.[36] The UW path makers claimed the ride from downtown to campus took only twenty minutes, though that was perhaps a bit of bragging since twenty minutes is a pretty good time even today with paved roads and modern bicycles. Then again, they didn't have any stoplights or car traffic to deal with.

Not all bicycle paths worked out for the path builders, however. A private company started work on a bicycle-only toll road from Seattle to Tacoma, building from both ends at the same time with plans to meet in the middle. Because the area south of downtown Seattle was tidelands at the time, much of the route was on wooden trestles that were expensive and time-consuming to construct. *The Argus* spoke with George E. Ames, the person in charge of the Seattle end of the path, in March 1897 to get an update on the progress. "We feel confident that the road will be completed and ready for travel by the 30th of June," Ames told *The Argus*. "Of course the road houses will not be completed at that time, but the road will be opened and the remainder of the work will then be pushed as rapidly as possible."[37]

However, that's not what happened. Less than a year later, *The Argus* spoke to John M. Bell, who was in charge of the Tacoma end of the project, and the paper reported that "in the first place, said Mr. Bell, the enterprise is a winner. It will go on to successful completion. Undoubtedly there has been mismanagement under Geo. E. Ames, who, as general manager, had full charge of the Seattle end of the line. The eight miles built yielded a gross revenue of $350 to $800 per month last year, quite sufficient to continue the work without going into debt. But Ames neglected his business and disappeared, and the company asked for the appointment of a receiver to get rid of the tangle that had been created. My active connection with the scheme, said Mr. Bell, was dropped last July, but I have every confidence that the enterprise will be carried to a successful completion and that no subscriber will ever lose a cent by it."[38] The company operated for a year before going bankrupt.

The Queen City Good Roads Club's most ambitious project after the Lake Washington Path was a route to Magnolia Bluff, then a mostly rural and wooded area that was not yet home to Fort Lawton and later Discovery Park. The bluff had a magnificent view from the north of Elliott Bay and the Seattle downtown waterfront. The route traveled north from the bluff down the Magnolia hillside before reaching sea level near Salmon Bay and the city of Ballard. The path, now Magnolia Boulevard, was stunning but also more difficult to ride. "The Magnolia bluff path has many beauties that cannot be duplicated in the Northwest," wrote a *Seattle P-I* reporter in 1902.[39] "Always a breeze is blowing from the

Sound, bearing the health-giving ozone from the salt waves. The view is magnificent. The rider commands a wide stretch of the inland sea, backed by the broken line of the cold-looking Olympics. You can see the ships and steamers far off plowing their courses through the waters to Seattle and other Sound points. The ride is one of the most refreshing that the brain worker can take."

The ability to explore such wondrous areas under their own pedal power and on their own time was a potent experience for a lot of people at the turn of the twentieth century. The irony is that as more people visited these areas, they became more developed and less wild. The old paths were doomed in part due to their own successes. Developing more of the city, especially the areas that were difficult to reach by streetcar, was a major reason why so many powerful people were such strong boosters and funders of path building from the start. They knew their paths were temporary because they were often constructed on private property, and that meant that property owners could displace the paths whenever they decided to develop the land they had claimed or purchased. For instance, cattle would often use the paths while grazing, a problem the Magnolia Bluff route frequently faced. When bicyclists complained, farmers could just build a fence across the path to contain their cattle, ruining the route.

The paths initially traveled through forests and other areas far out of town. But the paths themselves brought more people to these places, making them "somewhere" rather than the middle of "nowhere." The author of the 1902 *Seattle P-I* story noted that this was what happened in Magnolia, where the path to the bluff spurred development of whole communities. "When the track was constructed the houses along its route were so few and far between that they excited the curiosity of the lone wheelman. Since then, however, lots have been cleared, houses built and established communities have sprung into existence. The members of the good roads club point to this change as an evidence of the fact that the bicycle path is something of a pioneer for civilization."

Civilization is a loaded term, especially considering these paths and homes were being constructed on Duwamish tribal land that has been home to Indigenous people for millennia. The paths were helping the city's leaders and landowners expand beyond the original city center. The city of Seattle itself was part of the nation's westward expansion, a government-subsidized colonizing effort encouraged by the genocidal ideology of manifest destiny, which held that this land was ordained for white Americans (and maybe some white Europeans) to own and inhabit.

The core of Seattle's first permanent white settlers made claims to land in the 1850s based on the Donation Land Claim Act of 1850, which gave white male settlers significant plots of land (and an equal amount to their wives, though women could not make claims on their own) so long as they lived there for four years after making the claim. The act specifically did not allow Indigenous people already living there to make such claims, so the settling process was more akin to an invasion. The first settlers depended on local people to survive, and Indigenous people were the primary workers in the city's first white-owned businesses.[40] But people who already lived on the land and then helped build the city were not allowed to claim ownership of it. The Treaty of Point Elliott, signed by Duwamish (Dxʷdəwʔabš in the Lushootseed language) Chief Seattle (Si'ahl in Lushootseed) and many other leaders in 1855, was supposed to guarantee fishing rights and a reservation for the Duwamish people. White settlers broke both of these promises. When some Indigenous people attacked the city in the short 1856 Battle of Seattle, the US Navy fired cannons from a warship in Elliott Bay and struck the attackers' positions in the woods above the city. White theft of Indigenous land in Seattle was enforced by US military violence.

Within a decade, some white settlers of Seattle were looking for ways to rid the city of Indigenous people entirely. In 1865, Seattle's city government passed Ordinance No. 5, which stated that "no Indian or Indians shall be permitted to reside, or locate their residences on any street, highway, lane, or alley or any vacant lot in the town of Seattle."[41] The wording of the law betrays the double-sided relationship the city's white residents had with their Indigenous neighbors: they wanted a whites-only city, but they also relied on the labor of the Indigenous people. Despite the law, Indigenous people never left Seattle.

In 1866, white leaders in Seattle—including many men whose names have been immortalized on street signs such as Terry, Denny, Stewart, Van Asselt, Horton, Maynard, Ballard, Holgate, and more—signed a letter opposing plans for the promised Duwamish reservation along the Black River south of Seattle in modern-day Renton, Tukwila, and Skyway. Their argument was that the reservation was "of little value to the Indians . . . whose interests and wants have always been justly and kindly protected by the settlers of the Black River country."[42] The Duwamish Tribe does not have a reservation to this day, and the federal government refuses to officially recognize the tribe.

The letter opposing the reservation was about protecting white land claims, which early settlers hoped would someday pay off big if the city managed to grow into a thriving city and region. Those claims were like all-in bets for the white people who made them, and they were determined to maximize their profits. Many early city-building decisions were based around the same goal. City engineers led huge efforts to fill in tide flats, flatten hills, build railroads, and redirect waterways, projects that landowners hoped would make their claimed or purchased land more valuable.[43]

The early Seattle bike paths were no different. Like little Oregon Trails, the paths were constructed so that the growing population of Seattle could "discover" new parts of the city, opening those areas to development that profited the landowners. Expanding the scope and reach of the city was a motivating force for the Queen City Good Roads Club, whose membership included many of the very landowners who would stand to profit from the paths. George Cotterill told *The Argus* in 1896 before most of the first paths were even constructed that he saw the paths as "the first step in the direction . . . for a boulevard system."[44] He saw his engineering and road-building work in the challenging Seattle terrain as vital to the success of the still-young city. While traveling around Europe in 1902, Cotterill was especially impressed by the alpine roads in Switzerland, and he saw their potential as a tool to build out more of Seattle. "Our problem of road building and making in this Pacific Northwest, with the difficulties which are before us, is indeed one of the greatest, if not the greatest, problem which we have to confront and solve and overcome if civilization is to advance in this country as we all hope and believe it will," he said in a 1904 address to the Pacific Northwest Society of Engineers.[45]

Cotterill's guiding philosophy, as with many of the white people working to build Seattle, was based on white colonization rooted in Europe. In his convention address, he spoke of visiting Delft in Holland, "whence the Speedwell sailed two hundred years ago to meet the Mayflower at Plymouth, and subsequently giving to us the Plymouth Rock foundation of the land in which we live." He later wrote a long and very dry book titled *The Climax of a World Quest: The Story of Puget Sound: The*

Modern Mediterranean of the Pacific, in which he described his vision for a prosperous Seattle as the latest chapter in the centuries-long effort by European explorers like Ferdinand Magellan, Sir Francis Drake, and George Vancouver to discover sailing passage from the Pacific to Europe. In his book, he outlines his belief in the "destiny" of Seattle's place in America's westward expansion, calling it "the final frontier of western civilization":

> Ever westward, they swept over the newer Europe with twenty centuries of development; then, groping over unknown seas, revealed a New World which they dedicated to the great social enterprise. Through four centuries America has been in the making, and Humanity re-created in the expanding process. At first an Atlantic fringe of colonial development; then over the Appalachians to the great valleys and vast prairies of the interior; at last a rippling of the more ambitious and venturesome over the continental barriers of mountain and desert to the Pacific slope—the end of the long trail of the centuries!
>
> Unless Pacific America—and in a special sense the Pacific Northwest—is found wanting in those natural and social resources which provide sustenance and opportunity for human industry and happiness, the westward current of the ages will not reverse or divert until it fills this favored region to its utmost capacity for progress and prosperity.
>
> Where else can the "westward course of empire take its way?"
>
> This is the heritage of history, the goal of destiny![46]

This supposed destiny of white colonialism across the continent also applied to new Seattle neighborhoods. The Interlaken housing development, which included areas near Interlaken Boulevard and today's Montlake neighborhood, was made possible by the Lake Washington Bicycle Path and the boulevard that followed. "Every one in Seattle who was a resident here five years ago will remember the old bicycle path that formerly ran through this addition; the half way house, Cape Horn and the Crossed Logs—well, that path is the boulevard of today and that boulevard is one of the many things that will make Interlaken the most charming and popular residence district of the city," wrote the *Seattle Sunday Times* in 1906.[47] But as John E. Boyer of the Interlaken Land Company made clear in the article, this new community was for white people only. "In all the additions that have heretofore been put on in Seattle one essential has been lacking, for which nothing else will compensate," he told the *Times*. "This essential of a permanent home district is the lasting assurance of congenial neighbors. It might be said the Utopia alone can give this assurance, and that is all but true. The idea has been worked out in part in the beautiful suburbs of Chicago, New York, Boston and Los Angeles, whereas in Seattle it can be brought to its full realization." The *Times* reporter who interviewed Boyer noted that the effort was novel in Seattle, especially its goal of preserving the whiteness of the residents forever. "Things have been so arranged, by a simple and natural process of self selection—and this, not only at the start but for all time," the reporter wrote. "In fact it is to be doubted if there ever was a residence district that has been so carefully guarded as has Interlaken." Boyer's efforts to guard his white "Utopia" were advertised widely in newspapers that bemoaned how other neighborhoods could be rendered "intolerable by the introduction of new and inimical influences."[48]

The Interlaken development was one of the first in Seattle to attempt to codify race and class exclusivity covenants into the deeds of its residential properties. While the company took care not to explicitly specify race, perhaps out of concern that it might be illegal to do so, the scheme involved giving neighbors and the Interlaken Land Company the right of first refusal whenever someone tried to resell their property. As discussed in chapter 5, racially restrictive covenants became widespread in Seattle, King County, and communities across the country after the US Supreme Court allowed the practice in their 1926 decision *Corrigan v. Buckley*. The 1906 Interlaken effort was a precursor to the widespread use of such covenants, which were one potent tool used in Seattle to solidify racial segregation and white supremacy during the twentieth century.

The Bike Paths Become Boulevards, 1901-1905

By 1901, the city's bicycle paths were beginning to show signs of trouble. Path builders wanted them to encourage private development, and it worked. Unfortunately for people heading out for a ride, this meant that construction and development impeded many path segments. With more than twenty-five miles of paths, the sheer amount of work to maintain them stretched the abilities of the Queen City Good Roads Club thin.

"It is true that Seattle has not a decent thoroughfare for the accommodation of a man who wishes to ride to the suburbs on a bicycle," wrote the *Seattle Mail and Herald* in 1901.[49] "If he goes south it is at the peril of life and limb. West Seattle is out of the question. Of course the hills toward the lake are not to be considered; and First avenue to Denny way and the road on out to Interbay are worse than the 'Rocky Road to Dublin.' . . . On the other hand, our country towns and county precincts have planned their road and street work with a view to the convenience of wheelmen. Snohomish has reserved the center of her streets, planking them lengthwise for the accommodation of bikers; and bicycle paths skirt the roadways into the remotest corners of our rural districts. . . . If the Queen City Good Roads club does not look to the betterment of roads within our corporate limits before next year, or use its influence with the city council to that end, our bicycle dealers are bound to fare poorly, and there will be a noticeable advance in the price of horse flesh."

It became clear to city leaders and the Good Roads Club that the old paths had successfully run their course. Before leaving his job as a city engineer and his leadership role with the Good Roads Club in 1902, Cotterill urged the club to hand over trail maintenance duties to the city, which they did.[50] In 1903, Seattle worked to hire the Olmsted Brothers landscape architecture firm, run by the sons of the ailing Frederick Law Olmsted who famously designed New York City's Central Park among other iconic American parks. Seattle wanted the firm to design a series of new parks as well as a network of boulevards to connect their new and existing city parks. As Cotterill intended, the bike path network served as a great foundation for the boulevards. In addition to engineering permanent surfaces and bridges for these streets, the boulevard work would bring the routes fully into city ownership and serve the growing number of new conveyances arriving in Seattle, including motorcycles and automobiles. In 1904 voters in the city passed an initiative at the ballot box expanding the role of the Seattle Parks Department, increasing its taxing ability and giving it control of the city's "parks, squares, park drives, parkways and boulevards, play and recreation grounds." Voters liked the bike paths so much they passed a tax to expand them into public boulevards as part of a new park system.

The city and the Olmsted Brothers firm worked for the next four years to develop the boulevards and parks plan. The voters of Seattle supported the concept so strongly that they voted multiple times to approve a total of $3.5 million in public bonds between 1904 and 1912 to build out the vision.[51] That's about $90 million in 2020 dollars, adjusting for inflation. Seattle constructed dozens of parks and boulevards from the Olmsted plan, including Seward, Green Lake, and Volunteer Parks as well as Ravenna, Interlaken, and Lake Washington Boulevards. The result is the stuff of local legend and a revered part of the city's history, protected in current times by the Friends of Seattle's Olmsted Parks historic preservation board that meets monthly at the Seattle Parks and Recreation headquarters.

Seattle immortalized its first-ever bicycling boom through its boulevards. But by the time construction of the boulevards was complete, there was a new conveyance capturing imaginations in Seattle: the automobile.

In an effort to raise public awareness about traffic deaths, the Seattle Traffic and Safety Council erected a towering "death thermometer" in 1940 at the intersection of Fourth and West-lake Avenues downtown, the current site of Westlake Park. Museum of History and Industry, *Seattle P-I* photography archive, no. 1986.5.15092.

CHAPTER 2

After the Bike Bust

While people in 1890s Paris cruised their city's grand boulevards in automobiles, faraway Seattle was just starting to build its gravel bike paths and pave its downtown streets. As with the late arrival of the bicycle, automobiles were slow to make it all the way to Puget Sound. The first automobile ride in Washington State happened September 17, 1899, on the other side of the state in Spokane.[1] Seattle newspapers covered the automobile news from other cities closely, printing wire stories from Paris and London, then New York, then Cleveland, then Chicago. European fashion trends like the "automobile coat" and "automobile tie" hit Seattle years before actual automobiles rolled through town.[2]

The thunder of military bands rang through the streets of Seattle's Pioneer Square, playing proud patriotic music through the afternoon and into the evening before Independence Day 1900. As the evening grew late, several thousand people gathered near the band and started decorating and illuminating their bicycles. Illuminated bicycle parades had for years been one of the city's favorite ways to celebrate, but this parade had something special. Preceding the bicycle riders and the marching band was one of the first automobiles in Seattle making its ceremonial first drive. The parade processed north on Second Avenue to Pike Street, then east on Pike before stopping at Eighth Avenue, where the paved roadway ended.

The short trip demonstrated the challenge facing more widespread adoption of cars in the city: There were not many roads suitable for driving one, and cars were even worse at navigating dirt roads rutted by horses and wagons than people on bicycles were. Early cars did not have the engine power to climb many of the city's steep hills or the braking power to easily stop on the way down. "The hills of Seattle's streets offer one comforting assurance to its people," wrote the *Seattle*

Post-Intelligencer in 1902, "no crank possessed by the speed mania will ever be able to operate a racing automobile here."[3]

Still, the idea of the automobile was an effective marketing tool. The downtown department store Bon Marche announced in 1901 holiday newspaper ads that Santa Claus would be arriving in town in his new automobile, parading up and down the same paved downtown streets before holding court for Seattle children.[4] Toy autos were the hot holiday gift for Seattle's kids that year. Though there were few autos actively in use in Seattle, city leaders understood that they were the future. "The automobile will do wonders for good roads, taking up the work just where the bicycle dropped it," wrote the *Seattle Daily Times* in 1901.[5]

The Bicycle Fad Fades, 1903-1905

In the meantime, bicycles still had a few more years in the city's limelight. Through 1903, bicycling was still a favorite pastime in the city and the primary force behind path and road building. More than three thousand people turned out to ride in a July 1902 "twenty-fifth anniversary parade commemorating the birth of the bicycle in America."[6] But the bicycling wave had finally crested in Seattle. The sales of annual city bicycle licenses peaked at 4,698 in 1901, though the decline in licenses in subsequent years had a number of causes. New bicycles were typically sold with licenses, so the decline in new bike purchases led to a decline in those guaranteed license sales. People were supposed to buy a new license every year, but many people grew tired of paying the annual fee. The number of people who showed up to that 1902 bicycle anniversary parade outnumbered the bicycle licenses sold that year. But perhaps the biggest cause of the decline was a surge in roadway and neighborhood construction, which blocked the city's favorite bike paths in many places, including the Lake Union Path out of downtown. The same roadways the Queen City Good Roads Club had pushed the city to build often conflicted with the improvised bike-path routes the club had previously constructed.

With declining bicycle sales, some Seattle bicycle shops became the first to sell motorcycles and autos, and the growing number of car owners joined the bike groups in advocating for more and smoother roads.[7] Like early bicycle owners, early car owners used their vehicles mostly for recreation and to get out of the city. Due to the extraordinarily high cost of owning an automobile at the time, only the wealthy could afford them at first. The next group to get into auto driving were the former bicycle enthusiasts, including Harry Chadwick at *The Argus*. After he and a group of biking friends checked out a $650 gasoline-powered Oldsmobile in action in 1902, Chadwick declared that "it is a luxury to ride behind an Olds mobile."[8] A bicycle at the time cost between $25 and $60.

Chadwick's interest in autos became more and more apparent through 1903 and 1904. In one of his final Cycle Notes columns in September 1904, Chadwick wrote, "It is noticeable that nearly all of the machines in the city are owned by old bicycle riders. They know the roads surrounding Seattle, and know that a machine can be put to good use.... Automobiles are practical in this district, provided that the motors are powerful enough to climb the hills, and I believe that another year the number will be more than doubled."[9] In Chadwick's obituary in 1934, the *Seattle Daily Times* noted that "he was one of Western Washington's first motorists."[10] It did not say anything about bicycling.

After 1904, bikes became old news, and cars were novel. People still rode bikes, of course, but cars were the new fad. Seattle media mentions of bikes and bicycles went from the talk of the town in 1903 to a few murmurs by 1905. When new boulevards were opened, people drove cars at the front of the celebratory processions. Certainly people biked during these grand opening parties, but they no longer seemed worthy of mention in the newspapers. It was clear even then that cars were going to be the vehicle of the future, and many of the original bicycle riders and promoters expanded their calls for good roads to focus on automobiles.

The story of Seattle's first bike boom is not about how Seattle's bicycle culture began—it's the story of how Seattle's car culture began. The bicycle paths helped open more parts of the city to development, but automobiles were dramatically more effective at achieving this goal. While many core Seattle neighborhoods developed around streetcar lines, the mass adoption of cars would eventually allow for the development of suburbs with little or no transit access. George Cotterill even served as one of the first chief engineers for the Washington State Highways Department starting in 1916.

But some people in Seattle could see that building boulevards to serve cars meant giving up something special. "These systems of beautifying are carried out in every city sooner or later, and Seattle is of the wide-awake variety," wrote the *Seattle Mail and Herald* in 1905. "Her people shall have the best, which means they shall have space to breathe. A place where her population can get away from the pent-up stream of life flooding the streets between the 'skyscrapers' which are fast being built and bathe themselves in the fresh air and refresh their tired senses in the forest primeval, saved from the devastating hand of the landscape gardener. In the line of march of our city save some of the natural beauty of our country. As I write I am mourning the loss of the bicycle paths that have been obliterated, where we have wandered sometimes in the past. 'The world is forgetting by the world forgot.'"[11]

Giving Space to Automobiles, 1905-1940

From 1905 onward, cars were the transportation priority. Cities in the United States and many other parts of the world experienced a fundamental culture shift once they started making space for cars both physically within the city and within the laws and customs of the people who lived there. As Seattle learned in the coming decades, the public would need to invest unimaginable amounts of money to build the infrastructure needed to carry the number of cars that would soon arrive. Even the way people walked around their city would need to be turned on its head. Seattle would need laws telling people when and where they could walk, a major shift for people accustomed to walking to their destinations by the easiest and most direct paths, dodging whatever horse-drawn carriages or streetcars might be in the way. Collisions, injuries, and even deaths happened in Seattle streets before the automobile arrived, but autos dramatically increased the scale of that carnage and forced a cultural change ceding dominance of street space to vehicles.

While the early peak of bicycling was nearly over by 1905, bicycles did not go away. Aside from recreation and racing, bikes also served an increasingly important role in quickly moving messages and packages around the city. And perhaps the most successful messenger service in world history started on bikes in downtown Seattle. A nineteen-year-old Jim Casey and his friend Claude Ryan put their bicycles to work starting in 1907, delivering messages and packages around the city.[12] Ryan's uncle invested a hundred dollars and gave them a free office in the basement of a saloon in Pioneer Square. Because biking was fast and Seattle was small, the messengers were efficient and their business grew. Soon the American Messenger Service had a team of people making deliveries by bike, foot, and streetcar. The company didn't purchase its first automobile until 1913, a decision that set it on a different course. Six years later, they made the leap to doing business beyond Seattle when they bought the Motor Parcel Delivery Service and renamed their company the United Parcel Service, also known as UPS.

As the young century turned adolescent, bicycles faded more and more from the center of public conversation. Mentions of the term *bicycle* in Seattle's two biggest and most consistent daily newspapers, the *Seattle Daily Times* and the *Seattle Post-Intelligencer*, topped 16,000 between 1900 and 1910, according to the decade-by-decade snapshot in the NewsBank digital archive system.[13] This count includes both advertisements and news stories. But those mentions fell to 11,500 in the 1910s, then bottomed out at fewer than 8,000 in the 1920s. The number of bicycle references in Seattle newspapers would not again reach the level of the century's first decade until the 1970s.

For much of the 1910s, bicycle mentions in the media were either advertisements or stories about a bike theft. A 1919 story in the *Seattle Daily Times* noted that bicycle sales were on the rise due to increases in streetcar fares.[14] "As a means of getting back and forth from work, the bicycle seems to be winning back much of the prestige it enjoyed a score of years ago," the reporter notes. But this is not a trend that seems to have lasted very long, at least not for adults. The Yoo-Hoo Skin-Nay Bicycle Club was briefly popular in 1919 and 1920 among young people.[15] Hundreds of kids went on long bike rides across the city, and the club even held a major bike race on the streets around Green Lake.[16]

Around this time, another kind of bicycle story became increasingly common: people driving cars were injuring and killing people all over the place, which understandably alarmed Seattle's residents. The September 25, 1919, issue of the *Seattle Post-Intelligencer* noted that people driving cars had struck and injured five people in various collisions around the city in just one day, including one collision that caused serious head injuries to a thirteen-year-old boy biking at Broadway and Union in the densely residential Capitol Hill neighborhood east of downtown.[17] After striking the boy, the driver sped up and fled the scene.

The 1920s were more of the same. Ten-year-old Robert McNeil Jr. was seriously injured when someone driving a car struck him while he was biking at Sunnyside Avenue North and North Forty-Fourth Street in Wallingford in October 1929.[18] The next day, ten-year-old Ralf Backman was killed when a person driving a truck struck him in Renton. It was his first ride on the new bike his mother had given him the day before as a reward for helping around the house and being kind to his three little sisters.[19] The trend became clear during the '20s: kids, usually boys, were being injured or killed by people driving cars. The trend may have been especially prevalent at this time because so many boys had bicycle messenger and delivery jobs in the decades before passage of the federal Fair Labor Standards Act of 1938, which limited child labor like messenger work. "The FLSA and other failed federal labor regulations that eventually led up to the passage of that law were all influenced by bicycle messenger boys," wrote Chris Sweet in a 2018 article about the role of bicycle messenger boys in the passage of child labor laws. "The extent of that influence is certainly small, but messenger work of all types was a very common form of employment for boys in the early twentieth century. Messenger boys and newspaper boys would have been visible daily in any major city. It would have been easier for the average person to empathize with the plight of the messenger or newspaper boy than it would for those hidden behind factory walls or in rural fields."[20]

Seattle's total annual traffic deaths climbed from 48 in 1924 to a shocking 121 deaths in 1934.[21] To put that death toll in context, 12 people were killed in traffic collisions on Seattle streets in 2011, the lowest figure since the early days of the automobile. As more cars arrived on Seattle streets, people grew accustomed to the devastating amount of death and injury that came with them. Newspapers reported the steady stream of deaths as they happened, but the number kept rising.

With no relief from the traffic carnage in sight, the Seattle Traffic and Safety Council decided to try something new starting in 1939, convening what the *Seattle Post-Intelligencer* called "a council of war" to fight traffic deaths.[22] Starting May 1, they would publicly count the number of days since someone was killed in traffic as part of a large education campaign they called "100 Deathless Days." The goal was for everyone to work together to go a hundred days without a single traffic death. The city had previously gone thirty-eight days during the summer of 1937, but that was as good as it got. "Can the city do it?" asked a *P-I* editorial in May 1939. "The answer lies with motorists—and pedestrians." the *P-I* ran a "Daily Traffic Record" scoreboard tracking the number of traffic deaths and injuries from the day before. "Deaths . . . 1. Accidents . . . 16. Injured . . . 4. Reckless driving arrests . . . 3. Speeding and arterial arrests

. . . 59," the scoreboard read June 23, 1939. The *P-I* also regularly listed the names of every person injured under the headline "Traffic Victims Yesterday."

The city didn't make it to one hundred. By July 4, the city was already advertising "A New Start!" as the fifth Deathless Days campaign began.[23] The first campaign lasted forty-six days. The second lasted six days. The third lasted five days. Then Arthur Lubach struck and killed seventy-year-old Sena Seggelke while she was crossing Third Avenue Northwest in the Fremont neighborhood just three days into the fourth campaign. "These campaigns are not ridiculous efforts at reaching a hopeless goal," Traffic Sergeant C. A. Wilson told the *Seattle Daily Times* on the first day of the fifth campaign. "We members of the traffic division are not Houdinis that we can miraculously stop deaths. We can only strive with the cooperation of the public to hold them down." The education campaign was credited with a slight reduction in deaths that year. The sixty-one people killed in Seattle traffic was down from seventy-eight the year before. But it didn't last. Traffic deaths increased nearly 5 percent in 1940, and injuries increased 33 percent. As the *Daily Times* noted, it seemed to work at first, but then the effort "dwindled out."[24] Eighty-one years later, Seattle still has not gone one hundred days without a traffic death. The closest the city got was a seventy-six-day streak in the spring of 2017, but the city is getting closer. The four longest streaks were in 2017, 2018, and 2020.[25]

The 100 Deathless Days campaign in 1939 included public service announcements warning people to not be reckless, and the warnings were accompanied by police enforcement stings. Other than recommending that streets get more lighting to improve visibility at night, the campaign did not address the fundamental underlying dynamics that drove traffic deaths. The campaign did not highlight how the design of streets might play a role in traffic collisions, did not suggest that speed limits should be reduced, and did not talk of how to make crosswalks safer. The campaign did note that nearly 70 percent of the people killed were pedestrians, but they drew the exact wrong conclusion from that information: "We can't have the rest of the year deathless if pedestrians are going to invite death by jaywalking," Seattle Police Captain Joseph E. Prince told the *Seattle Daily Times* before a 1939 sting in which he told his officers that "pedestrians must share equal responsibility with drivers."[26]

This was also the opinion of the city's Traffic and Safety Council, the people in charge of the Deathless Days campaign, who went a step further and recommended that the city create a new "reckless walking" infraction that carried major penalties. "The pedestrian factor is the most serious one with which we have to deal in eliminating traffic fatalities," Traffic and Safety Council Manager Earl F. Campbell wrote in a letter to the city council.[27] One hundred ninety pedestrians had been killed between 1936 and April 1939, he noted. "We believe that an ordinance should be passed which will make possible just as high fines for careless pedestrians as are now given erring drivers. . . . It must be assumed that some pedestrians are just as reckless as any driver ever could be." The city council did not pass the reckless walking portion of the request, but they did pass a new requested ordinance making jaywalking illegal on every city arterial street rather than just in business districts.[28]

Seattle Police also took the safety council's advice and engaged in a series of jaywalking enforcement stings. Even when a collision was obviously the fault of the person driving, people walking were still targeted as at least part of the problem. A man driving a truck full of berries struck and killed a fifty-five-year-old man walking in the rain at Alaskan Way and Main Street near the Pioneer Square waterfront on June 22, 1939. The man driving the truck told police he didn't see the victim, and he was then charged with recklessness.

But in response to that incident, Seattle Police conducted what may be one of Seattle's first ever jaywalking stings. The lead story in the June 23 issue of the *Seattle Daily Times* proclaimed "16 Jailed In Drive On Jaywalkers!" and listed the names, ages, and occupations of everyone arrested. Of the sixteen arrested that morning, only five were able to post the five-dollar bail: clerks Carmen Lopez, Ruth Rackner, and Tyko Johnson, housewife Mrs. Gladys Wolfe, and tool grinder Holly Nichols. The rest were held until they could go before a judge in the afternoon, who fined them one dollar each: bill poster Edward Wickstrom, carpenter Jalmer Johnson (who earlier bailed out his son Tyko, but apparently did not have enough cash for himself), truck driver Victor Zabraska, salesmen Irving Gussman and Allison Raycraft, and laborer Ignacio Mirando. Five of the people arrested, all listed as laborers, chose to serve a few more hours of time in jail in lieu of the one-dollar fine: Vincenti Tulsvott, Pablo Domingo, John Soss, Ralph Oyen, and Arnold Kennedy.[29]

A couple of weeks after those sixteen people were arrested, police doubled the amount of bail before conducting another sting in their "war on jaywalking," arresting forty-seven people for jaywalking in just three hours.[30] But arresting people walking across the street and keeping the poor ones locked up all day did not slow or stop traffic deaths. In fact, nearly all the news stories from this era about the need for more jaywalking enforcement are accompanied by stories about drivers who injured or killed people walking around the city. Reading them side by side is dissonant. Rather than searching for ways to stop people driving cars from hitting people, the focus was on finding ways to get people walking to stay out of the way of cars.

Shifting Attitudes toward Pedestrians, the 1910s

How did Seattle's culture change so strongly in just a couple of decades that people killed while walking were consistently blamed for their own deaths? To get an idea, a look back at the 1910s reveals that a powerful new word had arrived in the city: jaywalker. The first Seattle newspaper mention of the word *jaywalking* was in a 1912 *Seattle Daily Times* editorial suggesting the term would be effective at shaming people who "cut corners" by walking through the middle of an intersection.[31] The editorial quotes a *Cleveland News* editorial at length, part of a trend across the country at the time to carve out more roadway rights for people driving cars. But originally, the term was based on a more common term: jay-driver. When cars first started arriving in cities, people didn't know how to drive them. People who drove on the wrong side of the road or otherwise broke the normal ways of city streets would be called a jay-driver, with *jay* meaning "a greenhorn or rube," according to *Merriam-Webster*.[32] It wasn't until the 1910s that the term was turned around to point back at people walking, and the effect of the term *jaywalker* was much more insidious. While a jay-driver might be someone who didn't know how to drive these newfangled cars, walking in streets was normal everyday behavior. If someone needed to cross the street, they crossed the street. If their destination was at an angle, they crossed the street on an angle. Why would they walk out of the way? But as more and more cars arrived, traffic quickly became a problem. These machines could go fast, but not if there were people in the way. So the cultural fight over control of the streets heated up.

Some cities, like Kansas City, took the drastic action of regulating how someone could walk on the streets. But such laws initially met tough public resistance. "Legislation of this sort rubs human nature the wrong way by seeming an arbitrary intrusion upon personal liberties," said the 1912 *Times* editorial.[33] "It's a challenge to free-born citizens to cross streets wherever and however they blooming please." And this is where the usefulness of the term *jaywalking* came in. "By the magic phrase, jay walker, the hurried business man . . . has been redeemed from his devious and kitty-cornered path and made to walk rectilinearly if not uprightly in the fear of ridicule." In other words, it was a shame campaign, and it worked. People walking were deemed in the wrong for doing what they had always done, and if they got hit by a car it was because they were a rube and were walking wrong. It took a while for this concept to fully catch on with the public, but as is clear in the present day, cars won this cultural battle over city streets.

Another term also played an enormous role in changing street culture as cars rose to dominance: pedestrian. A pedestrian is just a person moving around in their most basic state, whether by walking or using an assistive mobility device like a wheelchair. Or at least that's how the term is commonly used in transportation policy. The term is likely an eighteenth-century play on the word *equestrian* for someone riding a horse. In fact, the adjective use meaning "dull or ordinary" likely predates the literal use meaning "a person walking."[34] Compared to riding a horse, walking is rather dull and ordinary, the term implies. Riding a horse (especially for travel rather than labor) has long been a symbol of high status and importance, and the same went for cars when the expensive machines first arrived.

So the word *pedestrian* has always had a pejorative tint to it. By giving people this dehumanizing label, lawmakers, courts, and police could regulate the rights and responsibilities of pedestrians as a class of roadway user in relation to vehicle drivers. "Today is the last day of unrestricted liberty in the use of the public streets by those who walk—officially dignified by the term 'pedestrians,'" wrote the *Seattle P-I* on July 6, 1917.[35] "Tomorrow the new traffic code goes into effect and then and thereafter pedestrians must be as consistent in their conduct at intersections as automobiles are required to be." Before that day, there were no laws requiring people to cross busy downtown streets at intersections or to never cross kitty-corner. "He might be sent to the morgue, but not to jail," the *P-I* noted. Someone caught walking wrong under the new rules would be fined a minimum of $5 (about $100 in 2020 dollars) and could be fined up to $100 (about $2,000 in 2020 dollars). They could even "be asked to labor in the city jail for thirty days, without pay and under the careful vigilance of an armed guard," according to the *Seattle Daily Times*.[36] The new law "places the responsibility for the safety of a pedestrian largely upon himself," the *Times* noted before considering a grim scenario. "While he is lying in the hospital watching the various portions of his anatomy reunite some judge may decide that he was to blame for the accident. Then, along with the hospital, nurse, medicine and doctor bills he would have to contribute a small sum—even up to $100—for the privilege of being hurt." That still happens to this day.

The editorial board of the *Seattle Daily Times* was happy to see the new pedestrian rules, arguing that people who drive cars had been unfairly called "highway barons" for "lay[ing] claim to ownership of all the roads. . . . The man with an automobile doesn't get his greatest enjoyment out of running over somebody any more than does the pedestrian in being run over. Seattle is becoming a very large city and its traffic problem is becoming a serious one. There is no reason why the pedestrian should be granted rights that do not extend to the autoist."[37]

Giving people driving cars the primary rights to the roads and shifting the blame for the deaths and injuries they cause onto the victims they hit is one of the most fundamental shifts in the past century of American urban culture. People who were wealthy enough to own a car gained enormous power over others. The use and ownership of cars could never have increased the way it did if not for this vital change in urban street culture in the 1910s. Few people would have purchased a house in a suburb accessible only by car if they couldn't freely drive from that house into the city. And the public may never have learned to accept the crushing toll of deaths and injuries caused by people driving cars without a way to legally justify that carnage. Jaywalking was the perfect scapegoat.

"These individuals do not realize how difficult it is for approaching drivers to see them during dusk and at night," Seattle Traffic Engineer J. W. A. Bollong told the *P-I* in 1939.[38] "If the pedestrian is wearing dark clothing, less than 5 per cent of the light which falls upon him is directed back to the driver's eyes. Yet the light returned to the driver's eyes is all he has by which to see." As traffic engineer, Bollong's job was to design the city's streets and their safety features. He is perhaps best known for another effort he was working on during that same year: the initial plans for an elevated roadway on the downtown waterfront that would later become the Alaskan Way Viaduct.[39] The traffic engineer was perhaps the person in the best position to do something about the rising traffic carnage in Seattle. But while Bollong had grand dreams for how to move cars, his advice for preventing nighttime pedestrian deaths was for people to wear different clothes when walking.

This is an enduring black hole in the logic supporting car culture: the person controlling the fast-moving heavy vehicle is not responsible for the damage they cause so long as they were following the rules of the road when they caused the damage. Even if they are driving too fast to see someone walking in the dark, it's not their fault unless they were significantly exceeding the speed limit or recklessly impaired. Then if the person driving is absolved of responsibility, no responsibility falls on the transportation agency or traffic engineer who designed the street or set the dangerous speed limit. It's just nobody's fault, so nothing changes. Dangerous roadway conditions are often allowed to remain in place no matter how many collisions occur.

Nearly 3.8 million people died in traffic collisions in the United States in the hundred years from 1920 through 2020.[40] Tens of millions more have been seriously injured, often left with lifelong health challenges and disabilities. Driving cars is among our largest sources of greenhouse gas emissions, and huge swaths of the population live in communities that essentially cannot function without cars. The number of vehicle miles traveled in the United States doubled in the first five years of the 1920s. It doubled again five years later. Then it doubled again by 1950, again by 1960, again by 1980, and again by 2020. The damage caused by driving cars is not getting better. The number of annual traffic deaths is down compared to the horrifying totals of the 1960s and '70s, but the number is still on par with the hundred-year average.

Seattle's Bicycle Dark Ages, 1910–1939

As noted earlier in this chapter, Seattle newspaper mentions of the word *bicycle* plummeted in the 1910s and hit a low in the 1920s. I've started referring to the 1910s through the 1930s as "Seattle's bicycle dark ages" because there was so little media attention for biking during this time.

There was some interest in the sport of bike racing, but most references to bikes treated them as toys for children.

Seattle media mentions remained low in the 1930s in stark contrast to the rapid increase in bicycling on the other side of the Pacific. While this era may have been the bicycle dark ages in Seattle, this was not the case everywhere. Bicycle use in China had been rising quickly through the 1930s and 1940s, but the machines became nearly ubiquitous in urban areas once the Communist Party took control in the late 1940s. The party used state funding to subsidize Chinese-made bicycles for the proletariat as part of its centralized economic plan.[41] Bicycle production was nationally controlled, but its bike-making efforts could not keep up with demand. When the nation began to open its economy in the 1980s and relinquished national control of bicycle production, the industry took off. By 1987, China was producing 41 million bicycles per year, up from 8.5 million a decade earlier. This is how the nation became the so-called Kingdom of Bicycles by the second half of the twentieth century, probably the largest bicycle culture in history.[42] The People's Republic of China demonstrated a wide-scale, authoritarian example of using bicycles to achieve larger economic and social goals.

In Seattle, stories of people in cars injuring or killing kids on bikes remained common throughout the 1930s, and bicycle sales in the United States were as low as one bicycle per 500 people.[43] (For context, US bike sales in 2015 were estimated at one bicycle per 19 people.[44]) But with the world teetering on the verge of World War II, a new bike club filled with optimism and positivity formed on the University of Washington campus, and a major advancement in bicycle component technology made their mission possible.

Multigear Bikes Unlock a New Era of Bike Travel, 1939–1968

Bike sellers in Seattle knew that multigear bikes had a lot of promise in this notoriously hilly city as early as 1903. Gifford and Grant, a Pike Street bicycle shop that also sold fireworks, ran a series of newspaper ads for a Hill Climber bicycle that had "a changeable gear" and "can be ridden up any incline with perfect ease."[45] The technology promised to solve an issue that people who bike in Seattle today are familiar with. "No need to dread the hills now, it's a pleasure," the ads promised. It's not clear whether the Hill Climber bicycle used an internally geared hub, like British bike companies were starting to use at the time, or one of a countless number of design concepts engineers devised during this time for moving the chain to differently sized cogs. But since bikes were still rather heavy and gear-changing technology was in its infancy, the 1903 Hill Climber promises were likely too good to be true. (Luckily for Gifford and Grant, they had a backup plan and had recently become the first business in Seattle to sell a different type of vehicle: the automobile.)

Creating a reliable and easy-to-use gear-changing mechanism was a difficult engineering challenge, especially for changing gears while in motion. Some early designs required the user to move the chain while stopped, and it took decades and countless design attempts before French bike makers finally settled on a cable-actuated dual-pulley design similar to modern derailleurs (pronounced and often spelled "derailer" in English). Development of multigear solutions took off after World War I as European nations worked to rebuild their industries and residents sought leisure rather than battle in the countryside.[46] The few American bike makers still in existence mostly focused on single-speed bikes, often stylized to look like motorcycles. But European bike makers worked to unlock a new market for adult touring bikes. British companies largely focused on internal hub gearing, designing mechanisms enclosed within the rear wheel that function almost like clockwork to give riders two or three gears. At the same time, French and Italian bike makers worked on derailleur designs that moved the chain to differently sized cogs.

Design ideas developed during the 1920s became widely popular during the 1930s. Frank J. Berto, author of an exhaustive history of the derailleur called *The Dancing Chain*, dubbed the 1930s "the golden age for bicycle touring and derailleurs in Europe." French workers won laws mandating a forty-hour work week and fifteen days of paid vacation per year, freeing up a lot of people to travel by bike. The dual-pulley derailleur designs by companies like Le Cyclo and Simplex were perfect for extending the range and terrain that bike tourists could reach, and the industry thrived. At the same time, a youth hosteling movement grew across Europe, encouraging people to see new places and meet other travelers. Hosteling and bicycle touring were a perfect pair.

As with many other bicycling trends, the new European style of touring took a few more years to reach Seattle. With war breaking out once again in Europe, a group of University of Washington students and faculty members formed a local Youth Hostel Club in 1939. "When this club joined with a group of cyclists who had purchased English bikes at the Broadway Cycle Shop in Seattle, the Pacific Northwest Cycling Association was born," wrote Helene G. Ryan in her unpublished manuscript, "The Blowout," documenting the history of the PNCA.[47] The organization had a few members who had biked extensively, but most people were new to biking as adults. So their "first rule" for group rides was that "the party's pace is as slow as that of the slowest cyclist."[48] But the same edition of the *Seattle Daily Times* in May 1940 that introduced the organization to its readers also bore headlines about the German military breaking through the French lines. The PNCA was forming at a precarious time.

"A PNCA group was biking up Whidbey Island on the morning of December 7, 1941, when a farmer rushed out of his house, shouting: 'The Japanese have bombed Pearl Harbor,'" Ryan wrote. A few months later, charter member Bill Calder was killed near Manila. At least two dozen other PNCA members were drafted or enlisted. Those who remained continued organizing bike adventures, and the organization's newsletter posted the schedule as well as any news they received from enlisted members. One issue noted that due to wartime restrictions on materials that had made new bicycles difficult to come by, some members had been experimenting with making bikes out of wood. But gasoline rationing also freed up space on the roads as people kept their cars parked. As a 1961 *Seattle Daily Times* story about the PNCA noted, "The heyday of bicycling during the past 40 years, they all agree, was during the gasoline-rationing days of the Second World War."[49]

On September 17, 1945, member Russell Langstaff wrote a message from occupied Nagasaki, Japan, where he and the rest of the crew of his US Navy minesweeper were stationed. They had been through a hellish year, participating in the brutal battles of Iwo Jima and Okinawa. Only six weeks had passed since the United States dropped an atomic bomb on Nagasaki, but Langstaff made no mention of the devastation or ongoing suffering there. Instead, he wrote that western shores of Kyushu near Nagasaki reminded him of home:

> Dear Friends, It has been a long time since I have written, but the fact is that I have been pretty busy during the past several months. I often think about all of the good times we used to have on our

bicycles before the war. . . . The landscape is very beautiful here, and looks very much like the shores of Puget Sound. It seems funny to see men pulling rickshaws, and I have also seen many cyclists—one pulling a trailer behind his bicycle. It would take a book to tell all the experiences I have had, but they won't be able to send me back any too soon to suit me. Here's wishing you the best of luck and pleasant cycling. Russell.[50]

After the war, the PNCA continued hosting rides, but a couple of members decided to fully commit to the biking and hosteling life by buying a ninety-eight-foot decommissioned ferry and converting it into a floating hostel. Leigh Whitford and Rex Clark bought the *Atlanta* in 1947 and towed it to a moorage at the northeast end of Lake Union.[51] The *Atlanta* was a 1906 wooden steamer that had been used for decades on ferry runs across Lake Washington. It was also used to give tours of the brand-new Lake Washington Ship Canal and Hiram M. Chittenden Locks in Ballard when those opened. By the time Whitford and Clark bought it, it had no engine and was in sorry shape. They patched dry rot using concrete, connected it to city utilities, built a bike repair shop in the former engine room, and opened for business. "Boys topside, girls main deck, bike forward, and chow aft," wrote Ronald W. Gallup, who visited from Vermont and wrote about the trip for *American Bicyclist and Motorcyclist* magazine in August 1949.[52] It cost thirty cents per night to stay on board.

The *Atlanta* quickly became a hub for the local bike scene. It hosted bike repair lessons, bike club meetings, dances, and parties. It also became the de facto starting point for bike rides and tours. A hosteller visiting the city could get a place to stay and find good company to take them on a bike tour of the city. But since Seattle did not require houseboats to be connected to sewer lines until 1968, it was probably best not to go for a swim. Jean Whitford, a hosteller who met her husband, Leigh, on the *Atlanta* during her travels, wrote about her time living aboard the floating hostel for Ryan's "The Blowout." Jean said they referred to the waters near the houseboats as "Lake Cesspool." She also wrote about the trials of keeping the old boat together. During cold winters, the water connection froze. During the spring, the roof leaked. She plugged the holes with chewing gum. "But every time I had one plugged, another would burst forth; I had a busy afternoon before I ran out of gum and gave up," she wrote.[53]

The *Atlanta* operated as a hostel for three and a half years before it went out of service in 1938 and was sold at auction to someone who turned it into a large houseboat. "The Atlanta was sold at a loss, but Rex Clark described it as the 'most enjoyable loss' he ever suffered," Ryan wrote in a 1975 article for the *Seattle Times Magazine*.[54]

Freeways and Wide Roads Smother the Bike Movement, 1950-1961

John B. Speer provided an ominous explanation for the end of the *Atlanta* in a 1961 letter to the *Seattle Daily Times*, writing, "It went the way of other hostels with the decline of bicycling."[55] The Pacific Northwest Cycling Association continued to host events into the 1950s, but the city and state were developing their roadways with the rapidly increasing car traffic in mind rather than the needs of the bicycling public. Thirty-one adult PNCA members and twenty-two of their children met up in 1961 at Jean and Leigh Whitford's home (by then firmly located on dry ground) to celebrate the group's twenty-first anniversary, but none of them arrived by bicycle. The group still organized adventures together, though mostly by car. "Club members say it is the increasing number of automobiles that keeps bicycles off the roads, rather than apathy on the part of the cyclists," wrote the *Seattle Daily Times* in a 1961 profile of the group.[56] "The city-dwelling cyclists finally have conceded that traveling by bicycle in large groups is dangerous and the club no longer bicycles as a group."

By 1953, about 450 people were killed every year while biking in the United States, and another 25,000 were seriously injured. That staggering toll, as terrible as it was, represented a great amount of safety progress over the course of the previous decade when the number killed each year was about double. The majority of those injured were boys between the ages of five and fifteen, according to a special report in the *American Weekly*.[57] But blame for these deaths was still squarely centered on the victims rather than the people driving cars. Even a spokesperson for the Bicycle Institute of America, a bicycle manufacturing industry group, blamed the kids for breaking traffic laws or failing to maintain their bikes. By this time, there were almost no media references to bicycling that were not about a child, a race, or a theft. The Seattle–King County Safety Council partnered with Seattle Public Schools in the early 1950s to distribute bicycle safety material to every elementary school and to host a dozen bicycle safety "rodeos" across the city featuring a series of bicycle safety lessons for kids thirteen and under. Local Schwinn dealers donated bikes and bike lights for the winners.[58] Seattle Police also held bicycle safety roundups in which they would inspect students' bikes and give them a "Safety Inspected" decal if they passed.[59]

There was some truth to the "jalopy bike" problem during the mid-century. It was common for people back then to ride bikes with poor brakes or fixed-gear cogs in which the pedals turn with the rear wheel and can be stopped only by slowing the rotation of the pedals. This was especially problematic on Seattle's many steep hills. A scary news story from 1959 describes a terrible collision in which a thirteen-year-old boy was critically injured in Magnolia because he was trying to drag his feet to stop his bike, which didn't have working brakes.[60] He couldn't stop, entered an intersection, and crashed into someone driving a car. Washington State passed a massive traffic law in 1965 that included a section requiring bikes to have a brake "which will enable the operator to make the braked wheels skid on dry, level, clean pavement."[61] Bicycle brake technology has advanced immensely in the past century.

Bikes also rarely had reflectors and almost never had powered lights for visibility at night due to technology limitations of the time. Some very early bikes had oil lamps, though this was not really a practical solution for many reasons. Bike manufacturers experimented with many different designs for bike lights during the first half of the twentieth century, including electric lights powered by batteries or a dynamo generator powered by a spinning bicycle wheel. Washington State did not require nighttime use of a front-facing bicycle light until the 1965 law, but the state did not fully commit to an international movement to require bicycle lights. The Vienna Convention on Road Traffic in 1968 recommended that bike lights should be a mandatory feature of a new bicycle, and several nations enacted such regulations.[62] But lights still are not a standard required feature of bicycles sold in the United States.

Washington State's 1965 traffic law fundamentally changed how biking legally worked in the state. Some changes were good, such as requiring a light and working brakes. But some changes severely limited the rights of people riding bikes, and it would take decades of organizing work to reverse these changes. One change banned people from biking on a roadway wherever there was a "usable path . . . adjacent to a roadway." This sounds innocent at first, but the mandatory side-path law deeply divided the bicycling movement for much of the century. It pitted advocates fighting for people on bikes to have the full legal rights of vehicles against advocates fighting for more bike lanes and paths. Another provision of the 1965 law created confusion and conflict between people biking and driving. The law stated that someone biking "shall ride as near to the right side of the roadway as practicable." There is enough gray area in that sentence to drive a pickup truck through. For example, how do you define "practicable"? And according to whom? People biking could read this law as saying they could ride in the full lane if it would not be safe to squeeze to the side. But someone driving could read this law as saying that a person needed to bike as close to the side of the road as was physically possible. The law was also unclear about whether someone biking was allowed to move away from the right side of the roadway in order to make a left turn. It would take seventeen years before these rules would be partially clarified, then another thirty-seven years before the law would be further cleaned up to specify a driver's responsibility when passing someone on a bike.[63] Since 2020, state law requires someone driving a car to slow down to a safe speed and pass with at least three feet of separation, though this doesn't mean people will actually do so. It is easier to change a law than it is to change a culture.

Back at the PNCA anniversary meetup in 1961, the *Times* reporter captured an interesting conversation between an adult member and one of the kids:

> "All you do is talk about what happened a long time ago," one youngster complained. "Don't you ever talk about now?"
>
> Helene Ryan answered the youngster's question best, we think, when she wrote in the club's history:
>
> "When the time comes for bicycling again, there will be a few beautiful old roads to be found left high and dry by the freeways. Someday the 'PNCAer' may see his own youngster coasting down a mountain, saddlebags bulging, a glow on his face; see him chuckle through a thunderstorm, poncho spread wide, relishing an inconvenience that soon turns into an adventure; singing 'Tit Willow' around a fire with his neighbors from across the border—storing up treasures for a lifetime."[64]

The Seattle Freeway (now Interstate 5) is under construction
through downtown Seattle on February 25, 1964. Museum of
History and Industry, John Vallentyne Photographs collection,
no. 2009.23.130.

CHAPTER 3

Freeway Fighting

First, Aubrey Knoff noticed a funny new crack in the street in front of his home. His house on Bellevue Place East, located on the steep hillside on the western slope of Capitol Hill, was supposed to be safe from the major construction work happening below, where workers were digging a deep cut to make space for the Seattle Freeway. But then a water main broke, flooding his patio. Next, his house started to change shape. "Walking through his home became like traipsing through a fun house at an amusement park as doorways began to sag and lean," wrote *Seattle Post-Intelligencer* reporter Charles Dunsire in the first part of an investigative series into a megaproject that was becoming a boondoggle.[1] Knoff and his neighbors had to flee their homes because the hillside was collapsing from the construction work. The state highways department was forced to buy and demolish their homes as part of a wildly expensive reengineering of the hillside, including a towering concrete retaining wall that, along with other challenges, doubled the original cost estimate of the Seattle segment of the freeway project. The costs would continue increasing, and the central section of freeway scheduled to open in 1964 wouldn't actually open until 1967. The whole freeway area was a construction site for most of the decade.

Today, the area where Knoff once lived is a hilly park on the edge of Capitol Hill with a biking and walking trail connecting Melrose Avenue to Lakeview Boulevard just east of the freeway now known as Interstate 5. His home was part of a story that would be repeated many times throughout Seattle's freeway construction efforts. The city's many iconic lakes, bays, and glacier-carved hillsides make Seattle among the most expensive and impractical places to build freeway infrastructure. Engineers have consistently underestimated the challenges their projects would face, leading to huge cost overruns due to engineering mistakes, unexpected soil conditions, and overly rosy cost estimates. The land itself seems to resist freeways. Even after they are completed and opened, the land and waterways work together to destabilize them. The 1953 Alaskan Way Viaduct, which towered loudly over Seattle's downtown waterfront, was seriously damaged during the 2001 Nisqually earthquake. Studies suggested that the structure would collapse in the event of another earthquake, but people drove about ninety thousand vehicles daily on the troubled structure for another eighteen years before it was finally replaced, although over budget and delayed by years, by an underground freeway tunnel. People normalized the danger.

The route of I-5 through the heart of Seattle was an enormously consequential and damaging project for a city with a long history of major land and waterway engineering projects. This is a city that spent thirty years removing Denny Hill from Belltown and filled in the Duwamish tideflats south of downtown with nearly 22 million cubic yards of fill to create SoDo. Even some people who worked on those early major engineering projects thought the I-5 routing had serious issues. A retired George Cotterill said in 1955 that a freeway through the heart of downtown would be "a destructive monstrosity."[2] Cotterill was an engineer with extensive experience working along the steep hillsides of the planned I-5 route. After all, he was the person who had surveyed and planned the old Lake Union Bike Path along the same route more than half a century earlier. "Making a great cut through the city on a side hill, where there is a rise of 30-feet on average between 6th and 7th Avenues, would be disastrous," he said. Cotterill died in 1958 before construction began.

But Cotterill was no freeway opponent. As former head of the Washington State Department of Highways, he preferred routing the freeway down Martin Luther King Jr. Way (known then as Empire Way). This route would later be planned as an elevated freeway named in honor of Cotterill's old boss R. H. Thomson. But we'll get to that later in this chapter. Seattle and Washington State engineers chose the downtown route in 1951, and Seattle City Engineer Ralph W. Finke sold it to the public by declaring that it would somehow simultaneously fix downtown traffic congestion and increase traffic to the business district. "It will solve many of our major traffic ills," Finke told the *Seattle P-I* in 1951.[3] "It will furnish a means whereby traffic through Seattle can escape the downtown bottleneck, relieving congestion there, and it will enable much city traffic, by using the freeway, to get to and from the central business district." Of course, it couldn't both add traffic downtown while also relieving traffic congestion downtown. Only one of these predictions could come true.

It added traffic. To this day, freeway access is the primary cause of traffic backups in downtown Seattle.

"What a Pity Progress Has to Cost So Much," 1959-1967

Another reason the downtown route was chosen for I-5 was because it was initially intended to be a toll road, and the central route would generate more revenue. "When the project was being planned as a toll road, it was considered necessary to locate it close to the business district to collect the maximum income from tolls," the *P-I* reported.[4] But a few years after the route was selected, the Washington Supreme Court ruled the state's toll-roads law to be unconstitutional. This was only a short setback because the Federal Aid Highway Act of 1956 stepped in to fill the funding gap. With the federal government footing 90 percent of the bill, there was no need for tolls. Rather than reconsider the freeway route, planners erased the toll booths but kept the rest of the downtown design.

In total, the Seattle Freeway required the state to acquire 4,500 parcels of land, and the government condemned about 450 of those parcels from owners who wouldn't sell.[5] The land where the freeway ran was not empty. People lived, worked, and played there. Even historic buildings, like the 1881 Hotel Kalmar, were demolished, much to the dismay of preservationists like architect Victor Steinbrueck. Though Steinbrueck lost the preservation battle against I-5, he would continue fighting against freeway projects and for historic preservation. One of the designers of the Space Needle, Steinbrueck helped lead successful historic preservation efforts in Pioneer Square and Pike Place Market. After his death in 1985, Seattle named a park near the market in his honor.

But the impact of Interstate 5 goes far beyond the loss of a few interesting structures. Some people never recovered from the displacement. Zoë Dusanne opened her art gallery on the hill overlooking South Lake Union in 1950. Dusanne, who was a founding member of the Seattle chapter of the National Association for the Advancement of Colored People, is considered Seattle's first modern art dealer. But her gallery, which was also her home, stood in the way of the proposed freeway. The state paid her far less for her property than what she had paid to build it. Though she tried to reopen her gallery in a different location, it never regained its original popularity. "I'm a great fan of progress," she said in a 1959 *Time* magazine story about freeway disruption. "But what a pity progress has to cost so much."[6]

Cutting a trench through the middle of the city wounded it in a way that has never fully healed. Stand near I-5 and your ears are filled with the endless roar of traffic and your nose is filled with toxic exhaust. Trying to get from one side of the freeway to the other is often difficult and uncomfortable. What used to be a short walk a few blocks downhill from the densely residential Capitol Hill neighborhood to the Cascade and South Lake Union neighborhoods north of downtown became a long meandering journey to a busy bridge crossing with dangerous intersections at each end. The result is that people stopped making these treks if they didn't need to, so neighborhoods were divided. In the twenty-first century, South Lake Union became the fastest-growing employment center in Washington State, and Capitol Hill is the state's densest residential neighborhood. But there is only a single bridge over I-5 that directly links the two neighborhoods, and the intersection at the base of it was twice voted Seattle's Worst Intersection by readers of *The Urbanist* (2017 and 2019). Contest organizer Troy Heerwagen summed up the feedback from readers by writing, "The intersection fails everyone."[7]

But as destructive as I-5 was for Capitol Hill, it was even worse for Beacon Hill south of downtown. A 1956 street map from before I-5 construction began shows dozens of streets connecting the mostly residential Beacon Hill to SoDo, the jobs-filled industrial district to its west, though it is not clear how many of these streets were actually usable due to the very steep hillside.[8] But freeway construction left only three accessible places to cross I-5 in the more than 6 miles from Interstate 90 in downtown Seattle to the southern city limit. The worst stretch, from South Holgate Street to South Lucille Street, forms an uncrossable barrier 2.3 miles long. Since the early 1960s, people living on Beacon Hill have been able to see SoDo and the West Seattle waterfront, but they haven't easily been able to walk or bike there.

Most of this stretch of Beacon Hill is among Seattle's historically redlined neighborhoods. Redlining refers to a systemic and racist practice by the real estate and banking industries to purposefully disinvest in neighborhoods where people of color lived, a practice that was largely legal until 1968. Redlining paired effectively with racially restrictive covenants on home deeds that outright banned people of color from owning a home in many neighborhoods. This racist housing practice was legal in Seattle until City Councilmember Sam Smith successfully led an effort to pass an open housing measure in 1968, just weeks after the assassination of Dr. Martin Luther King Jr.

For most of the twentieth century, people of color were able to live in only certain parts of the city, and financial institutions would either refuse to invest there or offer unfair terms. Perhaps the best visual of this practice is a now-infamous 1936 "security map" of Seattle created by the Home Owners' Loan Corporation under the supervision of state and federal appraisers.[9] The map color-coded neighborhoods based on how "desirable" they were for investors, capturing a snapshot of how the real estate industry treated neighborhoods differently. The whiter neighborhoods received better ratings. Beacon Hill was mostly given the lowest rating of "hazardous."

When designing I-5 two decades later, engineers included eleven freeway crossings in the 2.5 miles of "desirable" neighborhoods north of the Lake Washington Ship Canal, but zero crossings for a nearly equal distance next to "hazardous" Beacon Hill. The consequences of this act of state-sponsored racism are still felt today. Freeway projects across the nation were often sold as "urban renewal" projects, and the displacement of lower-income communities of color was intentional. Highway planners would "renew" neighborhoods by demolishing them. But in the 1960s, people started to fight back.

Seattle Neighbors Revolt against Freeways, 1960-1972

In the early days of freeways, the selection of routes was largely made by engineers at the State Department of Highways (one of the agencies that preceded the Washington State Department of Transportation) or the Seattle Engineering Department (an agency that preceded the Seattle Department of Transportation). A 1947 state traffic study for the Seattle area formed the basis for the freeway network plans that followed.[10] Seattle and Washington State conducted a series of studies during the 1950s that formed many of the specific route plans, including I-5, the R. H. Thomson Expressway, the Bay Freeway along the south end of Lake

Union, and I-90. But it wasn't until President Dwight D. Eisenhower's Federal Aid Highway Act in 1956 promised to cover 90 percent of the cost of qualified highway projects that development of these freeway plans accelerated.[11] Suddenly many different freeway projects all were moving at the same time.

The next year, Seattle developed a comprehensive plan that included these major freeway projects, and voters approved a bond measure to fund them. Seattle voters would approve another roads funding package in 1960, including funds for the Thomson Expressway and the Bay Freeway. Not only were there many new freeway plans at this time, those freeways also grew bigger and wider. Nobody knew how long the federal highway funding would last, so states and cities across the nation raced to build as many major freeways as they could before the flow of cash was cut off. Seattle and Washington State were no exceptions.

But as details about the expanded plans started to come out, opposition formed. The R. H. Thomson Expressway (initially called the Empire Expressway) was especially damaging to neighborhoods the length of the city. It would tear a north-south path through the eastern part of the city, including Rainier Valley, Judkins Park, the Central Area, Madison Valley, Montlake, and the Washington Park Arboretum, before crossing under Union Bay in a tunnel, resurfacing on the University of Washington campus, and cutting through Ravenna in the north end. The Thomson Expressway would displace as many as eight thousand people in addition to paving over acres of parkland.[12] The first significant acts of resistance came from a handful of Montlake residents, a representative from The Mountaineers—a Seattle alpine club and conservation organization founded in 1906—and architect Victor Steinbrueck, who all opposed plans to destroy ninety-one homes in the Montlake neighborhood to build the Thomson. They voiced their concerns during a 1961 hearing, but their complaints were ignored. The city council voted to approve the home-destroying route in 1962. That's when neighbors filed the first lawsuit against the freeway.[13]

But while the lawsuit would force the State Department of Highways to host another public hearing, it did little to change the plans or the pace of the planning. The mid-1960s saw an enormous amount of freeway planning and construction in Seattle. Construction crews were busy for most of the decade tearing down neighborhoods in the path of I-5 and building its complicated structure. The State Route 520 bridge was completed in 1963, connecting Eastside communities across Lake Washington to the center of Seattle. The bridge included ramps leading to the future Thomson Expressway, though neighbors along its path continued to sue to delay the project. Opponents packed four hundred people into one 1963 hearing at city council chambers. They also packed a series of hearings in 1965. But the demonstrations of public concern didn't stop the plans, and the city council voted in 1965 to approve the controversial Thomson route. Neighbors kept suing and were able to delay it many times.[14]

In 1966, newspapers published concept images depicting a massive trench cutting through the Mount Baker Ridge to carry the future I-90 into the city, complete with a large interchange with the Thomson and another large interchange with I-5.[15] With I-5 construction nearly complete and the extent of its destruction clear, the concept images helped to grow public opposition against freeway projects. Highway planners still tried to move their projects forward, but they were increasingly met with resistance. When the city tried to hold a hearing about the Bay Freeway in 1967, Steinbrueck drew a sketch of the planned freeway in what is now South Lake Union that depicted the elevated structure blocking the view north from downtown, complete with squiggly lines representing the exhaust from all the cars rising into the sky. The sketch was published in the *P-I* in 1967 with a headline calling it the "Concrete Curtain."[16] Central Area neighborhood groups and the Urban League started organizing efforts against the I-90 and Thomson plans in the neighborhood, which was the heart of Black community in the city. The Urban League hosted a forum in 1967 called "Third Bridge . . . Southern Wall to the Ghetto?"[17]

The political pressure led Mayor James d'Orma "Dorm" Braman and Governor Daniel Evans to support a redesign of the I-90 and Thomson interchange.[18] A new regional transportation plan was released that, while maintaining the freeway routes, added rapid rail transit to them. Mayor Braman also tried to build support for scaling the Thomson back from an expressway to a "parkway," but these changes would also have cost the project much of its federal funding because it would no longer meet the necessary qualifications. Regardless, none of these proposed changes slowed the growing opposition to the freeways. Instead, the freeway revolt spread across the region from neighbors in Lake City and Bothell fighting freeway plans for State Route 522 to Eastside communities organizing as the East Side League to fight plans for an Interstate 605 connecting Auburn to Bothell.

Back in Seattle, anger and frustration boiled over. "The citizens' freeway revolt broke out again yesterday," wrote *Seattle P-I* reporter Shelby Scates on October 14, 1969. Twenty community groups were again protesting against plans for a third bridge across Lake Washington designed to carry I-90 into downtown Seattle. Protesters argued in a letter that the new bridge, along with the rest of the freeway connection, would "divide and probably destroy the established residential communities of the city it passes through."[19]

But freeway opponents at this time did more than write letters. Thousands of people marched down Azalea Way through the arboretum in May 1969 to protest plans to destroy part of the beloved park in order to build the Thomson. The *P-I* published a photo of a child holding up a sign nearly as big as they were that said Keep the Arboretum Green with a picture of a flower. Other signs said Stop the Freeway Invasion, Sink the Fourth Lake Bridge, Plan for People Not Just Cars, Don't Pave Our Birds, Our Right to Breathe, Parks Not Parking Lots, and How Much Is a Park Worth?[20] Speakers at the rally, called Save, Don't Pave, included a deputy mayor, two state representatives, and Central Area community organizer Flo Ware. Ware was a foster parent who volunteered an enormous amount of her time working to improve schools and parks in her majority-Black community, which had long been neglected. She also helped lead the effort to convince Seattle to buy and renovate the building that would become the Central Area Senior Center, an important community institution to this day. A small park was named in her honor shortly after her death in 1981, located just one block from the planned route of the Thomson Expressway.[21]

People also gathered in significant numbers in the Mount Baker Ridge area to organize against the I-90 plans to cut a huge trench through the neighborhood. They fought the entire concept of a freeway that entered Seattle at this point, arguing that interstate traffic could take I-405 on the Eastside to bypass the city.[22] But as 1969 turned into 1970, many people were growing impatient with asking nicely for change.

"Disenchanted youth was in the front ranks of the outcry," wrote a *Seattle Daily Times* reporter following a June 1970 design hearing about the Seattle I-90 plans.[23] "The attack by the young was as unconventional as their mode of dress. Wearing sandals and paint-splattered jeans, young persons burned paper money and read passages from pocket books. They talked about the threat from carbon monoxide and hydrocarbons. They grilled E. I. Roberts, district engineer, like a swarm of 1930-circa detectives belaboring a murder suspect. They engaged in shouting matches with highway officials. They jolted and they offended." Some of the young people fighting the freeway plan were members of the Seattle Liberation Front, a fiercely anti–Vietnam War group created following the 1969 dissolution of Students for a Democratic Society. The short-lived SLF was best known for helping to lead a protest at the federal courthouse in Seattle earlier in 1970 that turned into a riot when police arrived. That protest led to the high-profile mistrial of the "Seattle Seven." But this time they weren't protesting the federal case against the "Chicago Eight" or the US invasion of Cambodia or the massacre at Kent State. They were protesting plans for a racist freeway.

At the same time, I-5 itself became a controversial protest ground. Students outraged by the Kent State killings took over UW campus before marching through the streets of the University District and then onto I-5 via the Forty-Fifth Street ramps. Protesters disrupted freeway traffic and made it all the way to Capitol Hill before police confronted them with tear gas and batons. Police beat students who were protesting police violence against students, which inspired more protests, including more protests on I-5. Though no organizing body claimed the I-5 march to be their idea, the action drew the city's attention. It was the focus of news reports at the time. The freeway was a symbol of the powers that be, making it a potent if not dangerous place to protest.

Most of the organized opposition to freeways in Seattle was not quite as brash as the SLF. But after witnessing I-5 construction carve a grim path of destruction through the city, the movement to stop the other planned freeways kept growing. "Unless the present trend here is stopped, this scenic area will be covered by a vast grid of bridges, freeways, traffic interchanges, cross-linkages and access roads," wrote Maynard Arsove to Governor Evans in 1968. Arsove had recently formed Citizens Against the R. H. Thomson (CARHT), and the group got to work building political power to "revolt" against further freeway projects in the city. They looked at Los Angeles, which had "surrendered 70 per cent of city land to automobiles" and rejected that future for Seattle.[24]

But stopping the Thomson was going to be difficult. For one, it was already partially constructed during the building of the SR 520 bridge that opened in 1963. Ramps to and from the Thomson were tied into the interchange, including an overpass that crossed part of Union Bay. The State Department of Highways was so confident that the Thomson was coming soon, they built these expensive sections even before the Thomson was officially approved and funded. Additionally, the Department of Highways had already purchased properties that were in the path of the Thomson. The department had even demolished the structures on a few of them. This triggered a deterioration of property values all along the corridor as people prepared for their homes to be purchased and destroyed, too. Many owners stopped investing to maintain their houses, assuming they were about to be bulldozed. People who wanted or needed to move found that nobody would buy their homes, putting pressure on the state to buy the troubled properties. After all, the decrease in marketability was the state's fault. The state and city were burning through federal highway funds buying houses for a project that was facing increasing public opposition. One of CARHT's first wins was to get the state to stop buying homes along the corridor while the freeway was still up for debate.

In 1967, the freeway resistance had no choice but to get political. Montlake neighbors lost a years-long lawsuit against the Thomson when the court determined that neighbors couldn't sue the city for planning the freeway through their neighborhood because the route was only a plan and wasn't officially confirmed yet. But that was the puzzle for neighbors. The public hearing for the project had already occurred, and this was the time to take legal action. But how were they supposed to take legal action against a project if they didn't have the final details of that project? Over the next several years, the rise of the environmental movement combined with local concerns about the lack of public participation in major infrastructure decisions, and the result was the creation of Washington's State Environmental Protection Act in 1971.[25] SEPA would require public agencies to develop documents outlining project details and the anticipated impacts it would have on people, places, and ecosystems. The act would also ensure that the public was involved in the process before final decisions were made.

But Seattle's freeway revolt did not have the luxury of waiting for SEPA. If they were going to stop the Thomson, the Bay Freeway, and a third bridge across Lake Washington, they had to gather a wide coalition of support and work to change the conversation and mindset around freeways in the city. They had to change the city's culture, which had until that point largely accepted the need for more freeways as a fact of life in a modern city.

The Racism of Freeway Culture, 1956-1972

The pursuit of improving the flow of car traffic had been the goal of cities, states, and the federal government almost since the vehicles had first arrived in cities at the very start of the twentieth century. After World War II, the United States turned much of its military infrastructure into a cars, freeways, and suburban development machine. President Eisenhower, a general during the war, championed the 1956 Federal Aid Highway Act in large part as an act of national security. Highways would facilitate evacuations and make it easier to move military personnel and equipment around the country. They would also be wide enough to land airplanes if needed. He saw Germany's limited-access autobahn highways at the end of the war and was convinced the United States needed something similar. But while the federal government's massive investment in freeways provided the means for building them, highways also had powerful political forces behind them. The highway building and automobile manufacturing industries were powerful lobbyists and major employers. Suburban developers grew increasingly powerful as a real estate gold rush kicked off on land near cities that had previously been too far away to be practical locations for neighborhoods. Highways enabled farmland and forests to become suburbs.

Changing the region's car-oriented culture was going to be a monumental task for the freeway revolt movement. They quickly formed alliances with other movements in the city, including the increasingly powerful historic preservationists like Victor Steinbrueck. Steinbrueck's 1967 "Concrete Curtain" sketch of the planned Bay Freeway in South Lake Union framed the project in a rather potent way. The elevated freeway blocked the view north from downtown,[26] and the reference to the Cold War's Iron Curtain tapped into the feeling that the freeways were constraining the city rather than freeing it. By placing the viewer on a city sidewalk facing the concrete expanse, the sketch directly confronts all the auto industry marketing depicting happy, free people cruising down the open road. Freeway planners at the time were so focused on the goal of moving traffic around the city that they were willing to force major sacrifices onto people and neighborhoods.

Before I-5 was constructed, freeway supporters downplayed problems like ugliness, noise, and a lack of crossings. But after I-5 opened in 1967, this was a difficult case to make, though some still tried. "The argument about harming neighborhoods by cutting them up with a freeway doesn't deserve refutation—a neighborhood is just as cut up by a four-lane road as by a 10-lane road . . . and the noise is about the same," wrote *Seattle Daily Times* copy editor Dick Hubbell in a 1970 op-ed piece arguing for a "really adequate Interstate 90."[27] But public opinion was shifting. The impact on neighborhoods was huge, and people could see that clearly. A group of twenty city organizations sent a letter to the State Highways Department (and the region's newspapers) questioning "whether the redevelopment of the city is the proper provenance of the State Highways Department."[28] By December 1967, Seattle Mayor Braman had shifted his stance in the face of mounting public resistance to the Thomson Expressway. The project was crumbling under its own weight—then the people of Seattle stood up and gave it a final blow.

"You are bringing a major arterial highway into an overcrowded city," said Central Area Citizens Committee member Ed Banks during a 1970 hearing about the planned Thomson and I-90 projects. The Central Area Citizens Committee oversaw creation of the Central Area Motivation Program, which is now known as Byrd Barr Place and is still serving the neighborhood as a food and housing safety net and advocacy organization. "And it don't make sense to me that you, having run one ditch right straight through the city," referring to I-5, "that you allow another major 8, 10-lane highway to be brought into the city as a means of transporting cars. I don't see it, and I don't understand it." The crowd gathered in the room cheered wildly in support of Banks's comment. An estimated nine hundred people had shown up to the hearing to express their opposition to the major freeway projects and to vow to continue organizing to fight them. Their voices were captured wonderfully in the 2018 documentary *Ramps to Nowhere* directed by Minda Martin, who dug up powerful audio recordings of the hearing.[29] The audio captured a moment that was the result of a huge and wide-ranging organizing effort by a lot of people in a lot of communities. In a contemporary interview for the documentary, Dan Gibbs of CARHT stood in front of a house in Montlake and talked about the organizing effort. "In this living room, we had one of the strangest coalitions you can imagine. We had the Bellevue Garden Clubs and the Black Panthers all meeting in the same room planning."

Though the city's antifreeway movement may have started simmering in living rooms in Montlake, it boiled over in the Central Area and Judkins Park. "The thing that should be made clear right quick is that the freeway is a big trick by Tricky Dick, the big man, to divide the Black community," said Elmer Dixon during the hearing. Dixon was a founder of the Seattle Chapter of the Black Panther Party, which organized to inform the community about the destructive freeway plans. "It happened in Chicago. They built a freeway called the John F. Kennedy Freeway right down State Street. It split up the Black community. They're trying to do this in all the major cities across the nation to divide Black people. When they subpoena the people and ask the people, 'Can we build the freeway in your community?' tell them to stick their subpoena up their ass. Period."

The speakers at the hearing didn't just see a freeway in the plans, they saw a pattern of mistreatment. "It's very important for people to understand the priorities involved," said Kathy Howlett, another member of the Black Panther Party. "In fact the priorities involved in this community concerning the highways are just a microcosm of the priorities pushed forth by this country pertaining to the welfare of the people. It's very important that you understand what priorities are pushed and for what reasons. . . . The only people being served by this freeway in the long run are the people in power, and the people being affected by the freeway have not been asked about it, the people in the Black community have not been consulted about it." Another speaker at the hearing declined to give his name, then made it clear that the community was not going to allow these freeways to happen. "I'd like to go down on record now that there are certain elements in the Black community prepared and ready to deal with this situation by any means necessary. They can go over, around, under, but they are not coming through the Central Area."

Much of the community opposition was organized by a handful of people who set out to knock on the doors of people living in the path of the proposed freeway and tell them about it. Door after door, they found Black residents who had no idea their house was all but slated for demolition. One of the organizers was Larry Gossett, a life-long community organizer who would later serve on the King County Council for twenty-seven years. "As often occurs in cities across our nation, the intersection of freeways was often in low-income, inner city ghetto communities like the Central Area was in the '60s," Gossett told Martin during a contemporary interview for the documentary. "People felt it was unfair that the burden and primary sacrifice for the creation of mobility for middle class whites was the loss of homes and neighborhoods of working class or low-income Blacks. We did not think it's fair that 'urban renewal' essentially in this country was beginning to mean 'Negro removal,'" he said, paraphrasing the great James Baldwin.

When a highway agency digs a trench or constructs an elevated viaduct to carry a wide, loud, and polluting freeway through a neighborhood, the walkability of that existing neighborhood is demolished along with any homes and businesses that used to stand in the way. The effect this had on Black economic progress in the middle of the twentieth century was immense. For example, just look at three different neighborhoods that called themselves Black Wall Street in the first half of the twentieth century, a time when Jim Crow laws enforced segregation. Black Wall Street in Tulsa, Oklahoma, was the site of a horrific 1921 massacre in which a mob of white people murdered three hundred Black people in a thriving majority-Black neighborhood and business district, then burned down the homes and businesses of thousands more. But try to find Black Wall Street today, and you'll instead see the fate that followed the massacre: Interstate 244, the Crosstown Expressway. It was constructed right on top of the neighborhood.[30] Jackson Ward was also once known as Black Wall Street in Richmond, Virginia.[31] The Richmond-Petersburg Turnpike flattened a path the width of a full city block when it was constructed in the early 1950s, destroying homes and businesses as it tore through the neighborhood.[32] Black Wall Street in Durham, North Carolina, was a major financial center for Black community and businesses for decades during Jim Crow. The nearby Black neighborhood of Hayti was dismantled through a series of "urban renewal" projects that demolished businesses and homes starting in the 1950s and culminating in the construction of the Durham Freeway (NC 147), which flattened a huge swath of the neighborhood and separated it from the city center.[33]

The pain wasn't reserved for only Black people. In Seattle, I-5 destroyed large parts of the Chinatown–International District, especially Nihonmachi (Japantown) centered around Main Street. This neighborhood destruction followed the shameful and racist incarceration of anyone of Japanese descent during World War II. "I don't think it was ever really a Nihonmachi any more after the evacuation," Sally Kazama told the *Seattle Daily Times* in 1976.[34] Kazama grew up in Seattle's Japantown and turned twenty-one the day Japanese and Japanese American people on Bainbridge Island were forced into internment camps. Kazama would later be forced to join them, as she detailed in her testimony to the Commission on Wartime Relocation and Internment of Civilians in 1981.[35] When residents returned after internment, they discovered that part of the old neighborhood had been turned into a development called Yesler Terrace to house wartime workers. Then about fifteen years later, the neighborhood was split in half by construction of I-5, an act that faced little resistance because "it was before the vogue for social protest," according to the 1976 article. "Japanese-Americans were too busy struggling to survive."

Gossett and other organizers were trying to prevent the same fate for the Judkins Park and Atlantic neighborhoods, which were going to be destroyed by the planned interchange of I-90 and the Thomson Expressway. Few of the residents there knew about the state's plans when Gossett started knocking on doors, as he told Martin in the documentary. "[Judkins Park] was the primary community that was supposed to be taken completely out if the R. H. Thomson had gone through and the I-90 had gone all the way through. And the only reason there was a compromise to build a lid over that whole area and still allow housing is because of the door-to-door work in all the local houses in the Judkins community.... In the '60s very little attention was ever given to it because most people were working class or very poor that lived there. But we decided to go door-to-door and mobilize people there against the freeways because they were the most directly impacted." So many people turned out to that 1970 hearing that it was extended over multiple days.

The result was not just that elected officials finally had to embrace the freeway opposition; the organized efforts also built a voting majority against freeways in Seattle. In 1972, the projects were put to a vote of the people. The dual referendums were the final chances for the Thomson and Bay Freeways to stay alive. Seattle City Council was joined by 71 percent of voters in rejecting the Thomson, and 55 percent of voters overrode the city council's support for the Bay Freeway in South Lake Union, rejecting that project as well.[36]

People who lived in the Central Area and other neighborhoods in the path of freeways stood up and said that their neighborhoods had more value than a freeway. They called out the racist ulterior motives behind the plans, and they saved their communities from destruction. In the process, they educated the public and helped form a voting majority. In other words, they changed Seattle's transportation culture.

But while Seattle's runaway car culture, drunk on federal highway funding, was knocked down, it was not out for good. Those freeway projects were defeated, and the speed of building freeways slowed way down, but they didn't stop. The fight against I-90 ultimately failed, but it delayed the project by two decades and won some significant revisions to the original plan. The state agreed to construct a lid park over the freeway through the Judkins Park neighborhood rather than leave an open trench as originally planned. And because there was no Thomson Expressway, there was also no sprawling interchange. Instead, the neighborhood got a park, home to a major section of the I-90 biking and walking trail linking Beacon Hill, Judkins Park, and Rainier Avenue to a unique trail tunnel through Mount Baker Ridge. The lid park opened in sections in the late '80s and early '90s, and the city named it in honor of the late councilmember Sam Smith in 1998.

Riding through the bike tunnel today is a magical experience, and I love showing it to people. Emerging from the east portal and seeing Mount Rainier beyond vast Lake Washington is one of the most surprising bike-riding experiences anywhere. It doesn't offset the harm caused by the freeway, but it is special and a symbol of the significant wins the neighborhood earned even as it ultimately lost the fight. Decades later still, this lid park is set to cover not just I-90 but also Sound Transit's light-rail line to the Eastside. Judkins Park Station is under construction at the time of this writing. Where the state originally planned a massive cloverleaf-style interchange of two freeways, there will instead be a trail connecting homes to a light-rail station. That's a big difference. "We wanted to stop all freeways completely from that area, we were not successful at that," said Gossett in the documentary, "but at least the lid you see there, the playfield you see there, exists because of the struggle at that time."

Forward Bust: The Freeway Revolt Struggles to Boost an Alternative, 1968-1971

As difficult as it was, fighting freeways was the easy part. The freeway revolt movement found many eager allies inside homes on the ground wherever highway planners had drawn thick lines on a map. But people did need to get around in the growing region. Organizers knew they couldn't just be against freeways; they also needed to support a different way to move people and goods. The CARHT campaign's ask in 1968 was to halt freeway expansion in Seattle until a mass transit system could be constructed either alongside or in place of the automobile routes. CARHT's worry was that without transit, the freeways would turn Seattle into a city dependent on driving.[37] Thanks to the imposing and troubled construction of I-5 during much of the '60s, it wasn't terribly difficult to convince people that freeways could be at least as negative for the city as positive. But it would prove much more difficult for transit supporters to build a successful voting bloc for a freeway alternative, especially because state law was stacked against them.

The effort to build a rapid transit system in the Seattle region kicked off around 1965 as one part of a package of civic investments known as Forward Thrust. The rapid transit system included a forty-seven-mile, thirty-station train system as well as a major expansion of bus transit service. The transit section of the plan was estimated to cost $1.15 billion, but the federal government was prepared to cover two-thirds of that. That's less than the 90 percent that the federal government covered for freeway projects, but it was significant. Forward Thrust needed voters in 1968 to approve $385 million in property taxes (about $2.8 billion in 2020 dollars). People were increasingly against freeways, but were they in favor of transit? "The only way we can fail safe is with arterials, expressways, and a modern bus system," wrote Bellevue developer Vick Gould, leader of the rail-transit opposition group Citizens for Sensible Transit, in a letter to the Municipal League before the vote. "Let us not financially cripple ourselves for the next 40 years for a system that all experience proves to be a loser."[38]

A majority of voters (51 percent) said "yes" to the transit investment, but it wasn't enough. State law at the time required a 60 percent majority in order to pass a property tax increase at the ballot. It failed, along with measures to invest in low-income housing, storm-water drainage, and community centers. A measure to build the Kingdome baseball and football stadium, along with a youth service center and money for parks, sewers, firefighters, and $82 million for arterial streets, passed on the same ballot.

But transit supporters weren't going down that easy. They tried a revamped and slightly larger version of the measure again in 1970, but this time the city's economy was in dire straits thanks to the 1969 "Boeing bust" in which tens of thousands of people lost their jobs at the region's largest employer as the company struggled to remain airborne.[39] Seattle's unemployment rate shot up to 10 percent in 1970, on its way to 14 percent in early 1971. Two real estate agents paid for a billboard that famously lampooned the economic mood at the time: "Will the last person leaving Seattle turn out the lights." This was a challenging moment to ask the region to invest in a future-facing transit system, and the measure received only 46 percent of the vote this time. Public support for transit had waned, and reaching 60 percent seemed hopeless. The federal funds set aside for the project went to the Metropolitan Atlanta Rapid Transit Authority's rail network instead. The defeats were a crushing blow to transit supporters. It is tantalizing to imagine what the region would be like today if those measures had passed.

Bicycle and unicycle riders on Lake Washington Boulevard during Bicycle Sunday in 1968, the first year for the car-free streets event. Museum of History and Industry, *Seattle P-I* photography archive, no. 1986.5.1050.

CHAPTER 4

Biking Is Reborn

The Boeing bust gave Seattle a head start on the national recession of the 1970s, triggered by the 1973 oil crisis. As Seattle would see again in the 2008 recession, people seeking ways to save money in difficult economic times found that and much more in the humble bicycle. The seeds of Seattle's 1970s bicycle movement had been planted in the previous decades. Bicycle sales grew throughout the 1950s and 1960s as lighter bikes with multiple gears and easy-to-use gear shifters and derailleurs became more widely available to Americans at the consumer level.[1] For a place as hilly as Seattle, it was a big deal to be able to quickly move a lever while pedaling to put a bike into a hill-climbing low gear. The Pacific Northwest Cycling Association had used these bikes to travel the region and support youth hostels. But by 1968, a new kind of bike-riding movement was ready to form, empowering advocates to push for bike-friendly changes to the city.

Some people had been trying to get the city to build bike paths, especially a bike path in Washington Park Arboretum, since the start of the decade. And there were a few cycling groups, such as the Boeing Employees Bicycle Club, which had about a hundred members as of 1968. But a much larger number of people who owned bicycles were not yet organized. Harry Coe, Northwest Vice President of the League of American Wheelmen (now known as the League of American Bicyclists), told the *Seattle Daily Times* in a June 1968 feature about the rise of bicycling that there were an estimated hundred thousand bicycles in King County. "Coe and other wheelmen recognize that Seattle's hills and physical layout present special problems for cyclists not found in all cities," wrote reporter John Haigh. "But the main problem is automobile traffic, and the difficulty of avoiding it."[2] Coe expanded on this point in a 1968 letter to City Councilmember Sam Smith, writing, "The continuing expanding development of freeways has made it increasingly more difficult for bicyclists to go anywhere." But by developing a system of designated bike routes, the city could create "a happy marriage of the auto and the bicycle."[3]

The new bicycle movement was very different from the city's first bike boom. At the turn of the twentieth century, the wealthy and powerful saw promise in the bicycle as a way to unlock land value, and the city sought to create paths and roads that privileged bicycle riding. That first bike movement morphed into an automobile movement as soon as cars arrived, and Seattle has been under the spell of car culture ever since. In the 1960s and 1970s, the new bicycle movement grew within the context of car culture, and people were biking on streets where cars were undoubtedly the priority. The movement was at times subcultural, attempting to exist within a dominant car culture, and at other times countercultural, challenging or subverting elements of car culture.

"Car culture is something we're all forced to participate in because it's so big," said Dr. Adonia Lugo in an interview for this book. Lugo is a cultural anthropologist who has studied bicycle cultures in many places, including LA and Seattle. "Those of us who bought into the idea that it would be a good thing to have ways to get around other than driving, we're trying to change the culture. . . . That's where you can see these cultures revealed; when they're in conflict with each other."

Unlike the first bike boom, in which seemingly every little detail about bicycling was chronicled in newspapers, the number of people biking grew quietly throughout the 1960s. The Mountaineers lobbied the city of Seattle to build a bicycle path from Seward Park to Green Lake, noting in a 1965 letter to the Seattle Parks Department that "Seattle has upward of 120,000 bicycles and no special facilities."[4] The club proposed "a network of bikeways and bike routes that ultimately will cover most of the city. . . . Recreation for young and old, as well as commuting safely on bicycles to school and work, will be our goals." While the letter suggests that at least some people were aware of the growing popularity of bicycling, the bicycling public did not have much political power. The Parks Department did not take action on the letter's requests, but the idea stuck around.

Finding Each Other at Bicycle Sunday, 1968-1980

The moment that propelled bicycling into the civic spotlight was the brainchild of a woman who didn't even ride a bike. It rained all day November 16, 1967, which is to say that it was a very typical Seattle evening when Mia Mann walked into the regular meeting of the Seattle Board of Park Commissioners with a simple idea that would change her city forever. Mann was active on city and nonprofit boards, especially in support of city beautification and arts efforts. She seems to have mostly stayed under the radar. But she was a major force behind at least two beloved and iconic Seattle ideas. In 1966, she led a successful campaign to convince Seattle City Council that the Department of Engineering needed to hire a professional arborist to run a street tree program. The council agreed, and that program still exists today, overseeing about 40,000 of the city's 130,000 street trees. Seattle's lush, tree-lined streets are iconic and treasured, and much of that greenery is thanks to Mann and the street tree program she helped start. Her husband, Frederick M. Mann, was an architect for the University of Washington who laid out the famous cherry trees in the quad and helped design the park grounds in Discovery Park, so the two of them were a potent power couple for Seattle's trees.[5]

Following her street tree success, Mia decided to push another idea being tried out in her hometown of Minneapolis: a car-free streets event.[6] Mia wrote a Seattle City Council resolution to create such an event, which included the clause "Whereas: The tyranny of the automobile must be offset in present and future urban amenities."[7] Her use of the word *tyranny* here suggests that she did not see her idea as existing in "a happy marriage" with automobiles. Instead, she was proposing a way to subvert car dominance. Mia Mann's idea met resistance from those in charge. First, the Parks Department tried to ignore her, but she would have none of that.[8] Then the Parks superintendent said they couldn't do it because it would interfere with vehicle traffic and because the Parks Department didn't have jurisdiction to close streets.[9] Mia still refused to give up. Eventually, she got a powerful city councilmember named Myrtle Edwards involved. Edwards was responsible for major parks efforts, including the city's acquisition of a closing gas plant at the north end of Lake Union that would one day become Gas Works Park. Edwards ran with Mia's open streets idea, gathering council support and convening multiple city departments to make it happen. Her support was more than enough to win approval from the Parks board. They agreed to hold a trial event in the spring just to see how it would go.[10]

The plan was simple: put up signs closing a two-mile stretch of Lake Washington Boulevard to cars starting at Seward Park in South Seattle and heading north. They then invited people to bike freely on the boulevard and on the forested roads through Seward Park without fear of cars. The whole thing cost the city less than $500, and Mia Mann, Harry Coe, and coaches from Rainier Beach Cottage School volunteered to carry out much of the organizing and promotion. "People have to get hold of their lives and get out in the open," Mia told the *Seattle Post-Intelligencer* before the first Bicycle Sunday event. "The automobile just isn't doing this for us. I haven't ridden a bike in years, but I'll be out there."[11]

Nobody, it seems from news reports, expected the number of people who showed up April 28, 1968. An estimated five thousand people brought their bikes to Lake Washington during the seven hours the road was closed to cars. The sole food vendor was completely overwhelmed by the number of hungry event goers and sold twice as much food in one day as they did in a typical week. The forty-eight bikes available to rent were all claimed before the event even officially began. The few restrooms available "were in rather sad shape by mid afternoon," according to the city's follow-up evaluation of the first event.[12] In other words, Bicycle Sunday was a smash hit. "Originally it was thought that several hundred would be the basis of a successful operation," wrote Parks Superintendent Edward J. Johnson to Mayor James d'Orma Braman. "In this respect the turnout was overwhelming." City leaders clamored to show their support for the popular event and call for more. Soon the city was hosting Bicycle Sundays several times a month in locations across the city. More than half a century later, the Parks Department still hosts Bicycle Sunday on the same stretch of Lake Washington Boulevard.

But Bicycle Sunday did more than just create a fun space for a few hours during the summer. The simple act of kicking cars off a street for a few hours demonstrated to people the benefits of public spaces. In the city's deeply entrenched car culture, getting out on a bike on a car-free street could be a radical experience. Riding down the centerline without any fear of death was liberating and empowering, and people who experienced Bicycle Sunday pressed local leaders to hold more car-free bike events in other areas.

The Bicycle Sunday concept continued to be popular, and within a few years other nearby communities, including Mercer Island, hosted their own Bicycle Sunday events.[13] But the most ambitious leap came somewhat unexpectedly from the Washington State Highways Department. In July 1974, the state decided to open the Seattle express lanes of Interstate 5 for a day to people on bikes. It was a major hit. People could bike in the car-free lanes more than four miles from Cherry Street near City Hall downtown to the Northeast Forty-Second Street ramp in the University District, and a *P-I* reporter said the only complaint she'd heard was that the route should have extended another three and a half miles, to Northgate. She asked a state highway engineer about extending the route, and he replied that they were concerned about there being less separation between the express lanes and the general freeway lanes. But he unfortunately continued talking, saying, "We're also concerned about the rubbernecking motorists not knowing what's going on and gawking at the girls."[14]

The state opened the express lanes to people biking again in May the next year to kick off Seattle's third annual Bicycle Week, an effort to encourage people to try biking to work.[15] Bike Week was also a hit and is still an annual tradition, though it has since grown to span the whole month of May. The 1975 express lanes event was extended a couple of miles farther north to include the Ravenna Boulevard and Northgate ramps. No crashes from gawking motorists were reported.

Bike Week had become so popular by 1976 that major politicians— including then-Washington Attorney General Slade Gorton and Seattle City Councilmembers John Miller, George Benson, Tim Hill, and Paul Kraabel—led a big celebratory group bike ride from Seattle Center to Pioneer Square.[16] After a demonstration from unicyclists and old-timey high-wheel bicycle riders, people who were heading back north could take the car-free I-5 express lanes. Most of these politicians were Republicans, and all went on to have long political careers in city, county, state, and federal governments. Gorton would lead a similar ride each May for years to come. In the mid-1970s, Seattle's Democratic Mayor Wes Uhlman was building bike lanes and trails while Republican leaders were holding mass bike rides through downtown and on the I-5 express lanes. Biking was strongly bipartisan.

In 1978, Bike Day on the express lanes was delayed because the Seattle Supersonics were playing a home game in the NBA finals against the Washington Bullets that day (a heartbreaking game-four overtime loss). The express lanes Bike Day was held the following month.[17] Bike Day on the I-5 express lanes continued as an annual Bike Week tradition for fifteen years, but it declined by the late 1980s. For a couple of years near the end, the express lanes were closed to cars for KidsDay, a day of free activities for children all across the city, such as free entrance to museums and the Space Needle.[18] In February 1991, while US troops were fighting in Iraq, the Seattle Coalition for Peace in the Middle East hosted a bicycle rally on the express lanes to promote energy conservation and peace.[19] After that, special events would make use of the express lanes from time to time, such as 1995's Beat the Heat fund-raiser bike race to benefit the Special Olympics and time-trial bike races in the mid-'90s.[20] But the memory of Bike Day faded away.

The start of Bicycle Sunday in 1968 was something of a coming-out party for Seattle's growing bicycle revival. Politicians saw that many people were deeply interested in biking. People with bikes realized they should use their numbers to get organized and start asking for better conditions for biking, and people who didn't bike saw the crowds and thought it looked like fun. Within weeks of the first event, Harry Coe of the League of American Wheelmen was rallying political support for a citywide bike route network. Basically, he was asking the city to put up signs to help people find the best side streets to use to get around on a bike while avoiding busy streets as much as possible. Whenever a bike route crossed a busy street, signs would alert people driving cars to look out for people biking. The signed bike routes were a small step, but they could be done quickly and represented perhaps the first time since the turn of the twentieth century that the city's Department of Engineering was tasked with thinking about how someone on a bike might get around town. Each sign was estimated to cost seven dollars, but there was no bike budget at all before then. The department had to start somewhere. "That is also the reasoning behind the bicycle days and the bikeways proposed by Seattle's 'bike lobby,'" wrote the *Seattle Daily Times*' John Haigh in a June 1968 feature on the city's cycling comeback. "They've suffered in silence for years, and they think the time has come to speak up."[21]

Coe had indeed waited a very long time. He was a runner for Team USA during the 1908 London Olympics and had biked all over Seattle as a child. "You could ride downtown without much competition from automobiles," he told the *Seattle Daily Times* in 1968. Coe also wrote a letter to the *Seattle Post-Intelligencer* around the same time saying that the first Bicycle Sunday reminded him of those early days. "It was a day which will be long remembered as one of Seattle's finest for a lot of people who too seldom get together at one place to enjoy something which they all have in common, namely, love of bicycle riding," he wrote. "Without a doubt it was one of the largest groups of bicyclists ever assembled on a single day since the 'Gay Nineties.'"[22] He was eighty-three in 1968 when the city started putting up his long-sought bike route signs. The sheer number of bicyclists who participated in the first Bicycle Sunday gave the plan the popular push it needed to win approval. Signs started going up within months of the first event, and fifty miles of signed bike routes were installed across the city in the first year. Some of these weathered green signs are still in place, bearing a pictogram of a bicycle and reading simply "Bike Route."

But some people wanted more than signs. They had their sights set on something far more ambitious, expensive, and politically difficult. While stepping carefully between railroad ties on family walks along the nearly abandoned train tracks in northeast Seattle, a handful of people got a radical idea: what if this seemingly useless railroad were a biking and walking trail instead?

Saving the Railroad That Saved Seattle, 1970-1980

The railroad line through northeast Seattle had not always been as quiet as it was in the 1960s, with only a few train runs a month. Neighbors at that time got used to walking along the rails without much concern that a locomotive might come barreling down on them. Most rail traffic had been routed to other lines with more capacity and faster routes to major port terminals. But without those rails, Seattle as we know it today might not even exist.

Much of the early white settler investment in Seattle had a major prize in mind: the port terminus of Northern Pacific's transcontinental railroad. Northern Pacific had indicated that it intended to terminate its transcontinental line in Tacoma instead of Seattle, so settlers gathered resources to build Seattle's first railroad in an attempt to connect the line to the south of the city. But the narrow-gauge Seattle and Walla Walla Railroad never made it anywhere close to Walla Walla as the name suggested, instead barely making it beyond the Seattle city limits by reaching Renton and Newcastle to the south and east of Lake Washington. Though much of the route would eventually become a major rail corridor, at the time it was not enough to change Northern Pacific's decision to make Tacoma their primary terminus and run only branchline service up to Seattle.[23]

So Thomas Burke and Daniel Gilman launched a rather desperate plan to take their city's future into their own hands. Rather than try to hopelessly lobby Northern Pacific to change its terminus plan, these men founded the Seattle, Lake Shore, and Eastern Railway in 1885 to either force Northern Pacific's hand or go broke trying. They immediately got to work investing a significant amount of their own money, gathering contributions from other area settlers, and raising investment funds from people back East. The plan was to build a railroad north from the downtown waterfront to the nearby industrial town of Ballard, then head east across the city and around the north end of Lake Washington. From there, the line split into two directions. One line was supposed to head north to Canada via the town of Snohomish while the other headed east to Snoqualmie Pass via the town of Gilman (now known as Issaquah). Seattle provided space along the waterfront for the railroad, then the boosters worked to convince settler landowners along the planned path to donate the land needed for the railway.[24]

Communities and industry popped up and grew all along the new rail line, helping to further grow the city and region. Though the railway didn't quite reach Snoqualmie Pass as originally planned, it was enough. Northern Pacific needed the Seattle, Lake Shore, and Eastern Railway to maintain its hold on the region amid incoming competition from the Great Northern Railway, so Northern Pacific bought Seattle's line in 1892 and connected it to the transcontinental lines. The Seattle boosters had won, and Seattle became the major port they'd hoped it would be. "The city of Seattle should always retain a warm place in its municipal heart for the little railway that came to its rescue in the darkest hours of Seattle's history and fought for Seattle in its commercial supremacy against all powerful odds," said Burke after the railway's sale to Northern Pacific.[25]

In the late 1960s, Estell Berteig and some other northeast Seattle neighbors dug up this forgotten story about the defunct railway that ran through their neighborhood. It was hard to imagine that this quiet, overgrown railway had once saved the city's business ambitions and transformed the region. They were inspired to reclaim the story and the railway for the people of the city. Berteig and a group of neighbors and advocates got together to promote a new vision for the railway that would make it the central artery of the city's walking and biking network. And their history research gave them a name for their idea: the Burke-Gilman Trail. As bold and transformative as their idea was for

Seattle, it would also reverberate throughout the country, inspiring and setting legal precedents for the national rails-to-trails movement.

The idea for the trail bounced around for a couple of years in the late 1960s, and a group of organizers formed the Burke-Gilman Trail Park Committee. Berteig was a founding member, along with Jim Todd, Sandy Wood, Mamie Rockafellar, Nancy Todd, Merrill Hille, Frank McChesney, and Robert Metz. Berteig, Wood, and Hille gave a lecture in 2018 that went into details about all the work they put into the effort.[26] The committee's work turned into a full sprint in 1971 when the group of organizers found out that the newly formed Burlington Northern (the result of a major railroad merger) was planning to abandon the rail line. They thought that maybe they could get the railroad to simply give the railway to the city. "People who were investing in land north of the city gave a piece of the property to help save our city," said Berteig of those original land donors back when the railway was first constructed. "Well, if our upright citizens donated land at the time to save our commercial possibilities, why can't Burlington Northern donate [the railway] back?"[27] It turned out the railroad wasn't going to just give away property for free. But couldn't they at least give the city the first crack at buying it? The committee contacted both Burlington Northern and the city of Seattle to suggest the idea and encourage them to negotiate. But capturing the city leadership's attention required an unconventional method.

A month after news broke that the railway would be abandoned, Berteig and a few other committee members brought some brochures and information to Seattle Center for an environmental fair. They had their information and sign-up sheet on their card table as they spread the word and explained their idea to attendees. That's when Berteig saw Mayor Wes Uhlman making his way through the fair. "Under the card table was our sleeping two-month-old," said Berteig during the 2018 lecture. "So I pushed her out in the way of the mayor. I didn't trip him. He stopped and he said, 'Who's this?' And I said, 'It's a little girl who's gonna need a bicycle trail.'" Then Berteig and Nancy Todd started talking about the project and mentioned that many of the properties had been donated. "That got his attention, and he said he was really interested in this project." They followed up with a meeting, and he made the project a priority. He penned a letter to Burlington Northern expressing interest in city ownership of the railway, and the railroad said they would sell it at fair market value.

Mayor Uhlman told the committee that if they were going to pull this off, especially in the midst of the Boeing bust recession, they were going to need to gather a lot of support and show it in a big way. So committee members, led by Merrill Hille, got to work organizing a huge public show of support they called a "hike-in," a play on the "sit-in" protests of the time. The plan was to get as many people as possible to join two simultaneous walks along the railroad tracks, one from the north and one from the south, that would converge for a rally at Matthews Beach Park on the Lake Washington shore just off the railway.

None of the Burke-Gilman Trail Park Committee members had ever organized an event like this before, so they reached out to the antifreeway organizers for advice. In the 2018 lecture, Hille recalled Margaret Tunks telling her, "stopping is different than starting." Tunks was an organizer of Citizens Against Freeways, focused on stopping the R. H. Thomson Expressway and the freeway planned for State Route 522 in North Seattle and the suburbs around the north end of Lake Washington. In fact, some people who were against the freeways were also against the trail.

A photo from 1971 depicts a group of maybe fifty people holding signs protesting the plan for the Burke-Gilman Trail. One sign says, "Enjoy But Who Pays?" Another sign noted in a news report but not shown in the photo said: "Yield to private property owners. We don't walk in your neighborhood. Save our privacy." Yet another sign said "Welcome Hell's Angles [sic]."[28] Some people opposed the trail because they wanted to acquire the property to expand their adjacent lots. One neighbor told the Seattle Daily Times that he wanted to turn it into a car parking spot. Others wanted to run trains on the line, though nobody proposed a clear business model for doing so. But others were afraid of the trail, arguing that it would bring crime to their quiet neighborhood and property values would drop. There just weren't many precedents to help people understand how such a trail would affect a neighborhood. It was a new idea. The Burke-Gilman Trail would need to be a test case for the city and the nation.

This is a phenomenon that shows up again and again in community organizing. Coalitions against change can form quickly. Fear of negatives, both real and imagined, can easily outweigh the potential benefits in people's minds. When trying to create something rather than stop something, however, organizers find that they need to gather support almost person by person. Community members need information about why a particular idea would be good for the city, a process that takes a lot more time and effort than a "Save the [fill in the blank]!" campaign. But this community education and movement-building process is vital because the supporter group has to be strong enough to overcome the push-back that every significant change faces.

To gather support for the 1971 hike-in, trail organizers called as many elected officials as possible and printed twelve thousand flyers to hand out and post around town. They even arranged extra city buses to help with transportation. More than a thousand people showed up. Many volunteers helped lead the hike-in, including famed mountaineer Tom Hornbein, who a decade earlier was on the first team to climb Mount Everest via its very challenging West Ridge.[29] Though the hike along the nearly flat railway was certainly easier than climbing the tallest mountain on earth, the political and legal fight to build the trail would prove to be a formidable challenge despite the strong demonstration of support. During the rally at Matthews Beach, trail organizers presented Mayor Uhlman with a petition in favor of the trail that already had sixteen hundred signatures. In addition, they had letters demonstrating bipartisan support from state legislators, Republican Governor Daniel Evans, and Democratic Senators Warren Magnuson and Henry "Scoop" Jackson. Mayor Uhlman and King County Executive John Spellman both spoke at the rally. Mayor Uhlman was so impressed by how it went, he sent a glowing letter to organizers shortly after the event:

> Too often in recent years visible demonstrations of group feelings have had counterproductive results, alienating the broad majority whose support must be won for any cause to succeed. This has been because of poor planning and lack of attention to important but bothersome technical matters, or because of hostile and embittered attitudes among the participants. Sunday's march triumphed over both of these possible pitfalls. . . . The benefits of this success are twofold. First, a large number of people throughout the Seattle area have become familiar and involved in a most favorable way with our efforts to create a linear park. In addition, the vigorous show of support on Sunday has strengthened our bargaining position with the railroad. No longer can it be alleged that this facility is desired by a small or homogenous group of people.[30]

But despite an overwhelming amount of support for the trail, there was still a long and difficult battle ahead. Though organizers didn't know it at the time, the first section of the trail wouldn't open for another six years. While they were hard at work organizing public and political support, the trail committee was also fighting legal battles to make sure the city would even have a chance to acquire the land in the first place. When Burlington Northern decided to sell the rail line, it was required to seek approval from the federal Interstate Commerce Commission (ICC). Because railroads cross state lines and have national importance, many of the laws and regulations governing them are federal. So even though the railway went through Seattle and ran behind people's backyards, the decision about how it could be sold would be made in Washington, DC. The ICC quickly approved the abandonment of the railway in 1971. To prevent a sale on the open market and to save the trail park vision, the local chapter of the Sierra Club and the Burke-Gilman Trail Park Committee challenged the ICC's decision and demanded that the agency study alternative sale options by drafting an environmental impact statement (EIS), a relatively new requirement established by the 1969 National Environmental Policy Act.[31] (Decades later, irony would strike when trail opponents used a similar EIS process to delay completion of the Ballard missing-link segment of the Burke-Gilman Trail.)

The ICC decided the trail committee was right and quickly issued a very short EIS that did not change the agency's decision. So with the help of donated legal services from the Sierra Club, the trail committee filed a brief arguing that the EIS should study more options, including one to prefer railway sales like these to the public. After many months of waiting, the ICC sided with the trail committee, setting a precedent that public agencies should have the first opportunity to purchase abandoned rail rights-of-way for creating public parkland. The decision would have enormous ramifications across the nation. "That opened the door, actually opened floodgates, to the future of rail-to-trail conversions across the country," said trail committee member Wood during the 2018 history lecture.[32]

The decision snowballed as communities across the nation sought to acquire defunct railway lines and turn them into trails and parks. Hidden within a major railroad deregulation act in 1976 was funding for rail-trails, and the rail-trail process would become standardized and protected in 1983 when Congress created *rail banking*. Under rail banking, so long as an agency is willing to take on the maintenance of a rail corridor, the railway land cannot be sold to private landowners because it is not considered "abandoned" even if the tracks are removed. The act has preserved an enormous number of railway corridors across the nation, creating opportunities for trails that would be impossible or impractical otherwise. As of this writing, there are nearly twenty-five thousand miles of rail-trails in the United States, with another nine thousand miles identified for future projects, according to the Rails-to-Trails Conservancy.[33]

The story behind the Burke-Gilman Trail offers many lessons for people organizing community projects of all kinds. Wood summarized what she and the other organizers learned:

> We focused on a clear goal and gave it a name and identity right away. We organized ourselves, formed committees, and easily found consensus. We reached out for support, especially of trail-side residents. And we proactively addressed our opponents' concerns. And all along the way we emphasized the positive. We learned how to grow and corral support. We contacted the appropriate government agencies and media. We learned a lot about how governments work. We presented testimony at a hearing, and wrote brochures and letters. We learned to present our ideas with a very coherent message. And most of all . . . we showed that meaningful change can come from the bottom-up. It comes from the folks. And we discovered that the impacts of our work had implications and effects far beyond just the Burke-Gilman Trail.[34]

The first section of the trail was officially dedicated in August 1978 along with Kenmore's trailside Log Boom Park at the north end of Lake Washington.[35] A decade later, Seattle Department of Engineering staff telephoned residents near the trail, interviewed real estate agents selling homes near the trail, interviewed Seattle Police Department officers about trail-related crime, and studied real estate listings for properties along the route.[36] Almost everyone had a glowing opinion of the trail. Nearly all properties for sale proudly listed proximity to the trail as an amenity, residents loved it, and there was no known property crime increase. In fact, SPD officers interviewed said property crime is most common in places with car access, since burglars can carry more stolen goods in a car than on a bike.[37] The car-free nature of the trail made it resistant to property crime. One resident they interviewed even told them she had totally changed her mind about the trail. "I was involved in citizens groups opposed to the trail," she told the interviewer. "I now feel that the trail is very positive." Not a single resident interviewed said conditions were worse with the trail than they were before.

Cascade Bicycle Club Forms, 1970-1990

At the same time that the Burke-Gilman Trail Park Committee was first getting started with its campaign, two bicycling brothers on quiet Mercer Island in the middle of Lake Washington were dreaming of better bicycle paths. Mike and Rick Quam put out a call in July 1970 for people to join them at a Mercer Island elementary school for the first-ever meeting of the Cascade Bicycle Club. Thirty people showed up to their first meeting, but membership quickly grew to a hundred as the club set out alongside the Boeing Bike Club to organize Mercer Island's first Bicycle Sunday in September 1970.[38]

It was a great time to organize a new cycling club, as Harry Coe from the League of American Wheelmen was in his mid-eighties and deserved a well-earned retirement from Seattle bicycle advocacy. Coe largely stepped away from bike advocacy leadership around 1972. He had successfully bridged Seattle's turn-of-the-twentieth-century bike boom with the birth of Cascade Bicycle Club, a remarkable accomplishment in the history of bike advocacy in Seattle. Coe surely had a lot of lonely years in his long mission to grow cycling and build better bike routes during the decades when seemingly few people in power were giving such ideas any serious thought. "As Barry Fairfax of the traffic engineering department put it, 'Mr. Coe is very persuasive,'" wrote the *P-I* in 1968. "What he means is that Harry bugged the city until it capitulated."[39] By 1972 the bike movement was finally growing like Coe had dreamed, and it was time for new leaders. He passed away in 1977 at the age of ninety-one.

Soon Cascade was throwing their support behind the Burke-Gilman Trail project, but they were also organizing a ride that would become an icon for the club: a wintertime ride around Bainbridge Island appropriately named the Chilly Hilly. Thousands of riders still pack the ferries between downtown Seattle and Bainbridge on one day every winter for this cold and difficult ride, which has become something of a celebration of winter biking in the Puget Sound region. Photos of hundreds of people biking off the ferry in full rain gear never get old. Cascade Bicycle Club grew both ends of its organization at the same time. As it added more members, the club wielded more political power to support bike-friendly projects and policies at the local, regional, and state levels. The club also focused on expanding its schedule of rides and events, which increased local interest in recreational bike riding and eventually became a valuable source of reveue.[40]

I spoke with former members of the club's Bicycle Action Committee, Amy Carlson and David Moser, as well as other early Cascade members during a meetup in 2022 to get an idea of why and how the club grew in its early years. One of the biggest advocacy focuses for the club in its early years was making sure the state's planned bridge across Lake Washington for the future Interstate 90 had a quality biking and walking path. For many early club members, the bridge was a major organizing goal that inspired many more volunteers to get involved. Frustrated that the State Route 520 bridge four miles to the north was constructed in the early 1960s without a path for walking or biking, people were determined to make sure they could safely bike across the new bridge. As discussed in chapter 3, the bridge was delayed for many years due largely to neighborhood opposition, and Cascade Bicycle Club used those delays to continuously improve the bridge designs for people walking and biking.

"It seemed like every year it got delayed, we got another foot added to the path," said Moser during the meetup. The path was initially just a few feet wide with little separation from traffic. By the time plans were finalized in the late 1980s, it was nine feet wide and separated from general traffic by a concrete barrier.

Then in 1979, the club created the event that would put them on the international map: a two-hundred-mile ride from Seattle City Hall to Portland City Hall. A dozen people met in member Jon Jacobson's living room one day to discuss the ambitious idea, and they all left with responsibilities and tasks to help make it happen. About a hundred people started the first-ever Seattle-to-Portland ride, but only sixty-nine people finished. The STP was originally billed as a race, won by one of the organizers, Jerry Baker. "The first year, there was a headwind and wet almost all the way," said seventy-three-year-old Baker during a KUOW radio interview in 2015.[41] "I'm surprised it ever happened again." Baker was a mechanical engineer who was laid off from Boeing when the federal government pulled the plug on the supersonic transportation program in 1971. He then dedicated himself to a number of bicycle-related community and business ventures. Baker went on to complete the STP thirty-six times in a row before passing away in 2015. During the KUOW interview shortly before he died, the interviewer asked him what his favorite part of the ride was. "Finishing," he replied. Baker had become such a force for cycling in the region that the velodrome in Redmond's Marymoor Park was renamed the Jerry Baker Memorial Velodrome in his honor.

Some STP riders go for the full two hundred miles all in one day, while most break it up into a two-day adventure. The one-day ride is a major challenge even for fit and experienced riders, and even the two-day ride pushes many people's limits. It's an event people train for and aspire to complete, and it draws riders from all over the world. It is something of a bucket-list goal. It's also a great excuse to visit the Pacific Northwest and tour the countryside in addition to visiting the region's two largest US cities. The second STP was canceled when Mount Saint Helens blew its top in 1980. A club member at the 2022 meetup brought an old T-shirt that said "Seattle to Portland CAN-CELLED 1980" alongside a drawing of a bicyclist holding onto their helmet as a volcano erupts. But club members just turned their wheels north instead and created the Ride from Seattle to Vancouver and Party (RSVP), a slightly shorter (one hundred seventy miles) though arguably more scenic ride into Canada that also became an annual staple for the club.

Meanwhile, the growing club advocated for trail and bike lane projects across the region as well as a major Washington State bike law in 1983 that solidified the bicycle as a legal vehicle with all the rights and responsibilities of any other vehicle. This vital law prevented cities from banning bikes from streets and clarified to all road users that people biking on the roadways have a right to be there. That might not sound like much today, but it was very important at the time.

Barbara Hershey learned this the hard way in 1976. She was biking on Greenwood Avenue North near North 112th Street in Seattle when a police officer pulled her over and ticketed her for slowing the car traffic on the street down to ten miles per hour. "Do you think it's fair for a

$100 bike to hold up five big cars?" Hershey recalled the officer asking her.[42] "If you can't ride your bike at the speed limit [thirty-five miles per hour on that particular street] you shouldn't be riding it on the road." Seattle Police Chief Robert Hanson had his officer's back and went a step further. "Laws prohibiting bikes on public thoroughfares, except sidewalks and designated bicycle paths, would be welcomed by enforcement agencies," Hanson wrote in a letter to the Seattle City Council.[43]

With the help of the Cascade Bicycle Club's legal defense fund, Hershey fought the citation in court, hoping to clarify people's rights to bike in the streets. Unfortunately, Seattle Municipal Court Judge Vernon Towne agreed with the SPD officer and also had a bone to pick with young people. "Why couldn't you be riding your bicycle somewhere else?" Judge Vernon asked Hershey in court. "There's nothing that says you should be able to ride your bike on every street in Seattle." Hershey pointed out that there was no bike path there, but the judge didn't care. "I tell you I just don't understand what it is with you young people. I don't understand why I can't get through to you." He fined her twenty dollars. Hershey and Cascade appealed the decision, but the courts again decided against her.[44] Her case was one example of why the 1983 law was such an important win for cycling across the state.

The 1970s and 1980s were "a time of having to fight to make sure that the bicycle voice was heard," said Cascade's Amy Carlson in a 2015 profile on the club's blog.[45] That's why Carlson joined Cascade Bicycle Club and became the chair of the club's Bicycle Action Committee. After fighting for inclusion of a path on the I-90 floating bridge, Carlson was a founding board member of the statewide Bicycle Alliance of Washington (now known as Washington Bikes) in 1987.

Bike Shops Become Bike Advocates, 1970s-1980s

Amid the growing interest in bicycling during the 1970s and 1980s, demand also increased for the local bike industry. Longtime shops like Gregg's Cycle, founded in 1932, continued to serve the city while other institutions like Velo Bike Shop (1968), Alki Bike and Board (1971), Elliott Bay Bicycles (1973), and Wright Brothers Cycle Works (1974) expanded access to repairs and the ever-improving bicycle technology. But one couple that straddled the line between industry and advocacy started their relationship on a handmade tandem bicycle. "One day I made a tandem, and I had to ride it home past Carla's home," said Ángel Rodriguez in an interview for this book conducted over an internet phone line from the side of a volcano in Panama. He was talking about Carla Black, a Cascade Bicycle Club organizer who later worked for the city's bicycle program. Ángel continued, "[Carla] asked, 'Who are you going to get to ride on the back of that bike with you?' And I said, 'Somebody like you.'"

Rodriguez was studying marine biology and oceanography at the University of Washington, and he had started riding a bike "because I couldn't get between buildings on campus." He learned how to fix his bike and started teaching bike repair classes on campus. On a student trip to England, he visited a bike frame company and loved the idea of making bikes rather than just fixing them. He bought a set of bike-making tools and brought them back to Seattle. After a week working as a marine biologist, he quit because he did not enjoy all the time spent inside a basement lab. He was biking through the U District shortly afterward when he saw his sometime riding partner, Glenn Erickson, on the sidewalk and decided to pitch him an idea. "I said, 'Glenn, you want to start a bike shop?' And he said, 'Yes.'" R + E Cycles became a center of Seattle bike culture. Not only did they make custom bikes but they were a popular bike repair shop that organized events and published a minibook of local bike information called the *Seattle Bike Atlas*. They also provided Cascade Bicycle Club with space before the organization got its own office.

Rodriguez and Black were fully immersed in the Seattle bike scene for decades. "I would get up in the morning, go to the bike shop," he said. "Afternoons, I would go on a bike ride, go on a weekend century [hundred-mile ride], go to the bike club meeting, then go back to the bike shop. I just lived bikes." Rodriguez was mostly interested in the business of bikes rather than the craft of bike making or the politics of bike advocacy, he said. But he saw the obvious connections between them. "I learned early on that the only way to grow my business was to get more bicyclists. That's how I got into advocacy." He served on the Seattle Bicycle Advisory Board for years and supported the growing bike scene in any way he could. "It was the perfect business. You sold people bicycles, they had fun on them, there was no pollution. I wasn't working there for money. I was compelled to do it." When mountain biking exploded in popularity in the late 1970s and 1980s, R + E published the popular *Guide to Mountain Bike Riding in Washington* and started advocating for bike access in the state's natural areas.

Then one day, they were gone. Erickson had sold his share in the business to Rodriguez in the early 1980s, then Rodriguez sold the business in 1990 and he and Black sold everything they couldn't fit into an Airstream trailer. They then went on a decade-long adventure before settling on the side of a volcano in Panama, where Rodriguez started an internet service company as well as a low-cost seismometer company called Raspberry Shake.

Also in 1990, Cascade Bicycle Club's tenth STP was topping out at its ridership limits, which varied between eight thousand and ten thousand riders. That's a lot of people biking two hundred miles together. The club was able to maintain these numbers for decades while also adding more events to its annual schedule. With leadership from member Michael Abraham, who said he wanted to fight the annual bicycling "malaise" during colder and darker months, the club had also started hosting a wintertime industry trade show and party they called the Seattle Bike Expo. For twenty-six years the Bike Expo was one of the largest bicycle trade shows in the nation, but the club stopped hosting it after 2014, citing a decline in attendance.[46] This event income allowed the organization to start hiring permanent staff starting in the early 1990s, when they hired Chuck Ayers as the first paid executive director. Ayers would hold the job for more than twenty years, overseeing huge growth in membership, ride participation, and paid staff. With its uncommon mix of major events and advocacy work, Cascade continued to grow through the 1990s and 2000s to become a uniquely large regional bicycle advocacy organization. Only bike organizations in the biggest US cities, like Transportation Alternatives in New York City, could compare to Cascade's size.[47] And it became a political force to be reckoned with.

But as exciting as the rebirth of cycling in the 1970s was, the 1980s saw gas prices plummet and a massive expansion of car-oriented suburban sprawl across the nation. Biking had asserted itself as a part of Seattle, but the cultural momentum was still overwhelmingly in favor of driving cars.

Ed Ewing wears a Major Taylor Project jersey with project students, July 2016. Photo by C. B. Bell.

CHAPTER 5

Bike Culture Grows in the Shadow of Freeways

With the end of the oil crises in the 1970s came a nearly twenty-year oil glut starting in the mid-1980s. Electricity production steadily shifted from oil to natural gas, coal, and nuclear, and many old oil furnaces in homes and businesses were replaced with natural gas and electric heating. Global oil demand decreased just as domestic oil production increased, creating a lengthy period of low gas prices in the United States. To help the trend continue, US lawmakers have not increased the federal gas tax since 1993, and the tax is not indexed to inflation. That means the United States has effectively lowered the gas tax every year since 1993.[1]

US urban regions responded to cheap gas prices by doubling down on the suburban sprawl that began en masse following the end of World War II. States invested massive sums in new and expanded freeways to and through their major cities. Increasingly, they focused on beltline freeways so people could get around sprawling communities without needing to go to the city at all. Large malls and big-box stores flourished. Most of these new places were built assuming that nearly everyone would get there by car.

In a walkable neighborhood, homes are within an easy walk of people's necessities, like groceries, business districts, and schools. Walkable neighborhoods also have quality transit service to jobs and other necessary or desirable destinations the city has to offer. The most bikeable cities in the world also have very walkable neighborhoods. But these were not the kinds of neighborhoods the United States was building in the late twentieth century.

Car Culture Continues Expanding, 1980-2000

The expansion of the United States' sprawling suburbs following World War II was not an accident or a natural population-growth pattern. It was engineered. Landowners, developers, automakers, energy giants, and politicians all worked to pass policies that would prioritize these new communities. Often, these investments came at the expense of existing communities in cities and in nearby rural areas. Transportation was the key to making it all work. The public, mostly through federal and state tax dollars, would fund expensive big freeways to help people access land that previously was too far away from jobs and destinations to be a desirable location for a new community of homes. With the new freeways in place, that formerly cheap land became desirable and valuable.

The idea of investing in transportation to enable housing development wasn't inherently new to cars and highways. Many of the preautomobile streetcar lines in cities were created by private companies as a way to sell homes in developments beyond convenient walking distance from major city destinations and jobs. But streetcars still limited the extent of sprawl because they were costly to build and operate, giving developers a clear incentive to build dense neighborhoods around the streetcar lines to keep ridership high and land value at a premium. As noted in chapter 1, bicycle paths in Seattle were initially seen as a way to increase access to land, and neighborhoods started developing around the paths. When automobiles arrived, the bicycle paths were turned into boulevards, which accelerated city development.

The creation of highways and freeways enabled wide swaths of land far beyond the city to be developed into suburbs. Because individuals who could afford cars were expected to drive themselves around, any plot of land connected to a road could be developed if the drive time was quick enough. It wasn't the developer's problem whether transportation to these places was sustainable or efficient, especially not in the long term. The city, county, and state were responsible for maintaining the roads. Developers could build and build, making a lot of money and creating homes that were relatively affordable, especially for how much more square footage people could get outside the old city. There was little incentive to build densely spaced tall buildings in the city since it was easier to just build more houses farther out.

The costs and liabilities of sprawl are difficult to comprehend. In suburbs where housing is widely spaced, just about every piece of infrastructure costs more per resident to build and maintain. A mile of sewer serves a fraction as many people. The same is true for electric lines, roads, sidewalks, garbage collection services, and fire stations. Fewer homes are located within walking distance of schools, parks, grocery stores, workplaces, community centers, and business districts.

And sprawling communities would not be possible without one commodity: oil. People must burn oil to close the gaps between homes, jobs, destinations, and services. Because of this complete reliance on a single commodity, these communities are not resilient. Burning oil for transportation is responsible for about 28 percent of the United States' greenhouse gas emissions.[2]

Private cars are not the only way to move people distances longer than a walk. But while vast sums of public money were poured into freeways from the 1950s onward, transit was left with the table scraps. By the early 1980s, few transportation professionals gave biking any thought, and those that did often bought into a concept called *vehicular cycling*.

Bicyclists against Bike Lanes, 1976-2000

For decades leading up to the turn of the twenty-first century or so, the focus of mainstream bicycle advocacy across the United States was to protect people's rights to bike on public roadways and to advocate for turning defunct rail lines into trails. But bike advocacy and planning made a wrong turn in the 1970s, 1980s, and 1990s by focusing bicycle safety efforts on user education and the philosophy that rather than change car-oriented street designs to be safer for people biking, people biking should learn how to ride a bike as though they are driving a car, which does not require any special space on the roads. This concept, often referred to as "vehicular cycling," is good advice for able-bodied teens and adults trying to navigate the vast majority of American streets and roadways that were not designed with safe biking in mind: be visible and assert your right to occupy the roadway space needed to get where you're going as safely as possible.

But vehicular cycling grew beyond being a skill people could learn in order to navigate hostile traffic on a bike, morphing into a traffic engineering philosophy espoused in the late John Forester's 1976 book *Effective Cycling*.[3] This philosophy spread widely throughout US departments of transportation big and small. For cynical transportation leaders, vehicular cycling was a convenient way to not have to do anything to help people bike on their streets. They could just design streets for cars, then tell people biking to act like a car. For politicians who didn't want to stand up for bike riding, it was a convenient way to appear as though they cared without actually doing much to help: just support the idea of bicycle education, then move on to funding the next major roads project.

Even many bicycle advocates—including the League of American Wheelmen, the largest national bicycle advocacy organization in the country—took the philosophy seriously and set out on a mission to grow cycling by educating the masses about how to bike like cars. The league even used the name of Forester's *Effective Cycling* for their programming. The American Bicycling Education Association runs a similar ongoing program called CyclingSavvy. The league still teaches bike education through their Smart Cycling program, but they also advocate for building better bicycle facilities.

The biggest problem with the vehicular cycling philosophy is that only a small percentage of the general population is ever going to choose to ride a bike mixed with busy motor vehicle traffic. When the typical person looks out the car or bus window and sees someone biking as fast as they can in a futile effort to keep up with the cars zooming by just feet from their handlebars, they say, "I'm never doing that." It looks scary and totally unappealing. So people choose to continue getting around some other way instead. In America, that "other way" is mostly by car.

The Seattle Engineering Department Creates a Bicycle Program, 1984-2000

As a result of decades of car-oriented development with the help of the vehicular cycling philosophy, the raw number of people commuting to work by bike in the United States did not grow between the 1980 and 2000 US Census Bureau counts even as the population increased by about 56 million.[4] Meanwhile, the number of miles traveled by car or truck increased by 1.17 trillion during the same period, vastly outpacing population growth as more and more people moved to or (like me) were born into increasingly farther-flung and car-dependent suburbs.[5] Even Seattle, which had built a few quality on-street bike lanes in the 1970s, invested in the vehicular cycling philosophy. The city posted signs on busy streets all over town to designate them as bike routes, but from the late 1970s until the 2000s, very little new road space was designated for biking.

"Before we had a bike plan, our biggest partner was always the Parks Department," said Sam Woods, a Seattle Department of Transportation manager who led the city's Bicycle Program through a period of major growth. She spoke to me shortly after she retired in 2019. "We were a trails-oriented city. . . . We were known for having the Burke-Gilman Trail. Getting stuff done for trails was our biggest attribute for bicycling. I can't even tell you, in my tenure at the city, how many grad students wanted to do thesis papers about the Burke-Gilman Trail. . . . I think the urban trail network is what put us on the map for biking." But there are only so many defunct rail lines lying around waiting to be turned into trails, and they don't go everywhere people need to go. If rail-trails were designated as "linear parks," the Parks Department could handle much of the work to maintain and improve them. But to bike from homes to jobs, schools, transit, and other destinations, people needed to use city streets. The Parks Department didn't control the streets, though; the Engineering Department (and later Seattle Department of Transportation) did.

Before Woods, the head of SDOT's Bicycle Program from 1984 to 2009 was a Vietnam War protester from the Midwest who found himself among a small group of American urban planners in the 1970s who believed in cities that centered walking, biking, and transit as ways to create better places that build community. Pete Lagerwey created his own bicycle planning degree in Michigan, then worked for the regional planning commission in the Detroit area for a few years. In the early 1980s, he attended a meeting of bicycle planning professionals. There were probably fewer than twenty of them in the nation at the time. "It was a real 'Aha!' moment," he said during an interview for this book. The planners realized they were all hitting the same paradox: local traffic engineers wouldn't build anything that wasn't in a national engineering guidebook, and the creators of the national engineering guidebooks wouldn't include anything that didn't have local buy-in. So Lagerwey identified a handful of places that seemed willing to experiment beyond the guidebooks and decided to try to get a job at one of them. When an opening popped up in Seattle, he paid a thousand dollars for a last-minute plane ticket to interview. "They have a certain pride in not always following the rules," he said of Seattle's transportation philosophy even back in the early 1980s. And that's exactly what he was looking for. He got the job.

One must seriously adjust the definition of "success" when talking about bike infrastructure improvements in the 1980s and 1990s in an American city. These were boom days for driving. When Lagerwey arrived in Seattle, he walked into the end of a bitter loss for local bike advocates. The city had decided to build a massively expensive and tall bridge to the West Seattle neighborhood that did not have any space for biking or walking. In fact, it would be illegal to bike on the bridge, which was one of the only connections between "mainland" Seattle and West Seattle. "There was a lot of bitterness about that," he told me. But because the decision was made just before he got here, he was in a position to rise above that fight and look for ways to turn the defeat into future wins. "From then on, every time we built or rebuilt a bridge, there would be a bike facility on it," he said, referring to a new departmental rule that came out of the West Seattle Bridge debacle.

In hindsight, that rule has proven to be enormously effective. The trail across the West Seattle low bridge, the First Avenue South Bridge, and even trail connections to the Interstate 90 floating bridge were all given priority because leaders wanted to avoid a repeat of the West Seattle Bridge fight, Lagerwey said. That's a pattern that repeats through a lot of bike advocacy, especially in the late twentieth century: losing one battle now to win several later—or, better yet, losing a battle now but winning a lasting systematic change. At the time, it was hard to get a transportation engineer to even think about someone biking, let alone include dedicated space for bicyclists that might impact their traffic throughput goals or budget restraints.

The Bicycle Program's very small budget meant Lagerwey had to pick his battles carefully. Trails took precedence above all else, and he worked hard to secure the land and funding to build them. "Start with the trails, then you start connecting the trails, then you go beyond that," he said in our interview, describing the strategy at the time. Back then, the door was mostly shut when it came to bike lanes on busy streets. Before 2007,

Seattle had constructed more trails (thirty-nine miles) than on-street bike lanes (twenty-six miles), even though painting a bike lane on an existing street was dramatically less expensive than building an off-street trail. "They like trails, but they don't want you messing with the streets," Lagerwey said. "This is true of any department I've ever worked with that started a bike program." And he has worked with a lot of transportation departments. After leaving the Seattle Department of Transportation, he joined Toole Design Group and traveled to every US state consulting for different places on how to start making bike improvements.

Engineering isn't the biggest hurdle for making a city more bike-friendly. Politics is. Often, an engineering challenge is an easy excuse to justify a political decision. Cascade Bicycle Club was growing in size and political power throughout the 1980s, but the organization did not even hire its first paid executive director until 1997.[6] The power of the bicycling movement was nothing compared to the political demands of the ever-increasing number of people in the region who were driving cars. The population of the city of Seattle declined for about two decades from the mid-1960s to the mid-1980s, but the region's sprawling suburbs grew steadily during the same time.[7] Because households in these suburbs mostly relied on cars, the political mandate was to try to make traffic better even if that effort was futile.

While there was little public demand for on-street bike lanes near the end of the 1980s, demand for extending the Burke-Gilman Trail was strong. When a railroad giant made a sketchy land deal that threatened completion of the trail through Wallingford and Fremont, that deal blew up into a major scandal. Burlington Northern sold the abandoned railway right-of-way between Latona Avenue Northeast and Third Avenue Northwest to Dennis Washington, a Montana billionaire industrialist. Dennis Washington had a history of making land deals with the railroad, and the Seattle deal was made quickly and quietly. But contrary to federal policy, no notice was given to the city, which had long made it clear it intended to acquire the right-of-way and extend the Burke-Gilman Trail. Dennis Washington's intention was to lease the valuable property along the Fremont waterfront to the Fremont Dock Company and Quadrant, a company that wanted to develop an office complex that would later house offices of tech companies like Adobe and Google. The deal would have all but stopped the city from completing the Burke-Gilman Trail, which sparked intense public outrage.

One *Seattle Times* column in 1988 was titled, "Hostages! The Multimillionaire has our bike trail, and all we get are lame explanations."[8] A Burlington Northern memo released later confirmed that cutting the city out of the deal was explicitly part of its plan. "It is my intention to split the ownership of the BNRR right of way (between Gas Works Park and Third Avenue Northwest) between a developer, adjacent land owners and a parking lot operator," wrote a senior director of development for Burlington Northern's real estate business in a 1986 memo. "This 'split' disposition approach will best serve my business considerations and will also tend to diminish any thoughts that the city may have for extending the Burke-Gilman Trail, Linear Park or other public ways through the BNRR right of way properties."[9]

Seattle Mayor Charles Royer filed a complaint with the Interstate Commerce Commission asking the agency to investigate the potentially illegal sale. As noted in chapter 4, the long legal battle over the initial stretch of the Burke-Gilman Trail had set a national precedent within the ICC during the 1970s that gave cities the first opportunity to buy abandoned railways for the purpose of building a trail or linear park. Now a decision based on that precedent was needed to extend the same trail that had set the precedent. The threat of federal action led Dennis Washington to try to strike a deal with Mayor Royer that would allow Washington to maintain ownership of most of the land but give the city the land and rights they needed to build the trail. One of Washington's conditions during the "horse trading" was waterfront moorage for his 140-foot yacht *Lark*.[10] Royer told him he was "trying to horse trade with a stolen horse," then threw him out of the office, said Lagerwey, who was heavily involved in the city's efforts to obtain the land for the trail. Eventually, Washington gave the city the land needed for the trail without the yacht moorage agreement, and Seattle started building the trail as quickly as it could, breaking ground in May 1989.[11]

By the 1990s, one of Seattle's few remaining quality rail-trail opportunities was located along the south bank of the Lake Washington Ship Canal, just across the water from the Burke-Gilman Trail. Not wanting a repeat of the Burke-Gilman Trail fiasco with Burlington Northern, Lagerwey persistently pursued the Ship Canal Trail right-of-way. But even though the route was clearly abandoned, Burlington Northern delayed for years on making a sale despite Lagerwey's constant inquiries. Then out of the blue in 1993, a Burlington Northern executive called Lagerwey at 4:00 p.m. on a Friday and asked to meet with him. Like, immediately. Lagerwey had spent years working out the details of the complicated property transfer, but there was one document that remained unsigned. So he grabbed the papers and headed straight to Burlington Northern's Seattle office. "I've been dragging my feet," the BNR executive told Lagerwey, because he had worried that his superiors would dislike the deal with the city. There was just so much valuable land in the deal, and it all hinged on this document. "I'm retiring at 5:00," he told Lagerwey. "So I'm going to sign this at 4:59, and then I'm walking out this door and we never have to talk again." "I said, 'That sounds good to me.'" Lagerwey laughed while telling me the story.

The 1990s was a decade with a lot of bike route planning in Seattle, but not a lot of building. Seattle was finally growing again after a few decades losing population, and Mayor Norm Rice led the city's response to the state Growth Management Act mandating that every neighborhood should have a neighborhood plan. Bicycle advocates, led by the Cascade Bicycle Club, got organized and encouraged people to show up to their neighborhoods' meetings to promote better walking and bicycling conditions. "Of the thirty-five plans that had housing in them, I think thirty of them mentioned bicycling. And all thirty-five mentioned pedestrian safety issues," said Lagerwey in our interview. "Not a single plan said, 'Widen my street.'" This was surprising to many people working in transportation. "All of a sudden, [transportation planners had] this 'Aha!' moment realizing there was this huge gap between what the people who lived here wanted and what they thought their mission was. Nothing that the department did almost, other than the bike/ped program, was in these neighborhood plans."

At the same time, Seattle was reorganizing its transportation efforts and disbanding the old Department of Engineering. Initially named the Seattle Transportation Department, the agency had a wider view of transportation beyond just engineering, and it had new neighborhood plans that represented something of a mandate for better walking and biking conditions. SeaTran, as the department preferred to be called (later renamed the much more acronym-friendly Seattle Department of Transportation), went through all the neighborhood plans and made a list of everything people asked for, and for a while planners in the department had to demonstrate how its projects were part of a neighborhood plan if they wanted to get them approved. "It was one of those quiet things that I don't think ever made the news, but it fundamentally changed the thinking of the department," Lagerwey told me. "It wasn't 180 degrees, that would be an exaggeration, but it was the beginning of a longer turn that's never gone back."

Building on these advocacy successes, Cascade Bicycle Club also put a lot of effort into identifying boards and commissions in the city that could use a bicycle advocate, then they worked to get a bike supporter a seat. The simple act of being at the table changes a lot of small things in how a government operates. It's an important way to make sure bicycling is not forgotten or ignored.

But Seattle's transportation agency was only part of the problem. Funding is by far the biggest factor in deciding which projects the city will pursue. Federal funding was becoming more of a mixed bag, and projects that included walking and biking elements would often score higher in the grant-selection process than roads-only projects. The feds also started to consider walking and biking projects as transportation projects rather than simply recreation. This meant there was at least some money for the projects, a big deal for SeaTran's very low-budget Bicycle Program, now renamed the Bicycle and Pedestrian Program. "The battle got won at the federal level pretty easily, and it was a push but it got resolved here," said Lagerwey, talking about the effort to include bike transportation as a goal. "Where it got stuck was at the state level."

Transportation funds from Washington State always came with criteria that they must reduce car crashes or congestion. The state all but mandated that the majority of projects with state funding would be roads projects focused on cars and trucks. Washington State was far from the worst state in terms of prioritizing car movement above all else. In fact, it was consistently recognized as the most bike-friendly state in the nation, according to the League of American Bicyclists. No other state ever won the top spot in the ten years that the league published their list (2008–2017).[12] "Even though [Washington State] deservedly gets number-one rated, that just shows how bad the other states are," said Lagerwey in our interview. He said the state has the best design manual of any state and that other states often model their own manuals on Washington's. But the projects that received funding still came from a legislature that mostly prioritized freeways and large roads projects.

Even if Washington State remained reticent to change, the 1990s saw many changes to the formidable bureaucracy behind the nation's car culture. After the city's neighborhood plans and all the community organizing around them, biking and walking were finally important local political issues, and they would stay that way. "At the time, [the neighborhood plans] were game changers," Lagerwey told me. "They changed the direction of the department. They put bicycling and walking—and the biggest change was actually in the walking area rather than biking—they put it on the map. After that, when there was an election there could be a forum to talk about biking and walking issues, and all the candidates would show up. That never happened before."

But many people were tired of waiting for politicians and bureaucracy to get around to caring about bicycling, so they took matters into their own hands.

Critical Mass, 1996-2008

"Whose streets?" shouted someone. "Our streets!" riders responded as we rode through downtown Denver together, drawing the attention of crowds on the sidewalks and a police helicopter hovering overhead. It was 2008, and the Democratic National Convention just happened to be in town on the last Friday of the month, the designated time for Critical Mass. I had just moved to Denver after graduating college, and I had never seen this many people biking together before. Until I showed up, I had no idea what Critical Mass was. A friend said to ride my bike to Civic Center Park, so I did. It was quite the way to get to know my new home.

That slogan "Whose streets? Our streets!" lands differently depending on your perspective. For people biking that day, or at least for me, it meant that we had a right to bike on public streets. It was also a statement about democracy and the power of the people. While biking can be an intimidating experience on city streets for someone riding alone in car traffic, people can create a safe and fun bicycling space just by forming a large enough group. And while the cheers from onlookers suggested that many people also understood the phrase that way, the chant could come off as bicyclists saying they now own the streets to the exclusion of others.

Critical Mass was, and in many places still is, a powerful movement. It is an idea that started in San Francisco in 1992 and quickly spread across the world. There were no real leaders or official organization, just a bunch of people who showed up at an established time and place on the last Friday of the month to ride bikes together in their city.[13] It was a simple idea that directly challenged the order of how streets worked and who had power on those streets. Participants did not ask for space and wait for politicians and public agencies to provide it. They also did not pay for permits or provide the police with a carefully planned route. Instead, they took their space and rode where they pleased, even if only for a fleeting moment while they were together in large enough numbers to do so.

But when challenging the dominant culture, there is always push-back. Sometimes this came from news commentators, who accused the riders of being entitled and of making enemies of all the people they delayed with their bike ride. Sometimes the push-back was more direct and dangerous, such as a person behind the wheel of a large, heavy vehicle deciding to use it as a weapon. But perhaps the strongest push-back came from police, at least in some US cities during the 2000s.[14]

Critical Mass rides are not inherently dangerous. In fact, many people ride specifically because they feel safer as part of such a big group. But rides typically break some traffic laws, especially when they grow large. This is a necessary function of a large bike ride in traffic. It is safer and faster for everyone if Critical Mass rides run red lights, for example. Someone waiting for the ride to pass might not understand this, but it is clear when riding. The mass must stay together in order to be safe. Stopping for red lights splits up the group and can strand riders. It also introduces cars into the middle of the mass of people biking, which can create dangerous conditions.

A series of group bike ride tactics were developed during the early years of Critical Mass in the 1990s to help keep the mass together and to control intersections until the riders had passed. The most important tactic is called *corking*. As the mass of riders approaches an intersection, at least one person stops and stands with their bike in front of cross-traffic to make it clear that drivers should wait for the ride to pass even if their traffic light turns green. If riders do not cork an intersection, people driving may be tempted to try to squeeze through a gap in the group, which can be dangerous. Corking is a vital strategy for reducing confusion for people driving and for keeping riders safe and together. It is somewhat similar to how police officers on motorcycles control traffic along a parade route, motorcade, or funeral entourage. Except, of course, the people doing it are not police officers.

It turns out some police officers do not like it when non-officers take control of public spaces like this. As the idea of Critical Mass spread across the globe, police departments didn't always know how to respond. The events existed in a bit of a legal gray area. The heart of the event was completely legal. Unlike a protest march that defies laws against walking down the middle of streets, it is legal to ride a bike on a public street because bikes are vehicles. Police have a long history of taking violent action against people marching in protests, often citing "obstruction of traffic" as a reason. Critical Mass, on the other hand, was both a First Amendment free speech action and also not inherently illegal. Running red lights is illegal and people corking intersections don't have the authority to control traffic, but these actions are also in the interest of public safety. Is it really appropriate or a proper use of police resources to arrest people for taking actions to maintain safety?

As hundreds of people and I biked past the extensive barricades around the arena where the 2008 Democratic National Convention was meeting in Denver, I remember looking up at the helicopter following us and wondering why police were so afraid of people who were just out riding bikes. What I didn't know at the time was that there was history between Critical Mass and police forces guarding the major political conventions. In 2004, the Republican National Convention was in New York City to renominate George W. Bush. There were intense protests in the city against Bush and his wars in Iraq and Afghanistan, and the city's police force arrested about eighteen hundred people just for attending (or accidentally being near) protest actions, according to the 2008 documentary *Still We Ride*.[15] Hundreds of those arrested were on a huge Critical Mass ride. New York City would later settle a massive civil rights lawsuit filed over the unlawful detention of demonstrators, paying nearly $18 million. But the event put conflict between Critical Mass and the police in the spotlight across the nation.

"The police, on some level, as individual rank and file policemen, are offended by Critical Mass," said Chris Carlsson in *Still We Ride*. Carlsson was a cofounder of Critical Mass in San Francisco in 1992 and editor of several books about Critical Mass. Because Critical Mass is an inherently decentralized and leaderless event, the priorities of the people who show up for a ride can change the intent of the ride. If riders want to demonstrate against the police they can do that, but they risk losing riders who don't want conflict with police and may no longer feel comfortable. Police action itself can change the makeup of Critical Mass the next month. It's a constantly evolving concept, what Carlsson described in the documentary as "an organized coincidence." The ride can go for years without serious incidents, then a major news story about a conflict with someone on the road or the police will change the size and focus of the next month's ride. This is the power of the event, but also its limitation as a political statement. It's often difficult for the general public, who only see the big news stories about conflicts, to understand what Critical Mass is trying to say to them.

The event may be "an organized coincidence," as Carlsson put it, but it can take a bit of work to seed the idea around town before it grows into its own. Seattle had a Critical Mass ride for several years in the early 1990s, following the example of riders like Carlsson in San Francisco. But the Seattle rides dwindled out for a few years. I had posted a message online looking to talk to anyone involved in the 1990s start of Critical Mass, and several people pointed me toward a young guy who grew up biking in the Greenwood neighborhood and decided to try to restart Critical Mass in Seattle. Nic Warmenhoven, in an interview for this book, said he'd grown up biking to school and continued riding as he got older. He was in his early twenties when he and his brother decided in 1996 to print off a bunch of fliers telling people to meet at Westlake Park downtown the last Friday of each month for Critical Mass. The bulk of the people who initially turned up at Westlake were bike messengers who worked downtown, Warmenhoven told me. This time, Critical Mass stuck. The first handful of rides in Seattle were successful and relatively uneventful. A couple of dozen people dressed up in costumes for the Halloween ride, which became a long-lasting tradition and one of the most popular Critical Mass rides each year.

But on the January 1997 ride, a Seattle Police officer tried to stop at least one rider for running a red light, and a physical altercation broke out. Police claimed that the group of people biking assaulted seven officers, though riders disputed the official version and said officers instigated the violence.[16] Three riders were charged and later pleaded guilty to lesser charges.[17] Immediately after the conflict made the news, Critical Mass riders tried to recenter the event as an effort to bring attention to bicycling. "We're riding to make a peaceful and positive statement about bicyclists in Seattle," one rider told the Seattle P-I.[18] "We hope the public will get a better understanding of what we're about," said another rider. "We're peaceful people. . . . We wish no confrontation with the police. We wish to send a message to them they're welcome to come with us. We want to counter the negative impression of the earlier event and show solidarity for the people arrested, people we believe were wrongly arrested."[19] There were about fifty people on the January ride, but as news of the arrests went around, about two hundred people showed up to the next one.

"I remember being really psyched about the response of Seattle to this moment of police coming down ridiculously hard," Warmenhoven said in our interview. He didn't get a driver's license until he was twenty-four and is now a high school teacher living on nearby Vashon Island in Puget Sound. But even back in his early twenties, he might not have fit the mold of someone who would start a bicycle protest that would last more than a decade. In fact, there wasn't really any mold that Warmenhoven fit at that time. Unlike most of the early Critical Mass riders, Warmenhoven wasn't a bike messenger. "I came from the guerrilla theater side of activism," he told me. "I like to play within the rules as much as I can. At the very least I try to be respectful."

Critical Mass grew gradually throughout the 2000s and mostly avoided major conflicts. The rides faced some resistance from more established bike advocacy organizations like Cascade Bicycle Club, which never supported Critical Mass rides due to their disregard for traffic rules. Warmenhoven said a Cascade leader called him up in the late 1990s and said, "Stand down, you're giving bicycling a bad name." But Critical Mass was growing, and it was bringing more people into cycling, many of whom may not have been interested in Cascade's events or group rides. Critical Mass was different. It was culturally rebellious and subversive. It often pushed back against dependency on oil at a time when the United States had started a war in Iraq that many saw as a thinly veiled war over oil. People rode in Critical Mass for many different reasons. Some saw it as a political statement against oil, some saw it as a statement in favor of bike lanes, some saw it as a way to defy police and social order, and others were just there to have a good time riding bikes with a lot of other people.[20]

One month in 2006, Critical Mass in Seattle became about Susanne Scaringi. Scaringi was killed when someone driving a van turned in front of her while she was biking to work. The next Critical Mass transformed into a memorial for her. Friends and family, including her brother, gathered at the start to honor her, then the ride headed out to West Seattle to visit the location of the fatal collision. "You often mirror the people you are around," Scaringi's older brother James Neil told the *P-I* during the event.[21] "When you were around her and she started to smile, her personality was just so incredible you just couldn't fight it. She had that kind of presence." He rode with a large wooden cross attached to his backpack bearing her name.

The tragedy and the community's response put a spotlight on bicycle safety. It also brought mainstream bike advocacy and Critical Mass together for a moment. The movement for more and safer bicycling in Seattle had finally started to get real influence at City Hall. Within a year, Seattle wrote its first ever Bicycle Master Plan, and the city council passed a "complete streets" ordinance requiring SDOT to "plan for, design and construct all new City transportation improvement projects to provide appropriate accommodation for pedestrians, bicyclists, transit riders, and persons of all abilities, while promoting safe operation for all users."[22] Under the complete streets ordinance, the city must plan for the safety and mobility of all users whenever SDOT makes a significant investment in a street such as a major repaving project. Though there are loopholes in the law, it would prove to be an effective tool for safe streets advocacy.

But Seattle's final big Critical Mass news story was not positive. In July 2008, there was a chaotic conflict between someone driving on Capitol Hill and the Critical Mass ride that ended in violence. Even today, it's hard to piece together exactly what happened from the many conflicting reports. "A stopped driver caught in the rally refused to wait, reversing and then accelerating into at least two riders," the *P-I* reported.[23] "One bicyclist, whose leg was run over, said the driver was irate and aggressive, shouting at the cyclists for blocking his way. The driver, whose identity hasn't been released, has since said he panicked and did not intend to hit any riders. Riders attacked the man's Subaru station wagon as he tried to drive from the scene, police said. The driver was dragged from the car and struck in the head with a bicycle lock before police arrived." Though two of the riders were arrested, nobody was charged. The initial media report was about the assault on the person driving, and Seattle Police said they considered him the victim. It was a "Man Bites Dog" story because people are used to people in cars hurting people on bikes, but it is very rare for the violence to go the other way. Some riders and observers disputed this initial account of what happened and worked to counter the story and reclaim the event, but Critical Mass would not fully recover from the negative impression the story left on people. It's likely that if you ask someone who was living in Seattle in 2008 about Critical Mass, this is the story they will remember.

Critical Mass continued for years afterward and still sees surges of energy every once in a while. The rides are garnering renewed energy at the time of this writing, so who knows what the future holds. "Honestly, when I was doing it, I wasn't really doing it with a great critical understanding of privilege and vision and things like that," said Warmenhoven when we spoke. "I was doing it because it seemed like a good idea at the moment. . . . My sense is that lots of, I guess I'll call it "cousin activism" these days—direct action and marching and things like that—have a much more complete understanding of systems of oppression and things like that. I don't pretend that Critical Mass was a beautiful, well-thought-out attempt to remove bike oppression from the world. It just seemed like something I could do that was the next step to having some more fucking bike lanes."

The Solstice Naked Bike Ride, 1993-2003

Nic Warmenhoven not only helped kick-start the lasting Critical Mass tradition in Seattle, he was also responsible for another moment in Seattle bike history that would have long-lasting ramifications for biking and for Seattle's culture as a whole. "In college, I spent some time doing naked things, as one does in college," he said. "I remember talking to people and saying, 'Hey, we ought to show up and do a naked bike ride during the Solstice Parade.'" He floated the idea in 1997 but didn't get much traction and decided not to do it. But the idea stuck with him. So in 1998, he and a handful of friends got up the guts to do it. They stripped naked, hopped on their bikes, and crashed the annual Fremont Solstice Parade. The parade is a people-powered art parade held at the start of every summer as part of the Fremont Fair in North Seattle. Dance troupes, musical acts, creative costumes, and floats of all kinds show up in the parade. No commercial marketing is allowed in the parade—no written words of any kind—only art.[24] It moves slowly because people have to push or pull the floats, making it a sitting duck for some bike-riding shenanigans.

Warmenhoven and his friends riding naked were not the first people to bring nudity to the parade, and they weren't even the first people to bike naked through the parade. That would be Brian Nichols in 1993, who was featured in the excellent 2013 documentary *Beyond Naked* about the Solstice bike ride. "Originally it was a pretty innocent thing," Nichols said in the film. "It wasn't meant to be a political movement. It was just a couple of guys doing something wacky." The idea was a fusion of two ideas Nichols and some fellow students had the night before the parade:

> One night we were having a few beers, maybe a little smoke, maybe fifteen or sixteen people there that night. Some of the students mentioned that "wouldn't it be great if maybe we would streak in the Solstice Parade?" And someone else said, "Hey, we're mountain bike riders. Maybe we should ride bikes in the parade." And then somehow those two things merged. "Well, maybe we should ride our bikes naked." Everyone said they would do it. Then the next day, Gabe and I are the only ones that met at the specified time. . . . All kinds of thoughts are going through your head. "Should we really do this?" Or "What's going to happen when we do this?" And we just looked at each other and said, "Let's do this. Let's ride."[25]

Their decision to bike naked through the 1993 parade sparked something in Seattle, a city in the global spotlight at the time as the home of grunge even though that label didn't fit the city as perfectly as MTV wanted it to. But Seattle was redefining itself. After the population had peaked in the 1960s, the Boeing bust and the growth of sprawling suburbs led to two decades of population decline within the Seattle city limits. By the early 1990s, that pattern turned around and the city started growing again.[26] The Fremont Solstice Parade was essentially a gathering of artists, and artists throughout human history have captured and defined their moments in time. Riding a bike naked through an art parade was part of this 1990s Seattle moment, and it would inspire small groups of people to make it a tradition at each Solstice Parade.

But as Warmenhoven and his friends streaked through the 1998 parade on their bikes, their joyride was cut short by the long arm of the law. The crowd booed police officers as Warmenhoven was arrested, a moment captured in a photo published in the alternative weekly *The Stranger*. In the photo, Warmenhoven's hands were cuffed behind his back as two officers tried to help him step into a dress, the only piece of clothing he had with him on his bike.[27] "They took me to the police station, scared me for a few hours, then let me go," he said during our interview. "I remember going back to my dad's house and watching some of the World Cup and then going back to the Fremont Fair."

The arrest reverberated throughout Seattle, and though police did not charge Warmenhoven, all the attention around the arrest guaranteed a public response the next year. Sure enough, the number of people who showed up to bike naked in the 1999 Solstice Parade grew dramatically. About a hundred people arrived to bike naked, and many had painted their bodies before showing up. Some paraders painted themselves like police officers, chasing naked riders around like the slapstick Keystone Cops.[28] As the number of riders grew, pressure increased on the city to decide what it was going to do about it. The lead-up to the 2001 ride turned out to be the big showdown. The city was threatening that police would arrest anyone who showed up to ride naked in the parade, and these threats triggered a public backlash. The city wanted the Fremont Arts Council, the host of the official parade, to put up signs saying that naked riders would be arrested. But even though opinion within the arts council was mixed about the naked bike riders, they refused to put up the signs.[29]

City Councilmember Nick Licata spearheaded an effort among city leaders to oppose police action. The 1998 arrest and 2001 threat of arrests were a catalyst for the city to reassess its stance on public nudity and puritanical thinking in general. "In some ways it was a defining moment, I think, for Seattle," said Licata in *Beyond Naked* in 2013. "They were the edgiest expression of Seattle's creativity. And by tolerating them, I think we sent a message out that Seattle's a place you can come and literally be free." The documentary explains that days before the event, the city backed away from its arrest threat. Just like before, all the public attention and threats of police action guaranteed a big increase in the number of riders. After 2001, people got organized and started hosting preride painting parties, and by 2010 an estimated five hundred people were riding naked. By 2013, that figure jumped to as high as a thousand, though it is difficult to get an exact count since there are no sign-up sheets and riders tend to loop around and mix together.

The Solstice bike ride is a beautiful explosion of gutsy and joyful creativity. For many participants, it's one of the wildest things they will do in their lives. "You could ask every single rider in that parade what their reason is for riding, and they're going to give you a different answer," said Molly Meggyesy in *Beyond Naked*. Another rider put it well in the documentary: "I think this is one of the best Seattle traditions because it's great that we celebrate the sun even when it's not out." Other cities faced similar discussions about naked bike riding starting in 2003, when the World Naked Bike Ride started and quickly spread across the globe.[30] But the Solstice bike ride remains a uniquely Seattle take on the concept.

Finding a Black Bicycling Community, 1988-present

When Ed Ewing first arrived in Seattle to start a new job, his bike was still on the way from his hometown of Minneapolis. "I remember that my bike arrived two weeks later, and I remember how much I missed it," he said in an interview for this book. His was a biking family, and he had worked at a bike shop before leaving town for his first post-college job. But the Seattle area was unfamiliar, and in 1988 "there was no Google Maps," as he put it. But he had heard there was some trail nearby that should get him to the University of Washington and Lake Union, so he set out from his place in Bellevue to find it. "I didn't know it was called the Burke-Gilman or how long it was," he said. But he found it and started riding, figuring he would just go to the end and then turn around. "It kept going and going and going and going," and he was simultaneously wowed by the bike path and worried he would get lost. But he knew enough about the geography of his new home that if he just kept track of where Lake Washington was, he could find his way back.

As impressive as the trail was, he didn't see many other riders there who looked like him. Ewing is Black, and the North Seattle and suburban neighborhoods along the Burke-Gilman Trail were very white. This was not by accident. Many of the neighborhoods and properties near the trail, especially in northeast Seattle, had state-enforced covenants written into their titles during the first half of the twentieth century that required homeowners and renters to be white.[31] These covenants followed in the footsteps of earlier efforts to create white-only neighborhoods like the Interlaken development near the old Lake Washington Bike Path discussed in chapter 1. The 1926 US Supreme Court decision *Corrigan v. Buckley* affirmed that it was legal to attach binding documents to properties that restricted the sale or rental of residences based on race, and the practice was quickly adopted by white property owners and developers across the nation.

A typical covenant example from the Burke-Gilman-adjacent neighborhood of Windermere read, "Said property shall not be conveyed, sold, rented or otherwise disposed of, in whole or in part, or otherwise occupied by any person or persons except of white and Gentile race, except, however a domestic servant actually employed by the lawful owner or occupant thereof." Other covenants spelled out specifically which races were not allowed, like the restriction for the Westhaven subdivision in the trail-adjacent Sand Point neighborhood: "No part of said property hereby conveyed shall ever be used or occupied by any person of the Ethiopian, Malay, or any Asiatic race." Many of these covenants were collected by the Seattle Civil Rights and Labor History Project, which helpfully notes that in the racist colonial terminology of the time, "Ethiopian" meant anyone of African descent, and "Malay" included Filipinos. Other trail-side covenants outlawed sales or rentals to "Hebrews," "Negroes," "Hawaiians" (which almost certainly included all Pacific Islanders), or people of the Japanese or Chinese race (which almost certainly included all Asians).[32] It is safe to assume that the authors who wrote these covenants were painting with a wide brush when they described the nonwhite people that they didn't want around.

The project found two dozen of these covenants buried within property titles along the Burke-Gilman Trail route but noted that these are only a sampling of the records still available, which are likely also just a sampling of all the titles that ever existed. The practice of racially restrictive covenants was widespread and effective, one of the many reasons Black, Indigenous, Asian, and Pacific Islander Seattleites were concentrated in a relatively small area that included today's Central District, Chinatown–International District, Mount Baker, North Beacon Hill, and Duwamish Valley neighborhoods. In 1950, an astounding 99 percent of people living in northeast Seattle neighborhoods adjacent to the future trail were white.[33]

Even after the US Supreme Court's 1948 decision *Shelley v. Kraemer* struck down legal enforcement of these racially restrictive property covenants, it was still fully legal for property sellers and landlords to choose to discriminate based on race until 1968.[34] The impacts of segregation were further amplified by redlining, a real estate and financing practice that prioritized investments in white neighborhoods and discouraged investments within communities of color. People organized and fought for many years to pass an open housing ordinance in Seattle, and they got very close in 1963. When the Seattle City Council and Mayor Gordon Clinton tried to delay action on the ordinance, Reverends Mance Jackson and Samuel McKinney organized a march. Others held a sit-in at the mayor's office. On August 28, the Central Area Committee on Civil Rights held a Freedom March concurrent with the March on Washington on the other side of the country. The city council finally agreed to pursue the ordinance coauthored by Councilmember Wing Luke, the first Asian American to hold an elected office in Washington State and the first person of color to hold a Seattle City Council seat. But after a bitter debate, and over the objection of Luke, the council decided against including an "emergency" clause in the ordinance that would have protected it from a public referendum. The measure was put to Seattle voters, who struck it down by a huge margin: 115,627 to 54,448.[35] The city council would not successfully pass an open housing ordinance until 1968, taking action three weeks after the assassination of Martin Luther King Jr.

This legacy of racist housing practices has had long-lasting effects on Seattle. People writing and obeying these covenants further reinforced segregation in other aspects of urban life, leading to generations of inequitable access to education, mobility, clean air, healthy food, good jobs, sidewalks, safe streets, parks, bike trails, internet and cable infrastructure, and so much more. In the 1990 US Census, around the time Ewing biked on the Burke-Gilman Trail for the first time, nearly all Census blocks along the trail were around 90 percent white. Even in 2020, only a few trail-side Census blocks in northeast Seattle were less than 70 percent white. Resistance to desegregation is now legally embedded in more obscure ways, such as zoning laws. Most of the trail-side neighborhoods in northeast Seattle are zoned in such a way that more-affordable homes like apartments, condos, and duplexes, which allow two or more parties to combine their resources to share a property, are illegal. These zoning laws enforce an income or wealth barrier to moving into the neighborhood, which is also an effective racial barrier because of the financial legacy of discrimination.

The Burke-Gilman Trail was a unique opportunity for Seattle, but it's no coincidence that a very white part of the city got an amazing trail while neighborhoods that were home to concentrated populations of people of color were slated for demolition by freeway planners. Laurelhust got the Burke-Gilman Trail while Judkins Park, Atlantic, and the Chinatown–International District neighborhoods got Interstate 90. The trail became a beloved feature of the city that was a boon to property values and public health. I-90 tore neighborhoods in half and polluted their air.

Seattle's leaders did not typically view bike infrastructure as a way to maintain public safety and provide a mobility option to all residents; they saw it as a nice amenity for people who were asking for it. By 1990, Seattle had installed 13 miles of bike lanes and 41 miles of trails.[36] Of those, zero were in Rainier Valley. The only bike route in the Central District or Chinatown–International District was to the I-90 Trail (the South Dearborn Street bike route), but that project was tacked onto a major freeway project that caused irreparable harm to the neighborhoods. Of the 54 miles of bike lanes and trails listed, 37 miles were north of East Madison Street, the historic redline along the north border of the Central Area, and 5 miles were in or on the way to prosperous Alki along the West Seattle shore. The 7.6-mile Duwamish River Trail was the only project on the list that primarily served a historically redlined neighborhood. Seattle's inequitable rollout of the relatively few bike facilities it had was a reflection of who had power within bicycle advocacy, and it painted a picture of who bicycle lanes were really intended to serve. The poorest people are the ones most likely to ride a bike, and it's been that way for a long time. Bikes are cheaper to buy than cars and don't require gas or even bus fare. But Seattle wasn't building bike lanes for people who relied on biking; it was building bike lanes for people who were choosing to bike and had the time and resources to advocate for those bike lanes.

Inequitable distribution of bicycle infrastructure was just one of many ways that segregation and racism were systemically reinforced by infrastructure decisions. For example, a 2013 University of Washington study supported by Seattle Neighborhood Greenways and Bike Works measured the amount of time that traffic signals were programmed to provide for people walking across the street.[37] They found that the walk signals gave people in the wealthier and whiter Ballard neighborhood in northwest Seattle five additional seconds to finish crossing the street compared to people crossing a comparable street in the lower-income and more diverse Columbia City neighborhood in Rainier Valley. Not only that, but Columbia City residents typically had to wait longer for the walk sign after arriving at the intersection. Racism was programmed into traffic signal computers. Though walk signal timing was far from the only traffic safety problem in Columbia City, the traffic injury rate was six times higher at the Columbia City location than at the one in Ballard. The signal timing difference was part of a long-standing pattern in which Columbia City's roadways were treated differently than Ballard's.

Not long after his first ride on the Burke-Gilman Trail, Ewing moved across Lake Washington to Seattle. He then set out on a new bike adventure: find Seward Park. "So I was riding down Lake Washington Boulevard, and I saw all these cyclists, and one of the cyclists I saw was Lewis Rudd, the owner of Ezell's Chicken," Ewing said during our interview. "We both stopped and said, 'Wow, I didn't know you were out here.'" Rudd is African American, and he and Ewing bonded quickly. "It's one thing to find a bike community here, but it's another to find a Black bike community here, and someone that looked like me—especially then in the late '80s and early '90s in a town that I didn't know—that is out here doing the same thing that I'm doing."

In those years, bicycling for Ewing was all about racing and race training. He raced in the long-running Seward Park bike racing series, where he was one of just a few Black riders. "Back in the day, when I was racing quite a bit, my bike community was the bike racing team I raced for," he said. But around the turn of the twenty-first century, he started to see things change. The sport of cycling started to diversify, and he began to meet many more cyclists of color. But while the racing scene was changing, so was Ewing. "The less racing I did, the bigger the community I discovered." He was a spin instructor and started gravitating toward nonracers rather than his racing team. He got a job at Cycle University, a bike coaching organization that at the time shared an office building with Cascade Bicycle Club. One day, Chuck Ayers, the executive director of Cascade, walked over to the Cycle U part of the office and invited Ed to a breakfast with former King County Executive Ron Sims and Swedish Medical Center executives Dr. Rayburn Lewis and Dr. John Vassall.

"Ron had become a new cyclist, and when he would go on these rides he would say, 'Wow, there are not a lot of people on these rides who look like me.' And that was shocking to him," said Ewing. As county executive, Sims, who is Black, had led an effort starting in 2005 for the county to buy a rail corridor that ran through several Eastside cities with the intention of turning it into a trail that could rival the Burke-Gilman.[38] That project, now called the EasTrail, was under construction as of writing this book. At that breakfast meeting in 2009, Sims was transitioning from the county to become deputy director of the US Department of Housing and Urban Development under President Barack Obama.[39] Lewis and Vassall had cycled for many years, and they were familiar with being among the only Black people at a cycling event. Lewis has served on the boards of both Cascade Bicycle Club and Bike Works. They all saw a need for some kind of project to increase diversity in cycling.

With Cascade's resources and large member base, it seemed like the right organization to do something about it. At their breakfast meeting, they scribbled ideas on napkins, and the Major Taylor Project was born. Named after the legendary bike racer from the turn of the twentieth century, the first Black racer to win a cycling world championship, the Major Taylor Project would be a youth project of some kind serving lower-income communities of color in King County. Ewing was hired to lead the project. He had no previous experience developing youth programming or a curriculum, but he didn't see that as a big impediment. "I had my life lessons," he said. He knew that it would need to be "embedded in the Black and brown community touchstones, community centers, and schools." With Cascade backing him, he set out to talk to community leaders and teachers to figure out what was needed. "I would ask, 'What do your students really need? What's the best approach?' And whatever they told me, I just did," he said in our interview. "To me it was easy. They told me what to do, I did it, and it worked." The result was an after-school program that started in 2009 to provide quality cyclocross bicycles to students, teach them the rules of the road, and get them out biking together. Group bike rides create space for so much more than just a trip around town or some fitness, though they certainly do that. Bike rides can build friendships, give people a different and more intimate perspective about their own communities, and create space for deep conversations and personal exploration of all kinds.

In the project's early years, a student learned about Cascade Bicycle Club's annual Seattle to Portland ride and asked if they could ride it. "I said, 'Sure!'" Ewing told me. "I didn't know how we were going to do it, but, 'Sure!'" So they set out to start training for a ride 206 miles long over two days. Then they did it. "And people were like, 'Is this an activist program? Are you an activist, Ed?' And I was like, 'Yeah.' Major Taylor

[Project] students riding STP is very much a protest. It's very much a friendly, inviting protest. Because you have these kids that want to get out and explore and challenge themselves—they just didn't have the access to do it. And once they are given the access to do it, look! They knock down anything that's in front of them. By the time they get to STP, they would have already ridden four or five centuries.[40] They get done and go, 'So what else can we do?' Or 'How can a bike help me get into college?' or 'How can a bike help me get a job?' or 'How can a bike help me in school?' Or just plain, 'Wow, riding 200 miles in a weekend is really fun.' It shatters a lot of stereotypes, it challenges people with their thinking."

As big as all those ideas are, a lot of the truly hard work for Ewing happened back inside Cascade's offices. The historically white-led organization had never done anything like this before, and they had a lot to learn. In our interview, Ewing said he convinced Cascade leadership that "we have to go into communities and we have to manufacture and create demand for biking. Because we have neglected to do that in these communities. Because at the time, Cascade's programming was predominantly north of the Ship Canal. It didn't reach communities of color. In order to effect change and in order to affect behaviors, we need to embed ourselves in these communities, and we need to stay there. We need to be permanent. We don't need to be a well-intentioned nonprofit that comes in saying, 'You all need bikes. You need biking.' And I kind of innately knew that; however, I learned the most by listening to community leaders in White Center and in SeaTac."

Ewing also did not want the Major Taylor Project to be thought of as just another program in Cascade's lineup. "In my mind, a program is kind of plug-and-play, kind of cookie cutter, and it's finite," he told me. "An initiative is about a societal issue. It's something that's bigger than ourselves that will only succeed if other people and organizations are part of it as well. The initiative on the surface was to diversify cycling. In order to achieve that initiative, we had to address systemic racism. When you frame it that way, it becomes much bigger than one organization, much bigger than ourselves. And in order to accomplish that, you have to have multiple organizations' resources involved in doing so. It's not just up to one person. The project is dismantling racism and diversifying cycling, and we all get to work on that project. And then many different organizations and people can plug in and plug in their resources in an attempt to reach this higher and bigger goal. . . . I didn't want it to be watered down and become part of the soup of programming that Cascade offered. Again, great programs, but if you want an initiative like this to be successful, it needs to be front and center, and you need to support it with the resources that it needs. It can't be grouped into all the other programs because it gets overlooked, which is the problem and is why you have systemic racism anyway. Because people in those communities don't have a voice in the mix so they get underserved, under-resourced, whatever you want to call it."

Once the Major Taylor Project proved the concept in the first couple of years, it grew to more schools organically. "Pretty soon," Ewing said in our interview, "it just got this momentum where teacher friends of teacher friends of teacher friends would introduce us together, and they would say, 'I heard about this after-school program, and I want it at my school.'" Teachers and students also urged them to turn it into a year-round program, which they did. Students also learned to fix bikes in addition to riding them. "It wasn't just getting kids on bikes anymore, it was, 'How can the bicycle help them access opportunity and position them for the rest of their lives? Help these kids get access to what they want?'" With that realization, the project grew into more of an initiative the way Ewing had envisioned, with other major organizations getting involved. "That's when things really took off. That's when the phone started ringing from Tacoma and the Chief Leschi School in Puyallup Nation. They're looking at this like, 'We don't want to turn these kids into Tour de France riders, we just want to connect with them in a different way and use a bicycle to position them for success in their life.'"

By 2022, the Major Taylor Project was active in eighteen middle and high schools in King and Pierce Counties.[41] Ewing, who had left Cascade Bicycle Club in 2016, was named executive director of Bike Works in 2020.[42]

A Scrappy Bike Reuse Effort Grows into a Community Hub, 1996-present

In 2019, 2,197 young people and 1,041 adults in Seattle participated in the bicycle education and empowerment programs at Bike Works, a nonprofit organization with a packed schedule of after-school programs for students as well as education and volunteer programs for adults. The organization in Columbia City runs a popular Earn-a-Bike program in which students who put in the hours to learn how to fix a bike can graduate with a set of wheels they fixed up themselves. Bike Works also runs a community bike shop operating out of an iconic yellow house on South Ferdinand Street where community members can purchase affordable bikes and repairs. Beyond the day-to-day, Bike Works also runs a major bicycle recycling and reuse program that collected 8,038 bikes in 2019 alone, which they then fix up or strip for usable parts to support the shop and other programs. Add on a series of youth bicycle summer camps, community rides, and warehouse sales, and Bike Works is a large organization and a center of community.[43]

But the people who started the organization in 1996 that would become Bike Works had a much different idea in mind at first. "There was a meeting at the YMCA about creating a bike share program," said Suzanne Carlson in an interview for this book. Attendees included early volunteers, funders, and board members such as Richard Conlin, who would be elected to the Seattle City Council a year later. Carlson had grown up biking to get around town, and to this day she has never owned a car. She had just returned to Seattle after graduating from college, had a couple of part-time jobs, and was looking for a way to get involved. So she showed up to the YMCA meeting and volunteered to help lead the effort, which the group named Free Ride Zone.[44] She quickly rose to become the primary organizer while Chris Hellman took on much of the mechanic work.

From the start, the organization knew it wanted to provide "a way to recycle bikes and provid[e] affordable, environmentally friendly transportation," said Carlson. They were inspired by the 1994 Yellow Bike program in Portland, a free bike share concept in which volunteers fixed up donated bikes, painted them yellow, then placed them on the streets with signs instructing riders to leave the bikes on a busy street at the end of their trips so others could use them. But Free Ride Zone soured on the Yellow Bike idea before getting any bikes on the streets. "All these cities with Yellow Bike programs, all the bikes either ended up at the bottom of a hill at best or the bottom of a lake at worst," said Carlson. Indeed, Portland's Yellow Bike effort would end after only three years of operation due to ongoing theft and vandalism.[45]

Instead, Free Ride Zone decided to focus on partnering with other community organizations that could identify people who could use a free bike. For example, Carlson told me, they partnered with FareStart, an organization that provides food industry job training to people experiencing homelessness, to offer bikes to FareStart graduates who needed transportation. Free Ride Zone also established a community bike shop in Columbia City in order to help fill a large bike-shop void. At the time, there were no bike shops in the dozen or so miles between Capitol Hill and Renton, a gap spanning racially diverse and lower-income areas of South Seattle. Craig Lorch, who was a major early supporter of Free Ride Zone, sold his pedicab business in 1996 and used that money to buy a small house and retail space in the heart of Columbia City that a plumbing business had used to store toilets. Free Ride Zone transformed the house on South Ferdinand Street into the iconic and bustling headquarters for the organization. Lorch followed his interest in recycling by becoming co-owner of Total Reclaim, an electronic waste recycling company. However, that story is not as happy as Free Ride Zone. Lorch pleaded guilty in 2018 to fraud after exporting hazardous electronic waste overseas in violation of state agreements and altering records in an attempt to cover it up.[46] He was sentenced to twenty-eight months in prison.

Free Ride Zone soon found a natural partnership with the Seattle Kids Bike Swap, a large one-day event a group of parents started in 1997. Each spring, families would gather in Columbia City's Genesee Park to trade in their kids' old bikes that were too small for them, to offset the cost of a new-to-them bigger bike. It was an affordable, practical, and fun way for families to make sure their growing kids had bikes that fit them properly. Joel Horn, one of the primary swap organizers, connected with Free Ride Zone and eventually turned the event over to the organization.[47] Not only was the swap an important event, it also provided a basis for weekly adult volunteer repair parties. People could come to Bike Works and wrench on bikes to get them ready for the swap, developing community and learning repair skills at the same time.[48]

Free Ride Zone also started focusing on running an Earn-a-Bike program. "There were Earn-a-Bike programs starting up around the country at the time, and so we started the Seattle version," Carlson said in our interview. They partnered with the nearby Orca K–8 School to provide an after-school program and grew from there. After a few years, the name Free Ride Zone did not encompass everything the organization was doing, so they changed the name to Bike Works. The organization continued growing, developing new and innovative youth programs under the leadership of Tina Bechler. Bechler worked on youth programs for eighteen years before leaving in 2021. During that time, she led the development of the organization's 250-page Frameworks youth bike curriculum that is used by organizations across the nation.[49]

Carlson was Bike Works' executive director for seven years before heading to Chicago in 2003 to go to grad school. "The EDs that followed after me have done a great job and have really built the organization," she said. Under the direction of Deb Salls in the 2010s, Bike Works finally expanded beyond the yellow house by opening a much larger warehouse and classroom space nearby. The yellow house continues to serve the community as a welcoming and affordable bike shop.

PART 2

Seattle Enters a

Bicycle Renaissance

MIKE BIKES campaign poster from the McGinn for Mayor
campaign in 2009. Courtesy of Brice Maryman, McGinn for
Mayor 2009 campaign.

CHAPTER 6

Biking Tries to Go Mainstream

It wasn't the action of a single mayor nor the weight of a single moment that primed Seattle for a major shift in its transportation culture by the start of the 2010s but, rather, a decades-long struggle to push back against a cars-first mentality. Once the city was finally ready to start dedicating roadway space to biking, the Seattle Department of Transportation did not call up a concrete company and start pouring curbs to permanently protect the new bike lanes. Instead, Seattle got out the paint and redrew the lines or painted little pictures of bikes in the middle of traffic lanes. It was a sometimes timid yet important step for biking in the city.

But the city's interest in repainting the designs of its streets was not just about biking. Many of the new bike lanes were also about road safety for all users. Annual traffic deaths were down from their all-time highs, but they were stubbornly consistent throughout the 1990s. Seattle needed new strategies if it hoped to reduce the annual toll. Traffic deaths hit an all-time high on Seattle streets in 1934, when 121 people died in collisions. Seattle had grown from 43,000 people in 1890 to 365,000 in 1930, and the arrival of cars was devastating as the city tried to build out car infrastructure fast enough to keep up with its rapidly growing population and city limits. Safety was not high on the priority list, and an almost unimaginable number of people paid the price. The number of traffic deaths fell to around 50 per year during the 1950s, but the freeway boom years created a volatile pattern in the annual death count. For example, there were around 50 deaths in 1960 but more than 90 deaths in 1967 and 1968 each. Then Interstate 5 opened and Boeing nearly went bust, and deaths went down to around 50 per year again before climbing up to around 70 in 1971. From there, the trend settled into a gradual decline averaging around 30 deaths per year in the 1990s and around 20 deaths per year in the 2010s. The traffic death rate per capita in 1934 was 0.33 deaths per 1,000 residents. By 2011, that number had fallen to 0.02 deaths per 1,000 residents.[1]

In the years following those 1930s peaks, many of the nation's traffic safety increases came from manufacturers improving the effectiveness of car tires and brakes or government regulating car safety equipment such as headlights. Transportation engineers also started installing traffic signals at key intersections and illuminating busy thoroughfares with streetlights. The goal was not to reduce driving, it was to make driving safer, and engineers were partially successful. But while reducing annual deaths from more than a hundred in the 1930s to around fifty by the late 1970s was a significant change, that number was hardly anything to celebrate. These numbers represent human lives. Seat belts became mandatory in the early 1970s, then additional safety technologies like improved crumple zones, energy-absorbing car frame designs, air bags, and antilock brakes became standard during the 1980s and '90s to further reduce traffic deaths.[2]

Progress on US traffic safety was slow, but Seattle significantly outpaced the nation as a whole. The US annual traffic death count in the 2010s remained stalled at around an average of 35,000 lives per year, nearly the same as the average of 36,000 the nation experienced in the 1950s.[3] But Seattle's annual traffic death count in the 2010s was about 20 per year, far below the city's 1950s average of about 50 traffic deaths per year. Seattle did something right that most other places in the nation did not. Or perhaps just as importantly, Seattle did not do certain things wrong. Wider streets encourage more speeding and discourage walking, biking, and transit use. Many cities across the nation invested heavily in widening their streets whenever possible, often with the goal of improving traffic flow to and from freeway ramps. By successfully fighting several planned freeways as described in chapter 3, Seattle residents also prevented traffic engineers from widening all the neighborhood streets that would have accessed a freeway ramp. For example, major east-west streets in the Central Area like Union, Cherry, and Jackson Streets would have been freeway collectors for the R. H. Thomson Expressway ramps. If those streets had been widened as is standard for streets with freeway access, the number of traffic deaths and injuries in the Central Area would have been higher too. Fighting the Thomson didn't just save the properties directly in its path, it also saved the walkability and bikeability of all the neighborhood streets leading to it.

Widening streets and impeding walkability also triggers the phenomenon of induced demand. Creating more road capacity leads to more driving, which creates so-called bottlenecks of traffic backups elsewhere in the system. The very concept of a bottleneck is perhaps part of the problem. In this metaphor, there is a bottle's worth of cars trying to squeeze through the skinny neck, so it stands to reason that making the neck wider will allow all the cars to flow straight out. But this metaphor assumes that the bottle stays the same size. What really happens is that as the neck gets wider, the bottle also gets bigger, consuming more and more of the community and its walkability until there is little left other than street space and parking lots. Many places have been trying for decades to chase bottlenecks all over their cities, but widening roads often induces even more car trips, leading to backups in the same place or somewhere else nearby.[4] This is why so many of the nation's shopping districts that have streets six lanes or wider still experience traffic jams. By comparison, Seattle has been restrained, in part by choice and in part because the city's geography and development make widening streets difficult and expensive.

Seattle Paints the Town with Sharrows, 2000-2010

Perhaps as important, the city started actively calming many of its streets starting in the 1970s in an effort to reduce collisions and make it easier for people to cross streets on foot. These safety redesigns were low-budget improvements with huge payoffs. To give a common example, the city would repaint the lines on a four-lane street to instead have one lane in each direction plus a center turn lane. It was fast, as well as easy and cheap to implement, and the resulting street could move the same number of cars but with far fewer injuries and deaths. It also allowed the city to install more safe and low-cost crosswalks, a popular and high-demand request from residents and retail business owners. Safety redesigns also protected the walking-focused style of most of the city's neighborhood business districts and helped prevent the widespread adoption of strip-mall development common during the second half of the twentieth century. Seattle had completed safety redesigns on twenty-four different streets between 1972 and 2010, and until the 2000s, they were not overly controversial.[5] It's difficult to find any media coverage of the projects, suggesting that people mostly accepted the changes as just part of regular and unremarkable city maintenance.

But that changed in the early 2000s under Mayor Greg Nickels. Nickels was on the King County Council for all of the 1990s, and he came to the mayoral job as a big supporter of Sound Transit regional light rail, but he was otherwise not overly focused on environmental projects or cycling, at least at first. For example, one of the first major projects he oversaw after taking office in 2002 was a massive $14 million remake of the area along the west side of Lake Union. The project removed abandoned railway tracks that ran from South Lake Union to Fremont near the north end of the lake. But rather than build a trail where the former tracks had been, the project turned nearly all of the new public space into a 1.5-mile-long parking lot with 1,271 publicly owned, free-to-use car parking spaces.[6]

Nickels had inherited the project from outgoing Mayor Paul Schell, but he did not take action to fix the glaring problems with the project. People who biked were surprised to learn that the city was investing so much money in the only flat and connected piece of public land between the Fremont Bridge and downtown, yet was choosing not to build a pathway for biking. Though some tried to organize at the last minute to get a trail added, Nickels went ahead with construction as planned. The mistake would take fifteen years and millions of dollars to fix. But blowing such an opportunity to create a quality flat and direct bike route along the lake galvanized a new set of bicycle advocates, including future bike-commuting City Councilmember Mike O'Brien and future bike-commuting Mayor Mike McGinn.

As his time as mayor went on, Nickels found national success by making climate change a focus of his work. When George W. Bush won his second term as president, Nickels said that Seattle would meet the Kyoto Protocol's emission reduction goals that the Bush administration had abandoned, and he called on other mayors to join Seattle. The effort landed Nickels a spot in a *Vanity Fair* magazine spread for their Green Issue in 2006.[7] When the time came to develop a transportation levy to send to voters, bicycle advocates saw their opportunity to push for consistent funding of actual bicycle infrastructure work. But first they needed a way to generate and prioritize bike projects, so they worked with Nickels to create in 2007 the city's first modern Bicycle Master Plan.

"When I first started, you know what the budget was in the Bike Program? It was like $270,000 a year. It was nothing," said Sam Woods in an interview for this book. Woods worked for SDOT's Bicycle Program from 1990 until her retirement in 2019 and led the program for most of the 2010s. While that number may seem like a lot of money at first, it is pennies in terms of civil engineering. With such a low annual budget, the most the program could really do was paint a few lines on the road, create and print some bike maps, and put up some signs. "Before [the 2007 Bike Master Plan] we were more opportunistic," said Woods. "Like Dearborn," a busy, wide street just south of downtown Seattle. "We put these little four-foot-wide bike lanes because the road was really wide and you could still have eleven-foot[-wide] lanes and have four-foot bike lanes. . . . Doing that kind of striping, especially with a repaving job, is very cost-effective."

As the 2006 Bridging the Gap levy took shape, the proposed funding measure heavily favored road paving and bridge work. This concerned bike advocates who worried that bike projects were getting too small a slice of the pie, so Nickels oversaw passage of the city's Complete Streets ordinance, requiring the city to ensure safety for people walking and biking in every major paving project. Complete streets were not only the ethical way to design and fund transportation projects, the policy also made all the paving funding in the levy more palatable to the growing and increasingly organized safe streets movement. Seattle voters approved the Bridging the Gap levy in 2006, and within a year Seattle City Council approved the Complete Streets ordinance and the Bicycle Master Plan.

After voter approval, the city immediately got to work painting miles and miles of bike lanes and sharrows around town. They were not always high-quality bike lanes, and the lanes nearly always disappeared at busy intersections, but they were something. The strategy was quantity, not quality. But Nickels was also creating space within SDOT to change some of the long-standing ways the department had been thinking about streets, including bicycling. He wanted results, and he wanted the Bicycle Master Plan to be integrated into all the department's work.

"Under Mayor Nickels, more got done than under any other mayor," said Pete Lagerwey in the interview for this book, who led SDOT's Bicycle

Program from 1984 to 2009. "He really put the screws to the department to produce a certain amount of mileage every year." He would require regular progress reports from the department, checking to make sure the bike plan was getting completed. "The first Bike Master Plan, those were such exciting times," said Woods in his interview for this book. "We've got this adopted bike plan, and we've got the money [from the Bridging the Gap levy], and everyone was super jealous. Plus we had the political support for this. And we did a lot." The first three years after the levy was approved, the city painted ninety-two miles of bike lanes and sharrows. "We were energized," Woods told me. While many of those bike lanes were still a bit too skinny, provided no physical protection from car traffic, and disappeared before busy intersections, they nearly tripled the city's bike lane mileage in just four years and helped to increase the city's bike-to-work rate by about 52 percent, according to an annual US Census survey.[8]

"Eventually we picked all the low-hanging fruit, and then it got a lot harder," said Woods in the interview. SDOT quickly tackled the streets that could easily accommodate bike lanes without impacting any other mode of travel. The department also mostly avoided removing parking or reducing general-purpose traffic lanes from streets that were busy enough for anyone to notice a difference. The result was that a lot of projects really did help people get around by bike safely, but only to a point.

Perhaps no piece of "infrastructure" represents this phase of Seattle bicycle investment better than the *sharrow*, officially known as a "shared-lane marking." A sharrow is a pictograph of a bicycle with two chevrons ahead of it, pointing in the direction of travel, and Seattle often painted them in mixed traffic lanes on busy streets. Sharrows don't change any rules of the road. Instead, they are intended to remind people driving that people are allowed to bike on the street and that drivers should look out for them. It's a passive-aggressive way of reminding people of the rules of the road, like an unsigned note left on a smelly office refrigerator. SDOT painted ninety-one miles of sharrows all over the city between 2007 and 2012. They were cheap, easy to install, highly visible, and uncontroversial. They quickly became a symbol of Seattle trying to look bike-friendly while not actually doing the hard work needed to achieve that goal. When I started *Seattle Bike Blog* in 2010, I used the sharrow as the site's logo because it seemed to represent biking in Seattle at the time, though I turned it sideways and inverted the colors, like a black computer cursor prompt on a white screen.

The real test of a mayor's dedication to cycling safety and safe streets is how they handle a project that faces opposition. With the city suddenly painting bike lanes (and pictures of bikes) all over town, a backlash started to form. Even though the city had been conducting safe streets redesigns for decades, the addition of bike lanes to these safety projects and the growing political power of bicycle advocates were challenges to the car-dominant status quo. Whenever a dominant culture is challenged, the push-back against the new cultural idea can be fierce.

For example, in the early 2000s, Seattle planned a fix to Stone Way North, a busy street on the border of the Wallingford and Fremont neighborhoods in North Seattle. At the time, Stone Way had a mix of industrial businesses, housing, and neighborhood retail. It is also the least-steep street up the long hill from the Burke-Gilman Trail to the Forty-Fifth Street business district and Green Lake. Stone Way North had four travel lanes, two in each direction, and few safe crosswalks. Every year, several people were injured trying to walk across Stone Way. SDOT proposed a fix much like the one they had completed decades earlier on nearby North Forty-Fifth Street: repaint the lines to have one lane in each direction and add a center turn lane. But this time, they were also planning to paint a bike lane in the uphill direction, and that's when the fighting began. Industrial businesses and key landowners along the street resisted the project, claiming it would destroy their businesses. "We need the road. We need to move traffic, particularly trucks," Fremont business and property owner Suzie Burke told the *Seattle Times* in 2006. "It's not a good idea to narrow the street down because traffic will overflow on other streets. This is our arterial. We want the four lanes of traffic to be."[9] And with that, street safety redesigns became a political flash point in Seattle.

The fight over the way the lines were painted on the street became a symbolic proxy war about people's frustration with the direction their growing city was taking. You can see it in the words Burke used. Stone Way was "our arterial," she said, not the property of some person trying to ride a bike or walk across the street. This wasn't about traffic flow or safety, it was about who gets primacy on this stretch of public land. It was about power. Some industrial business owners and workers saw property values rising fast on both sides of Stone Way, and they feared their days on the street were numbered. Sure enough, Stone Way soon became a hot spot for housing and retail development, pushing out many of the more industry-oriented businesses there.

These changes were a product of economic forces in the growing city. Nearby property values were skyrocketing, so more-profitable dense residential and retail uses of the street were pricing low-density industry out of the area. I think most people can sympathize with the frustration of someone who owns or works at a business that is being priced out of an area, but the lines painted on the street were not responsible for this much larger shift in the neighborhood's economy. Trucks would still be able to use the street just fine with the bike lane in place. However, the lines on the street became symbols of the larger change, and they were something that city politicians could be held to account over. At the time, Critical Mass was peaking in popularity (see chapter 5) and Cascade Bicycle Club's political ambitions were growing. The bike movement was on the verge of pushing its way into the city's political mainstream and wielded some actual political power. Stone Way was a test both of Mayor Nickels's self-proclaimed dedication to improving cycling conditions and of the bike movement's political abilities.

Like so many Seattle bike lanes at the time, the planned lane on Stone Way was not a high-quality facility. It was skinny and went in only one direction, leaving people biking downhill to ride in mixed traffic on top of sharrows. But the street made a high-priority connection between the Burke-Gilman—the city's best bike trail—and the nexus of popular bike routes that converged around Green Lake. It was a must-win project and a potentially precedent-setting test of Seattle's new bicycling and complete streets policies. Losing this fight would have made a mockery of the brand-new Bicycle Master Plan, so the stakes for the bike movement were also much higher than just this one street. Cascade Bicycle Club, with Advocacy Director David Hiller leading the way, took a page from the Critical Mass playbook and organized a rush-hour protest ride in which several hundred people biked around Fremont and Stone Way to support the Stone Way bike lanes and encourage the city to keep the Burke-Gilman Trail open during nearby construction.[10] The message to City Hall was clear: back up your talk with action. Mayor Nickels and the city stuck to their original goal of improving safety on the street and went through with the Stone Way redesign. But the backlash left an impression, and Nickels put other bike lanes that were starting to face opposition on the back burner, delaying decisions about them until after his hoped-for reelection in 2009. SDOT kept its bike plan mileage goals on track by painting even more sharrows to make up for the delayed bike lanes.

Because Stone Way was such a hot-button issue, the city conducted a before-and-after study of the project. Just like SDOT predicted, the road became significantly safer while still carrying the necessary traffic. Collisions with people walking dropped 80 percent, total injury collisions dropped 33 percent, and bicycle trips increased 35 percent, the study found.[11] Though people feared the reduction in lanes would increase traffic on side streets, the study found that traffic levels actually dropped on side streets, perhaps because people could now more easily make left turns to and from Stone Way, thanks to the new center turn lane. Even with its lackluster ambitions and half measures for bicycling, the project was a success. It was better for walking with its safer crosswalks, it was better for biking up the long hill, and it was better for driving with fewer serious collisions and easier left turns.

Unfortunately, this was not the lesson many people in Seattle took away from the fight. Instead, the Stone Way fight became a template for intense political trench warfare over street safety redesigns for the next half decade. The city's most cost-effective tool for fighting traffic injuries and deaths—simply repainting the lines on the street—had become lines on a political battle map, and the young bike movement was drafted to the front. Some Seattle conservatives and media personalities even had a catchy name for the fight. Welcome to the "War on Cars."

The War on Cars, 2009-2011

At first, only a silhouette of a man was visible in the fog of war. But gradually, more details of this mysterious general emerged. He had a scruffy white beard, and his body armor was a suit coat he stuffed into a pannier on the back of his bicycle when riding from campaign event to campaign event. His path to power was not typical for a Seattle politician. He didn't have the support of the powerful Seattle Metropolitan Chamber of Commerce, and the city's labor unions were divided.[12] Instead, he was an environmentalist and neighborhood organizer who got his local political start trying to convince the city to build safer crosswalks in Greenwood, the neighborhood where he lived. His campaign handed out stickers that people slapped on bike racks across the city. It was a two-tone image of him wearing a rain jacket with a baseball cap under his helmet, and it simply said MIKE BIKES.

Mike McGinn shocked city politics in the late 2000s. He was a leader for the local chapter of the Sierra Club and had founded a nonprofit called Great Cities, which brought environmental and neighborhood groups together to promote better and more sustainable land use and transportation policy. He also biked to get around, which was not common for elected city officials at the time. McGinn had supported Mayor Greg Nickels in his two successful election campaigns in 2001 and 2005, and McGinn's job at the Sierra Club was to push Mayor Nickels to be an environmental leader. At the same time, McGinn had become a leader of his neighborhood community council in Greenwood and grew frustrated by how hard it was to secure money to build sidewalks and crosswalks.[13] He had made friends with the Cascade Bicycle Club through his Sierra Club work, and they successfully fought together against a 2007 ballot measure that tied a lot of highway spending to popular regional transit expansion plans. The loss was fairly shocking because the measure had wide support from business, labor, and the political establishment. Even organizations that were not particularly excited about the measure were hesitant to fight a plan with such widespread support. "The only other organization that joined us was the Cascade Bike Club," said McGinn during an interview for this book. But the Sierra Club's coalition, with some unwelcome help from antitransit landowner Kemper Freeman, led the fight against the measure by arguing that it would be expensive and make climate change worse. Sound Transit came back the next year with a transit-only measure, and it passed easily.

The cracks between McGinn's movement and Mayor Nickels grew during Nickels's second term. The 2007 and 2008 transit measures also revealed waning public support for the established political order and exposed the growing electoral space for politics that were more ambitious about climate change. McGinn then helped run a successful parks levy campaign. He also got involved with the People's Waterfront Coalition, which was fighting a new plan to dig a freeway tunnel to replace the aging Alaskan Way Viaduct, the elevated freeway along the downtown waterfront built in 1953 that was damaged in the 2001 Nisqually earth-

quake. Mayor Nickels supported the tunnel, going against the environmental bona fides he had gained earlier. "We have Greg Nickels who was
on the cover of *Vanity Fair* and he couldn't build a damn bike lane and
he backed the tunnel," said McGinn during our interview. Nickels was
not actually on the cover, though he was featured in a spread alongside
a handful of other mayors (see note 7 for this chapter). Nickels had also
constructed many miles of bike lanes after overseeing the creation of
the Bicycle Master Plan, as noted earlier in this chapter, though many
bike lanes were put on pause before the 2009 election. Nickels was backing away from some of his environmentally friendly and bike-friendly
promises, and McGinn was frustrated. So he wondered who was planning to run against Nickels. "I'm looking around, and nobody's running.
They all think Greg has it sewn up," he said. One day while riding his bike
into downtown, the idea hit him. "All of a sudden I realized I could win.
I could beat this guy. I could be mayor. . . . And I just said that to myself
over and over: 'I could be mayor.'"

Mayor Nickels was losing public support even before a major snow-
storm hit the city in December 2008. The snow wasn't his fault, obviously, but it took most of a week for the city to get the streets cleared
enough for buses and traffic to start moving again. Fair or not, Nickels
ended up taking much of the blame, a major political hit that would
make it even more difficult for him to turn his waning approval ratings
around.

McGinn wasn't the only one to challenge Nickels that year. A little-
known T-Mobile executive named Joe Mallahan also entered the race,
and he kicked off his run by putting $200,000 of his own money into
his campaign. Mallahan got a very slow and uncertain start, but he was
eventually able to gather enough support based largely on his history as
a business executive to edge out Nickels in the primary. Mallahan was a
fairly weak candidate whose campaign had spent money on confusing
ads attacking the type of paint the city was using for its bike lanes.[14] But
he still had the weight of the business elite behind him, as well as a big
share of the labor unions, often enough to win an election. Mallahan
spent nearly four times as much money on his campaign as McGinn did
on his, but Mike's grassroots style of organizing proved to be enough to
win 51 percent of the vote.[15]

The win was a huge moment for bike advocates in Seattle, who
had strongly supported McGinn's campaign. Someone who biked to

campaign events was elected mayor on a platform of bold environmental action, including strong support for investing in bicycling. It is difficult to overstate the importance of this moment for bicycling in Seattle, which had been largely ignored for decades and rarely received more than table scraps or broken promises from the city government. Bicycling was officially mainstream politics in Seattle. This is also the moment I started *Seattle Bike Blog*.

But as quickly as the political power of bicycling rose, so did the political opposition. One of McGinn's challengers during the 2009 primary was Elizabeth Campbell, who led several lawsuits against various large public projects. She had few if any wins to her name, but she was able to delay housing and transportation projects and was a thorn in the side of city leaders. During a campaign event in June 2009, she accused Mayor Nickels and the city of waging a "war on cars." It's not the oldest use of this phrase in local media, but it was the one that stuck.[16] A few days later, TV news station KING 5 asked Mayor Nickels if plans to discourage parking near light rail stations was "a war on cars."[17] Then alternative weekly newspaper *The Stranger* mocked the term a month later during its popular and humorous Candidate Survivor forum by asking candidates for Seattle City Council if they supported the War on Cars. Everyone on stage answered "yes."[18] But when McGinn won, the phrase became a refrain among people trying to argue for the preservation of the car-driving status quo. Initially the phrase was mostly related to increasing the price of paid parking, but it quickly grew to encompass bike lanes too. In October 2010, KING 5 News ran another segment dedicated entirely to answering the question, "Is there a war on cars in Seattle?" Mayor McGinn responded, "I'm sorry; that is just a silly question."[19]

Framing transportation policies as a war is silly, especially in reference to the city's efforts to reduce injuries and deaths. What exactly would winning this so-called war on cars look like for car proponents? People getting killed in traffic? More people driving cars and contributing to traffic jams? Those accusing the city of waging a war on cars typically didn't have any real solutions they were trying to encourage— they were trying to stop changes they didn't like. They were fighting a perceived incursion on the cultural dominance of the car and, in a way, acknowledging the emerging power of the local bicycle movement they had previously ignored.

Grassroots Groups Form as Cascade Struggles to Be Mainstream, 2010-present

"An April fundraising breakfast for bicycling advocates could have been a meeting of the Chamber of Commerce, with all the business leaders and elected officials eating eggs and waiting for the keynote speaker," wrote *Seattle Times* reporter Emily Heffter in 2010.[20] "The sixth annual Cascade Bicycle Club breakfast was proof, if you needed any, that a once-fringe activist group has landed squarely in the mainstream of Seattle politics. Sponsors included Vulcan and Starbucks, and the breakfast was attended by every member of the city council, as well as the mayor, county executive, [King] County Council members and state legislators." But the sudden rise of political power nearly broke Cascade, which seemed to collapse under the pressure of its recent successes. Seattle's new mayor moved forward with bike lane and safe streets projects that Mayor Nickels had delayed, such as safety redesigns on West Nickerson Street and Northeast 125th Street. But rather than revel in its new prominent position at the transportation policy table, the club's board fired longtime executive director Chuck Ayers, setting off a fight that some members called "a civil war."[21]

The dispute boiled down to a backlash from more conservative board members who wanted Cascade to focus on bike rides rather than leading provocative actions or engaging with McGinn's progressive politics. A group of members calling themselves the Bike Club Rescue Squad gathered member support to recall the board, prompting the board to resign en masse rather than face a membership vote. Seattle City Councilmember Mike O'Brien, a bike commuter, summed up the club's problems well in the *Times* story: "I think we've hit a critical mass, where bikes are transformed from this really fringe group to being a relevant part of the population," he said. "When you market to the folks that go to the Chamber [of Commerce] breakfasts, it creates a little tension with the activists."[22]

Meanwhile, a new kind of biking and safe streets advocacy was born in small coffee shops, microbreweries, and library meeting rooms across the city. In these spaces far away from catered breakfasts in downtown hotel ballrooms, the bike advocacy grass roots were growing stronger and deeper than ever. With Cascade embroiled in a "civil war" and loud bike lane debates in mainstream news media devolving into absurd arguments over a supposed "war on cars," neighbors in two different parts of Seattle were working independently on a deceptively simple idea that approached bicycling and safe streets from a very different point of view: a child's. While cross-city bike routes were great and all, what about people's needs to bike around their own neighborhoods? Where was the city's plan for helping kids bike to school? They turned the camera away from the bike commuter passing a line of stopped cars in rush-hour traffic and instead focused on an eight-year-old trying to shakily bike from home to a nearby park. From this perspective, Seattle's neighborhood streets appeared menacing, hostile, and immoral. But these groups also had ideas for how to make them right.

The first two neighborhood groups were Beacon BIKES (which stood for Better Infrastructure Keeping Everyone Safe, though later the name was changed to Beacon Hill Safe Streets) and Spokespeople, based in Wallingford. The work these groups were doing sparked a small revolution in neighborhoods across the city, and there was a simple type of infrastructure at the center of it: a neighborhood greenway.[23] Formerly known in Seattle as bicycle boulevards, neighborhood greenways are residential streets with slow speed limits that are connected by whatever infrastructure is needed to create a safe and complete biking and walking route. Both Vancouver, British Columbia, and Portland, Oregon, had been building neighborhood greenways for years, so Seattle's neighborhood groups had good models to emulate. Cars are still allowed on a neighborhood greenway, but steps are taken to limit the number of people driving there. Ideally, only people accessing a home on the street should drive on a neighborhood greenway. Significant traffic calming efforts are added, such as speed humps, to slow the few cars using the routes so that the street becomes comfortable for people of all ages and abilities to use. The surest sign of a successful neighborhood greenway is seeing a group of neighborhood kids playing in the street.

The most organized, energized, and immediately effective Seattle group, at least at first, was Beacon BIKES on Beacon Hill. They got tired of waiting for SDOT to get around to making their neighborhood's streets safe or adopting the Portland and Vancouver neighborhood greenway model, so they decided to apply for a grant from the Department of Neighborhoods to hire a professional transportation planning team to help write the Beacon Hill Family Bike and Pedestrian Circulation Plan.[24] "Beacon Hill residents are debuting a new form of transportation planning for their community," the plan declared.[25] SDOT embraced the planning effort and contributed to it, but the idea that it was not the lead agency in charge of a transportation plan was unusual. It was not an official SDOT plan, but it looked like one. It was intended to represent neighborhood priorities and influence SDOT's official transportation planning efforts. "Neighbors and advocates describe the process of creating the circulation plan as 'local destination-based planning,'" the plan's introduction said. "The community values continuous routes without gaps, so that children and adults can more safely travel the entire route to their destination. The goal is to enable families and children to travel to local destinations on continuous signed routes. Advocates believe that if a system is sufficiently safe for children to get to school, all Beacon Hill neighbors will be able to comfortably and more safely ride bikes on local trips to the store, to parks, and to visit neighbors."

The document was only part of the project's benefit. The process of creating the plan was a good excuse to engage neighbors in a conversation about biking, walking, and safe streets. They conducted a lot of community outreach, and because they were a group of neighbors rather than a city agency, they were able to reach people in a different way. For example, they invited the neighborhood to brunch one Saturday and spent hours going over table-sized maps to learn about people's different challenges and ideas for solutions. They also held a large community parade along one of their most promising routes for a neighborhood greenway. People walked, biked, and even rode on a large bicycle-powered parade float, which I can attest was extremely fun to help pedal. It was a neighborhood celebration that also helped teach people about what a neighborhood greenway is and how it could work on Beacon Hill.

When talking about transportation issues with neighbors, the group centered conversations around neighborhood destinations. So rather than asking, "How can people move through this corridor?" they asked, "How can people get to El Centro de la Raza?" Or to the Sound Transit light rail station or Kimball Elementary School or Jefferson Park or McPherson's Produce and so on. By framing transportation this way, they received different answers than might emerge from a more typical transportation plan. It forced people to think less from the perspective of someone traveling on a busy street and more from the perspective of someone trying to get across that same busy street. The Beacon Hill Family Bike and Pedestrian Circulation plan was completed in 2011, and

SDOT later constructed many pieces of it, including the city's first long complete neighborhood greenway, a route connecting from the I-90 Trail at the north end of Beacon Hill all the way south to Georgetown via Jefferson Park.

Spokespeople took a different angle. Founded by Cathy Tuttle in Wallingford, Spokespeople initially led a series of slow bike rides targeting beginners or people generally unsure about biking in Seattle. The goal was to just get people on bikes, starting with a short and easy-to-digest group ride on comfortable streets with slow speed.[26] After visiting Portland in 2010, Tuttle started working to convince the city to move quickly and test out the concept of a neighborhood greenway. Through Spokespeople, she applied for an SDOT neighborhood grant to build a fairly short one on North Forty-Fourth Street, a block south of the main business street in Wallingford.

The two groups were getting traction both with elected officials and with a wide range of people in their own communities. They had tapped into a big population of people who weren't necessarily interested in long rides or bike commuting but were interested in biking around their own neighborhoods and making sure their neighbors were safe. Combined with the existing bike advocates, the force for safe streets grew quickly. On *Seattle Bike Blog*, I wrote a series of stories in 2011 called "Neighborhood-Powered Streets" that highlighted the work of these two groups and suggested that readers could form similar groups in their neighborhoods.[27] Tuttle proved to be especially generous with her time and was happy to help new neighborhood organizers connect with each other and with other resources that could help them with their neighborhood's specific needs. Her work to help neighborhood groups get organized soon grew and turned into a new nonprofit organization called Seattle Neighborhood Greenways with Tuttle as the founding executive director. Greenways was a central hub designed to lead from the bottom up, meaning its mission was to support the efforts of neighborhood groups rather than direct the actions of those groups.

The early 2010s saw an almost frantic amount of organizing in neighborhoods across the city. Starting a neighborhood group was a lot of fun. As soon as someone suggested a new group on *Seattle Bike Blog*, their local news blog, or social media, neighbors would jump on board. Groups held lively brainstorming meetings where they laid big maps on tables and let people draw bike route lines or mark out problem areas. Certain ideas would come up over and over, and those became priorities. Often, people would show up to a meeting curious about the idea and leave with a leadership role and a list of responsibilities. I was involved in the founding of Central Seattle Greenways, and I was amazed how quickly the group coalesced and the way leaders emerged from the process. One person named Gordon Padelford immediately proved to be an exceptional organizer of the group, and Tuttle saw that too. She hired him to float around the city and give groups hands-on help getting organized. Several years later, Padelford became the second executive director of Seattle Neighborhood Greenways after Tuttle retired.

Because Seattle Neighborhood Greenways is designed to respond to and support community priorities, it is remarkably flexible and nimble. When times demand a certain focus, the organization is prepared to drop what it's doing and redesign its work to meet the emerging need. It isn't tied to a specific set of programming. For example, when the COVID-19 pandemic emerged in early 2020, Greenways quickly identified the public's need for a lot more open space as many other recreational opportunities shut down. So the group advocated for a network of car-free streets around the city that could provide more outdoor space for people even if they didn't live near a park or trail. SDOT's Stay Healthy Streets program was an immediate hit, and the city moved quickly to build twenty miles of them in 2020. At one point, expansion was briefly put on hold because SDOT had used every "road closed" sign it owned and needed to get more. Car travel on the already low-traffic residential streets decreased more than 90 percent in places, a sign that the program was working and that neighbors had embraced the concept. The number of people biking on these streets increased nearly 300 percent.[28] As soon as the "road closed" signs went up, people started walking right down the middle of the street. A Stay Healthy Street was an oasis of positivity during a grim and scary time.

As Greenways grew, the organization brought in a lot of people who weren't previously engaged in safe streets advocacy. Though Cascade's leadership may have gone through some turmoil, the organization's dedicated staff and volunteers were still a powerful political force. Together, Greenways and Cascade continued building a movement throughout the first half of the 2010s, solidifying safe streets and bicycling as a mainstream political priority. Cascade staffers Craig Benjamin and Max Hepp-Buchanan started an innovative and powerful program called the Advocacy Leadership Institute (ALI) in 2012.[29] The three-month program trained a small group of people about how their local power structures work and how to create and run an effective campaign based on personal stories. The program was entirely free, though participants were asked to commit to the full program if their applications were accepted.

The result was profound. People who graduated from the course went on to lead their local Neighborhood Greenways groups, started bike-to-school efforts at their kids' schools, joined political election campaigns, and created projects to make cycling more appealing to more people. My spouse, Kelli Refer, led the ALI program for several years when she worked at Cascade, and I was a regular guest speaker. My favorite aspect of ALI is that Cascade empowered all these people to become advocates and organizers in their own ways, even though much of what they went on to do didn't have Cascade's name attached to it. The project is inherently optimistic, investing in community members and trusting that they will then go out in the world and do good things that will ultimately make progress on Cascade's mission. Some stayed at Cascade and got more deeply involved in the organization (several graduates have served on the Cascade board of directors), but many go out and do things that ALI's teachers or Cascade staff never dreamed of.

For example, Merlin Rainwater was already a dedicated advocate for bike safety before taking the ALI program. She attended every monthly meeting of the Seattle Bicycle Advisory Board, a volunteer board launched in 1977 with appointees by the mayor and city council that advise all city departments on bike-related issues.[30] (Fun fact: Bill Nye the Science Guy was a bike board member in the 1990s.[31]) Rainwater initially attended as a member of the community and was often the only person other than me who was not a member of the board or scheduled to present. She later served the maximum of two terms as a member. A student in Chicago in the mid-1960s and a member of Students for a Democratic Society, Rainwater grew up as and remains a Quaker, and she has always ridden a bicycle as her primary means of transportation. Walking and biking "keeps us in contact with a place, that if you're walking or biking, you can stop and notice things, and you don't have to look for a place to leave your two-thousand-pound box that you're carrying around with you, and you can interact with people and the environment," Rainwater said in a 2018 interview with art and culture historian and self-described "performance geographer" Jasmine Mahmoud, then a professor at Seattle University. "I think that the world of cars has taken something really important away from us in these tiny everyday interactions that people have when they get around on foot," Rainwater added.[32] Rainwater became a strong community leader after graduating from ALI and retiring from her work in hospice care. First she joined Seattle's Bicycle Advisory Board, which was fitting after so many years attending from the audience. She has probably been to more Bicycle Advisory Board meetings than anyone other than SDOT's Bicycle Program staff. She also created a regular group bike ride called Senior Ladies on Wheels (SLOW). At first they were relatively short and, yes, slow bike rides to various destinations around town like a nice little park or coffee shop. But they evolved into much more. She started designing the rides both to be fun and to teach about city history.

As Rainwater was learning about Seattle's history of redlining, she got an idea while looking at a map of the old housing restrictions, as she told local National Public Radio affiliate KUOW: "You know, a map and a line? That could be a bike ride!"[33] So she created the Red Line Rides. She would lead people on a slow bike ride along the old lines demarcating the divides between segregated neighborhoods. The ride stopped often for Rainwater to talk about the history of each location and tell stories about how redlining worked and was enforced there. Rainwater is white, and she leads the rides because she believes it's important for white people to educate each other and learn a history that is far too easy for them to ignore. "The policies that created segregation have been so successful that, if you live in a white world, it's kind of hard to see out of it," she told Mahmoud. "You just have to learn to see it."[34]

Rainwater expanded on this idea in her interview on KUOW. "It really is white people's history," she said. "White people were the actors that developed and implemented the policies that led to segregation. And it's really inappropriate to, say, segregate those aspects of history that Black people suffered under and label those 'Black history,' as if they weren't relevant to the rest of us."[35] Her rides became very popular, and she soon developed walking versions to make them more accessible. They often fill up shortly after registration opens, a sign not just of the success of the rides but also of city residents finally thirsting for firsthand knowledge of how segregation worked in Seattle. And to Rainwater, biking or walking to see places for yourself makes the history much more powerful.

A spontaneous memorial for Sher Kung sprung up on August 29, 2014, near the site of her death. Within days, it was filled with notes, flowers, and a ghost bike. Photo by Tom Fucoloro, *Seattle Bike Blog.*

CHAPTER 7

Too Many

With Seattle and Mayor Mike McGinn facing accusations that they were waging a "war on cars," *The Stranger* wrote a staff editorial in 2011 facing the phrase head-on in a piece titled "Okay, Fine, It's War." "The mindless repetition of this 'War on Cars' falsehood—by car advocates harboring a phony, self-serving sense of victimhood—has led to a situation in which this 'War on Cars' is acknowledged by most Seattleites to be real," *The Stranger* staff wrote. "Because of this regrettable specter, it is high time that cyclists, pedestrians, and their transit-riding comrades openly publish their views, their aims, their tendencies, and meet this nursery tale of a 'War on Cars' with a manifesto of and by the nondrivers themselves."[1] The piece called for an end to subsidies for driving, putting most public dollars toward transit and protecting people biking and walking. The paper took a fighting stance, writing, "Seattle as a whole is now more and more splitting up into two great hostile camps, into two great classes directly fighting each other—car driver and nondriver." But the idea that drivers and nondrivers were locked in battle came crashing down to earth in 2011. It wasn't because of a war-posturing manifesto, but because something horrific happened. People died. After years of heated screeds about an imagined "war" over the streets, the city was overdue to confront the real-world impact of traffic injuries and deaths.

Seattle Finally Faces the Devastating Toll of Traffic Carnage, 2011-2013

People dying in traffic had been constant in Seattle ever since cars first arrived in town. During the early years of automobiles, each death was a major news story. But gradually, the public grew to accept the deaths as the cost of doing business in a modern city. One of the core tenets of car culture is that most traffic deaths are unavoidable accidents. If anyone is to blame, it's the individuals involved and not the roadway's design or the transportation system as a whole. But something switched in Seattle in 2011, not because that year was particularly deadly but because even a record-low number of traffic deaths was still too many. Though nobody could have known it at the time, 2011 was the safest year in a century of Seattle traffic. Twelve people died in 2011, down from a high of 121 deaths in 1934 and significantly lower than the average of 29 deaths per year during the decade prior.[2] Perhaps it was because there were relatively few deaths that each individual tragedy stood out so strongly.

Mike Wang was biking home from work to his wife and two children one Thursday in July 2011 when a man driving an SUV turned quickly in front of him and struck him, knocking him to the ground at the intersection of Dexter Avenue and Thomas Street in the South Lake Union neighborhood.[3] The man driving then hit the gas and fled the scene, driving over Wang's body and killing him. In that terrible moment, another tally was added to the city's annual traffic body count.

But Mike was so much more than a tally mark. He was a talented photographer for the nonprofit health organization PATH (Program for Appropriate Technology in Health) who got his start in documentary photography during China's Tiananmen Square protests.[4] He was also deeply loved. His wife, Claire Allen, wrote a letter to the sentencing judge one year later describing the loss her family experienced:

> I know that [Erlin] Garcia-Reyes has not been arrested for this before. But once is enough.
>
> Once was enough for me to sit in Harborview with my children and hear the weeping doctor say that my husband was dead. Once was enough for us to see his corpse, so clearly him and already, frighteningly, not him. When we got home (how did we even get home?) once was enough for my young son to ask, "So the guy that hit him just drove away? You can do that?" Once was enough for my young daughter to ask if Daddy was coming home. Once should have been enough for me to sleep without the man I've loved for 22 years. For me to look at the door at 4:35 every day and then remember he wouldn't ever come home again. For me to sit at my kitchen table surrounded by bills late at night, trying to figure out how we

would live without my husband's income. For my father-in-law to come to me weeping, asking how he could go on believing in justice. For my children to mutely slam doors, cry over nothing, rage over a broken pencil, be asked by their young friends what it is like to have a dead father.

But once isn't how often those things happen. They happen all the time. The world for us is divided now into Before and After. Michael was 44 years old. We'll never hear Michael laugh again, never know pure happiness again.[5]

Immediately after Mike's death, flowers arrived on the corner as his coworkers just blocks away mourned his death and tried to comfort each other. Then someone anonymously locked an all-white "ghost bike" to the signpost, a memorial letting everyone who passed by know that a person was killed there while biking. It was not the first ghost bike, and it wouldn't be the last. Ghost bikes are used all over the world as a way to memorialize someone who died while biking and to make sure that memory of their death is not erased from the place as soon as the emergency and cleanup crews leave.

Just one month later, Brian Fairbrother died after crashing his bike down an unmarked staircase near the Fairview Avenue East Bridge in South Lake Union.[6] His loved ones held a colorful memorial walk in his memory, creating art on the landing where he had died and adorning his ghost bike with orange flowers, his favorite. Then one month after Fairbrother died, Robert Townsend was killed while making a delivery in the University District.[7] He was headed down University Way Northeast—the Ave—when someone turned left in front of him at Campus Parkway and struck him. He was twenty-three.

The weight of one death after another after another within a six-week span was too much to handle. The old lie that traffic deaths are unavoidable accidents crumbled. The loss was too great to ignore the problem any longer. I had been writing *Seattle Bike Blog* for a year at this point, and it was clear that something different was happening in people's hearts throughout Seattle. People were angry, sad, and scared in a way I had not seen before. Friends Adonia Lugo, Davey Oil, and I decided to organize a memorial ride that would pass by each of the deadly sites before ending with a social speak-out. The idea was to honor those who'd died, to show support for their loved ones, and to create space for others in the community to talk about how they were feeling and to support each other. We called it the Safe Streets Social.

Before the ride, Claire reached out and said she and Mike's father wanted to be at Mike's memorial when we rode past. She had another request that I didn't fully understand: She asked us to yell out "Wang!" as we rode past. She said he would have loved that. So before the ride, we told the eighty or so people who showed up about the request. But as we approached the site and I saw Mike's family waiting, I couldn't say anything because I was crying. It seemed like nobody could say anything. It was silent. Then as our ride turned from Dexter onto Thomas, someone finally got the syllable out: "Wang!" The floodgates opened. More people started yelling it, "Wang!" "Wang!" His family was weeping, riders were weeping. I'm weeping right now trying to write this passage. The sound of everyone finally getting up the strength to say this one word that meant something to him and his family changed something inside me. I think it was the moment when I finally let myself embrace the extent of the wound that this one traffic collision left on our world and on this family. It's the difference between knowing something to be true and understanding that truth. It was radicalizing. Safe streets went from something I thought the city "should" do to being something the city "must" do. It wasn't just a good idea, it was a moral imperative. Mike Wang did not have to die. Nobody in that annual tally of traffic deaths had to die.

I was not alone. A lot of people during this time were going through similar experiences. At the end of the Safe Streets Social, the riders gathered on Campus Parkway near the spot where Townsend had recently died. Person after person took a turn sharing their personal story of loss while everyone else listened and consoled each other. Some told stories of loved ones who had died in traffic and how their lives had never been the same. Others spoke about their own injuries from a collision and the trauma they lived with ever since.

This was not just happening in this group of eighty people who biked together that day. Mayor McGinn responded to the deaths by calling for a Road Safety Summit, a series of public meetings in which people could work together to share stories and guide a new city effort to curb traffic deaths and injuries.[8] The meetings at City Hall were sprawling and sort of purposefully open-ended, but they were powerful. Importantly, safe streets advocates were not the only ones there. Representatives from major employers, public health officials and organizations, police, the American Automobile Association, and neighborhood councils were there too. Major local media organizations covered it.

At one point, someone got up and asked everyone in the large meeting room inside City Hall to raise their hands if they or someone close to them had been seriously injured or killed in a traffic collision. I was transported back to my youth in Missouri, remembering my childhood friend Ryan Devine, who had died in a car crash alongside his friend Greg when we were in high school. In elementary school, Ryan and I partnered to present a science report about high-jumping camel crickets, which stalked both of our basements. While I was focused on paging through the encyclopedia and learning how to pronounce *Rhaphidophoridae*, Ryan wanted to make sure we left an impression on the class. During our presentation, I read facts about the crickets while he got down on his hands and feet in the front of the classroom, humped his back up high, and leaped in the air in his best impression of what a camel cricket looks like in action. I'm sure he got reprimanded by the teacher, but I think about him hopping around in front of the class every time I see one of those bugs. Years later, he and some friends with fresh driver's licenses were driving too fast and crashed on a slick turn. Word spread to meet that evening in front of Lindbergh High School, where all of us sophomores tried to console each other, hold candles, tell stories about Ryan, and say prayers. No adult had any answers to make it OK. We grew up very fast that night.

So in that meeting room in Seattle City Hall a decade later, I thought of Ryan as I put my hand up. When I lifted my head to look around, I saw that nearly every other person in the room had their hand up too. The room let out a haunting, collective gasp. It was as though we had all been going through life thinking that our friend or family member who was killed or maimed in a traffic collision was simply unlucky. The finger of god came down and struck them, and it was just a freak accident. But it wasn't a freak accident. It was happening systematically within a transportation system that we designed, and it was impacting everyone's lives. If we designed it, then we can change it.

The Road Safety Summit led to a city policy document called the Road Safety Action Plan, which was Seattle's first attempt at a Vision Zero plan, though the document did not use that term. It stated that traffic safety is a public health priority and that "even one fatality is one too many."[9] It set a goal of zero traffic deaths by 2030 and outlined a strategy to get there. Making safety changes to the designs of city streets was at the center of the plan. The Road Safety Summit also highlighted the shortcomings of the existing Bicycle Master Plan. Skinny painted bike lanes were something, but they weren't necessarily changing the way a street functions or physically protecting people using them. Dexter Avenue had a painted bike lane, but that did not prevent someone from making a quick left turn into Mike Wang. The city had painted 129 miles of bike lanes and sharrows in the first five years of the 2006 Bridging the Gap levy, but it was becoming clear that bike lane quality was at least as important as quantity.[10]

The Road Safety Action Plan wasn't perfect. It put too much weight on education campaigns and relied on police enforcement for curbing driving mistakes. But it documented a turning point in Seattle's transportation culture, and the process of crafting the plan was almost as important as what it says. Though I didn't fully recognize it at the time, Seattle was confronting its deeply embedded car culture, and that was not a small feat. People were putting in the work to imagine a transportation system that had different and more humane values. Even the *Seattle Times* editorial board, which had been a constant force of opposition to Mayor McGinn, changed its tune, arguing that "Seattle should be in the vanguard" in building "a safe, comprehensive bike network."[11] That editorial was a symbol of how quickly and dramatically Seattle's culture had shifted.

The culture in Seattle had been turning for a long time, but it had been turning too slowly to be noticeable. This is often how culture change happens. Single minds are changed one by one until suddenly they represent the majority opinion and the walls supporting the old way of thinking seem to collapse all at once.

Living in Bonus Time: The Brandon Blake Story, 2013-present

Brandon Blake bent down on one knee and reached his careful hands to the floor, his fingers curled under the injured body of a small bird that his cat Lois carried in through the kitchen window and plopped into her food bowl. His eyes softened and he shushed comforting words into his palms as he rose to his feet and carried the bird out to the second-floor porch of his apartment, where he said some parting words and lightly let it go. "There you go!" The bird flapped its wings and took flight without hitting the ground. He turned back to me sitting inside, but his beaming face shifted as concern took over. "He probably won't last too long out there." Indeed the little bird seemed destined to join the estimated 2.4 billion birds killed by domesticated cats in the United States every year.[12]

Brandon sat back down on the bright orange sofa facing me and let out a shrug. "That's life with indoor-outdoor cats." But that shrug wasn't as easy for him as it might be for others, and just a few months earlier he might have broken down in tears. "I get so emotional about these little birds, these little consciousnesses," he said, gazing at his now-empty palms. Only a year had passed since Carmageddon on July 25, 2013, and Brandon was slowly discovering a renewed, yet somewhat different, consciousness inside himself.

Carmageddon is one name Brandon gave to the moment when a woman driving a car south on Dexter Avenue made a fast left turn at Harrison Street to try to squeeze through a break in traffic. Despite his yells and the twenty-foot orange skid mark his tire painted on the pavement as he slammed on his brakes, she didn't see him riding in the bike lane. Or so he was told. He doesn't remember it. But he vividly remembers taking his preschool class on a field trip to the Museum of Flight earlier that day. "And it was an epic field trip, Tom," he told me. He lightly closed his eyes and smiled as though he were reliving the trip all over again. "These kids are pigs in shit, they're so excited. We got to go in the space shuttle trainer, and they're just so happy. I remember getting on my bike, and I was two blocks from work at Uwajimaya. I'm on my orange Rodriguez, and I had this thought of, 'What a great day. That's why I do what I do.' Next thing I remember, I was waking up from the coma."

Sabrina Bonaparte, Brandon's spouse, did not find out about the collision from the police or the hospital. She was at a Seattle Reign women's soccer game when Brandon's bandmates called her asking why he hadn't shown up to MoreOfAnything practice. Then her friend saw a message I posted to the *Seattle Bike Blog* Twitter account saying that someone got hit on Dexter, and they started to piece together that it was Brandon.[13]

Once the hospital confirmed it was him, she rushed to Harborview Medical Center to be with him as medical staff rescued him from the brink of death. His face and his helmet took the brunt of the vicious impact, and the medics who arrived on the scene were shocked he was still conscious. His face was mangled and smashed beyond recognition. Fearing he would drown in his own blood, he was put into a medically induced coma and intubated for a day. He spent another two days in the intensive care unit after waking up, and doctors were worried about swelling and bleeding around his brain. They discussed brain surgery, but luckily the bleeding stopped on its own. Doctors reconstructed his face through hours and hours of surgery. Today, his usually smiling mug is held together by seven titanium plates. His gums and teeth were reconstructed by some miserable-but-effective dental work (he described the dental arch bars "like braces sewn into my gums").

A year after the collision, Brandon's recovery was his "full-time job," he said. He no longer needed to spend his days in near-silence with the window curtains drawn to block out the painful daylight, but when we got together in 2014 to chat at Lighthouse Coffee in Fremont, he had to sit facing away from the windows so I wouldn't be backlit by the sunlight. When the folks hanging out on the other side of the shop started to chat and joke louder, Brandon and I had to move outside because it was hard work for him to separate background voices from our conversation. But he was not dejected. He loved sitting on the cute little rocky spot next to the shop. That's one clear part of his personality that has absolutely not changed. "I was a ridiculously optimistic and upbeat person before Carmageddon," he said. "Having a near-death experience has amplified that part of me. That's one of the gains I feel like I've had."

He also knows it could have been worse. "The alternative is Sher Kung," he said, referring to the young mother and attorney who was killed while biking on Second Avenue in August 2014. "I could have been Mike Wang. . . . It was just one block away, two years later." Wang had been struck and killed in a very similar collision. Brandon considered himself "fortunate and privileged" to still be alive after a collision that could so easily have killed him. Sabrina would kiss her wedding ring when she traveled through that intersection. "It was miraculous the recovery that I made and that I continue to make every day," he said. "There's a principle that guides my life now, it's called Bonus Time. I should have died that day, but I didn't. From that point in time, I'm living in Bonus Time."

Brandon reached out to me one year after Carmageddon because he wanted to help make a difference on the streets of Seattle. "I want to go from being a statistic to being a face," he said. Earlier that year, he stopped by an on-street open house the Seattle Department of Transportation was hosting to inform the public about changes coming to the stretch of Dexter Avenue where Brandon and Mike had been struck. City staff had gathered data about collision history on the street that they were using to guide their street redesign, and they posted the data on a display board standing on the sidewalk. From 2011 to 2014, there were eighty collisions, ten of which involved a person biking and three of which involved a person walking.[14] "Those statistics they have on a board, those are people," Brandon said. "There were a lot of people who read about this accident last year. News reports said I was expected to make a full recovery. Well, here we are a year later, here's what that recovery looks like," he said during our first meeting. If he had not told me his story of trauma and recovery, I would not have been able to tell he had been through such a tough year. He looked right in my eyes while we spoke together and held a warm smile suggesting there was nothing in the world he would rather be doing than sitting right there chatting with me. "I'm a statistic, but I'm still here. What can I do to help others not become a statistic?" He paused, reached his hand out, and ran his gentle fingers through the fur on Lois's back. "Like that poor little bird."

Though Brandon replaced his destroyed Rodriguez bicycle with a new bright orange ride complete with his calligraphy scrawled down the side, he is not comfortable biking on city streets. He and Sabrina sometimes drive their bikes to a trail, but that's it. "To go from being cyclists that were so happy to be getting around on our bikes to not being able to bike around town, it was a huge change for us," he said. Maybe someday Seattle streets will have enough safe bike lanes that he can ride around the city again, but Seattle isn't there yet.

The woman who struck him with her car was charged with making an improper left turn and inattentiveness, and her tickets totaled just $325. But for all he has been through, Brandon doesn't hold ill will against the woman who made a driving mistake and struck him. "All it took was a split second of inattention," he said. "The more we all know about being aware of each other, the more people take that extra look over their shoulders," the more tragedies will be avoided. He initially shared his story back in 2014 because he hoped his experience could help convince others to take extra care. "Every moment of my struggle has been worth it if it helps others." But it's not just his story.

The woman who was behind the wheel also has a role to play, if she chooses to. While Brandon was recovering at home that first year, all the curtains drawn to keep out the light, he planned what he would say to her the day she inevitably called him up and asked him if there was anything she could do. He imagined how the call would go: "Why, yes, there is. You and I are going to partner up to spread bicycle and driving safety." Their story would be extra powerful because of the "unique position we have together" as both ends of a terrible collision. He is still waiting for her call.

Most of the time Brandon spent in the hospital immediately after the collision was understandably focused on the physical trauma and injuries, Sabrina said. But as he was being discharged, someone handed her a one-pager on brain injury. As his scars healed and the swelling receded, his short-term memory ability did not return to the way it used to be. Bright lights or too much background noise hurt his head. If there was too much stimulation around him, mental fatigue descended on him. And sometimes a somewhat small sadness, like a small bird dropped unceremoniously in a cat food dish, could take hold of his heart and come out as tears. "As crazy as all the face injuries were, it pales in comparison to the head trauma," he said. For the first couple of months of recovering from the physical trauma of the crash, when he was doped up on lots of pain medication, he and Sabrina noticed a difference in his mood and demeanor. "When I came out the other end, all the personality differences I had experienced weren't going away," he said during our first meeting. "That's when my wife and I realized," he paused a beat, "I have a brain injury." A year into his recovery, it was still difficult for Brandon to admit out loud that he had a brain injury. He grieved for the sometimes indescribable parts of himself that were not coming back, at least not the way they were before. Sabrina found resources for him, including a support group for people with brain injuries so he could talk to people who knew firsthand what he was going through. He became a fixture in these groups and later became a leader of a support group for young adults with brain injuries. But it wasn't just Brandon's life that changed that day. "Her life has changed too," Brandon said. "Living with a person with a brain injury is not always fun."

We were sitting in their living room in January 2020 as Sabrina talked about her memory of those first days following the collision. The light inside was soft, and it was quiet except for the moments when

Brandon picked up an instrument to play gentle background music while we spoke. The whole time she was talking about that traumatic day, he played repeating melodies on a hand-sized thumb piano called a *sansula*. "Even from a very early stage I noticed that if he's had a really hard day and he's exhausted and he can't think, he can always go play music," said Sabrina. She described it as "self-repairing." "In a lot of those instances, he will just write a new song. And he'll come back down and be like, 'I wrote a song.' And I'm like, 'How did you do that? Five minutes ago you couldn't even put together a coherent sentence, and you just went upstairs and wrote a new song. How is that possible?' It's almost like he has a separate brain for music. You know how you have a separate dessert stomach? He has a separate brain for music that's unaffected by his injury."

Previously a bass player primarily, Brandon found the *sansula* a few years after his collision and started to play it constantly. The handheld thumb piano is based on the traditional mbira from Malawi and Zimbabwe but with the metal prongs suspended on a drumhead. The sound of the notes is a gentle but resonant chime, and Brandon fell in love with it. Before too long, he started making modifications, adding a chain that rattles with the vibrations of the drumhead and other percussive elements that are sometimes found on traditional mbiras. He is comfortable with his customized instrument, playing with ease and proficiency as though it is an extension of himself. Brandon used his bass and *sansula* to record an instrumental 2018 album called *It's Bonus Time!* that is all about his collision and recovery.[15] The track list itself tells a powerful story:

1. Field Trip!
2. Dexter & Harrison
3. Glamorous Glennis
4. Harborview
5. Fading . . .
6. Keep Going
7. I Forgive You
8. It's Good to Be Here
9. Focus . . .
10. What's Next?

The album is an instrumental processing of a past trauma, but his musical journey with the *sansula* has also been about exploring who he is now and what it means to be living a life that almost wasn't. It's a message that has taken him places he'd previously only dreamed about, and it connected him to his childhood hero Victor Wooten. Wooten, a legendary bassist with a sprawling career, including decades as bassist for Béla Fleck and the Flecktones, heard Brandon play and was immediately interested. The two became friends. "The idea that my childhood musical hero would be in my life as a friend, as a mentor, as a teacher, and that he'll be wanting to collaborate with me with this instrument blows my mind, Tom. It's the pinnacle of Bonus Time," he said. "That's just an incredible gift that's been given to me."

Brandon first told me about Bonus Time during our first meeting, and it's a concept that has grown into something of a core principle that guides him. Bonus Time is about embracing and loving the person he is, including the effects of his brain injury. Empathy for other people and creatures is so powerful it can sometimes be overwhelming. But that powerful empathy is also beautiful, and it makes him who he is. He does struggle at times to find ways to cope with his emotions so that he can function and avoid falling into depression, but it's also not a bad thing that he cares so much. If he were a superhero and Carmageddon was his origin story, then having a conscience made of steel may be his superpower. He is no longer able to allow himself to do things that he knows deep down are unjust.

For example, he was a vegetarian before his collision, but he was eating lots of meat during the aftermath of his recovery. Then one day he opened his fridge, and he could no longer see sandwich meat and butter and eggs anymore. "I opened it and I looked at all these pieces of meat and in an instant I just saw it as body parts," he said. "I asked myself, 'Why did they have to die so that I may live?' It was a lightbulb moment, and I was like, 'Shit, this isn't congruent with Bonus Time.'" Caring for animals soon became a major part of Brandon's and Sabrina's lives. Shortly after his fridge revelation, they volunteered at Pasado's Safe Haven, a rescue and sanctuary for neglected or abused animals, and Brandon met someone that changed his life. "I had just made this amazing connection with this turkey." It was Bowie the turkey, Ziggy the turkey's brother. "We made this unbelievable connection, and I saw myself in his eyes, and I said, 'Shit. This changes everything.' Because I live so deeply the ideal of Bonus Time. It's not just a platitude." After his school closed for the COVID-19 pandemic shutdown in 2020, Brandon got a new job working at Pasado's. Throughout the pandemic, he made YouTube videos for children in which "Teacher Bando" read a storybook while sitting with a rescued animal. "I don't think pre-brain-injury Brandon would have done that," Sabrina said. "He's not the same person he used to be, and you have to respect that."

Sabrina has not only embraced the changed Brandon, but she has changed with him. "He's made me much more compassionate and kind," she said. "I've always been an extremely logical person, and I think without emotion a lot. I'm a data analyst, I think in numbers and absolutes and exacts. Whereas he thinks in emotions and abstracts. I think he's gone way more off to that side, and that's been a good complement for me because sometimes I need him to say, 'You should be angry about this. You should have emotions right now. You need to go through this.' I think that that's a good thing, I think that it's been helpful." She called herself an ally, ready to step in if Brandon gets overwhelmed by a situation for any reason. By embracing the way his brain works, she is able to see things that others often can't. "He seems, I would say 80 to 85 percent of the time, he appears to be totally fine, and no one would know. You don't see really any injury. I can see the scars on his face because I know where they are."

Sher Kung and the Immeasurable Potential We've Lost, 2014

Brandon Blake is one tally mark in Seattle's 2013 traffic collision statistics. He only just barely made the leap from the "deaths" column to the "serious injuries" column. His story is incredible in large part because it's not incredible at all. It's horrifically common. Brandon initially reached out to me and offered to tell his story after he heard the tragic news about Sher Kung. Kung was a young lawyer who was instrumental in the American Civil Liberties Union's pivotal and successful 2008 case *Witt v. Department of the Air Force*. The decision by the US Court of Appeals for the Ninth Circuit challenged the military's "don't ask, don't tell" policy, which discriminated against gay or bisexual service members. Kung was biking to work the summer of 2014 when someone in a truck turned in front of her while she was traveling down the old skinny painted bike lane on Second Avenue. She was killed at the

University Street intersection just across the street from the Perkins Coie law office where she worked.

Kung was "one of our brightest young lawyers," the firm said in a statement after her death, "an exceptional lawyer and a wonderful comrade, with boundless energy, legal brilliance, and relentless optimism."[16] A large memorial sprung up on the corner almost immediately, a coincidentally fitting location because it is also the site of the Garden of Remembrance, a memorial to Washington State service members who have lost their lives in wars since World War II. Kung was not a service member herself, but her work enabled service members to be themselves while serving. Major Margaret Witt cowrote a 2017 book about her case, giving an inside look at Kung's brilliant work. *Tell: Love, Defiance, and the Military Trial at the Tipping Point for Gay Rights* describes Kung as a "faithful guardian during the trial" and is dedicated to her memory. The book's epilogue ends by describing the aftermath of Kung's death:

> As word of the tragedy spread, dozens of bouquets, mementos, and notes were placed on and near the white bikes and then along the stone wall fronting the "Garden of Remembrance," a memorial to military veterans adjacent to the stairs leading into Benaroya Hall. Nearly all the broadcast and written tributes to Sher's lifework underscored her contributions to winning the Witt case. Among the flowers piled along the corner at Second and University was an ACLU poster with a handwritten message spanning two large Post-It notes. "Sher: Thank you for bringing your light and love to our community of Seattle LGBT attorneys and advocates for LGBT rights. You will be forever remembered for your contributions and positive spirit that you brought to us."[17]

The level of mourning following her death was unlike anything I had seen for any other traffic death in the city. One week after she died, a large crowd gathered at Westlake Park for a memorial ride for her and all other victims of traffic deaths. Before Sher Kung died, Seattle had gone fifteen months without a person on a bike dying in traffic. But the enormity of her loss demonstrated perfectly why the only acceptable number of deaths is zero. We will never know what else Kung might have done in this world. She became a tally mark in the "deaths" column of our traffic statistics, one of 32,744 people killed in US traffic that year.[18] Our world would be significantly different if that number were 32,743 instead. The scale of the loss is unimaginable, so our society often chooses not to imagine it. We will never know what a person killed in traffic was going to do with their life, the love they would nurture, the art they would create, the change they would make. We leave their family members and close friends to mourn in private and go about our days. Until we don't.

The response to Sher Kung's death was not large—the responses to everyone else's deaths were too small. Seattle stood together for a moment and said, "This is not OK. This price we are paying to preserve our existing traffic system is too high." Ten days after her death, Seattle demonstrated one part of the solution: a protected bike lane on Second Avenue through downtown and past the Garden of Remembrance. There was practically no opposition to the lane when it opened. People finally understood why we need bike lanes like it. Safe streets advocates were braced for another fight and ready to defend the new bike lane like they had fought to defend so many before, but nobody showed up on the other side of the battlefield. Because there is no War on Cars, and there never was. It was nothing more than an illusion, the belligerent bluster of people whose windshields obscured their views of what really matters in our world: the people we love.

Pronto! Emerald City Cycle Share bikes are docked on a rainy day near the newly opened University of Washington Link light rail station, January 2017. Photo by Tom Fucoloro, *Seattle Bike Blog*.

CHAPTER 8

Seattle's Bicycle Ambitions Grow

With the election of Mike McGinn in 2009 and the creation of neighborhood-based safe streets groups, Seattle's aspirations for bike infrastructure very quickly moved beyond the painted bike lanes and sharrows outlined in the 2007 Bicycle Master Plan. Evolving at hyperspeed, the bicycle advocacy movement steered away from the mentality that "we should take whatever scraps we can get" toward one of "we should ask for what we really need." If Seattle was going to have a bike network that was safe and comfortable for people of all ages and abilities to use, including children, then the city needed protected bike lanes and neighborhood greenways in addition to the already excellent trails. The city also needed a plan that considered both cross-city and intraneighborhood trips, as the recently formed Seattle Neighborhood Greenways groups demonstrated.

New Mayor, New Bike Plan, 2012-2014

The Bicycle Master Plan update process started in 2012, requiring massive outreach across the city, which the Seattle Department of Transportation and bike advocates used as an opportunity to teach a lot of nonbikey people about protected bike lanes and neighborhood greenways. The process set expectations among neighbors about changes that could soon be coming to their streets and allowed more people time to weigh in on those changes. The plan update also gave all those new neighborhood safe streets groups a chance to insert their priorities into an official city planning document.[1] But most of all, it created a project list that would require significant funding from the next transportation levy.

The Bike Master Plan update spanned two mayors and took more than two years to complete. Both of the major candidates for mayor in 2013 supported taking action to make streets safer. The question during the campaign wasn't whether Seattle should build bike lanes. Instead, the question was, Who will build them faster? McGinn lost to Ed Murray, a more mainstream Democrat with a long career in the state legislature. Though most bike advocates, including *Seattle Bike Blog*, strongly supported McGinn, the larger fight had been successful because both candidates were angling for support from people who bike. The city narrowly avoided a drawn-out legal fight over the Bike Master Plan update after the newly elected Mayor Murray negotiated a deal with a group that sued to stop the entire plan over their opposition to a single planned bikeway along the west side of Lake Union.[2]

In 2014, Seattle City Council unanimously approved the update to the Bicycle Master Plan. Because of the difficult public process the plan had gone through, it emerged stronger and with momentum. It also had the support of a new mayor looking to make a big splash and build support for a major new transportation levy in 2015. Mayor Murray was looking to earn the support of a formidable biking and safe streets movement that had largely backed his opponent in 2013, and he did exactly that. First, he negotiated around the bike plan lawsuit threat. Then he announced in May 2014, just a few months into his term, that he had secured Alaska Airlines as the major sponsor needed to launch the city's planned public bike share system, named Pronto! Cycle Share. "I made one call, and they said, 'Let us know how to do it,'" Murray told the crowd gathered for the bike share announcement and unveiling of the design. Alaska Airlines CEO Brad Tilden then took the mic: "This is a lot more people to show than we get to show up when we announce a new route or even a new order from Boeing."[3]

But the bike share announcement was not even the biggest bike news that week. The very next day, Mayor Murray spoke at Cascade Bicycle Club's annual downtown Bike to Work Breakfast, and he stunned the packed room with a series of announcements that few people, if any, were expecting. He announced that in addition to launching Pronto, Seattle would design and construct a protected bike lane on Second Avenue through the heart of downtown within five months (for details, see chapter 9). For a city that had just spent two years developing a planning document, constructing a major bike lane in five months felt like moving at light speed. Before we get there, though, we need to take a strange detour.

The Bike Share Idea Grows, 1965-2015

Though Seattle made a lot of progress on cycling infrastructure, there were missteps. But the city somehow found a way to pivot from its biggest bike blunder by positioning itself at the center of one of the most fascinating and strange bicycle experiments in American history. Seemingly out of nowhere, several companies were begging Seattle in 2017 to let them place thousands of bicycles on the streets that they would rent for only one dollar per ride. Seattle became the epicenter of private bike share in the United States, but only because the city had failed in its attempt at operating a public bike share system. How did Seattle get there? A little ride back in history shows that bike share is a fairly old idea that for decades was more of a dream than a practical system.

In 1965, the short-lived anarchistic, countercultural, and performative Dutch group Provo painted some bikes white and left them unlocked around Amsterdam. The idea was simple: If you see it, you can ride it. Just leave it outside when you're done so someone else can use it. The Provos publicized these bikes as part of their White Bicycle Plan, which would solve transportation in Amsterdam by banning all private motor vehicles from the city center (they decried the "terrorism of the motorized minority") and providing free-to-use shared bicycles to the public. The idea was just one of the group's White Plans, imaginative public policies the group published in its magazine during the two years it was active. Other White Plans included a White Corpse Plan in which any person driving who killed someone else would be required to dig the outline of the victim's body into the pavement where they'd died, then fill in the body outline with white concrete. The Provos also had plans for free women's health care, free child care, taxing polluters, reforming police, and more. The Provo manifesto suggests that the group considered its proposals and actions as "the inspirational source of resistance" and that "Provo realized that it will lose in the end, but it cannot pass up the chance to make at least one more heartfelt attempt to provoke society."[4]

Provo's White Bicycle Plan was very short-lived. There were only ever a handful of their bikes on the streets, and the police confiscated them shortly after they were released. But the action was a symbol of

Provo's opposition to the many problems of car culture, as shown in this text from the group:

> Amsterdammers!
>
> The Asphalt terror of the motorized bourgeoise has lasted long enough. Human sacrifices are made daily to this latest idol of the idiots: car power. Choking carbon monoxide is its incense, its image contaminates thousands of canals and streets.
>
> Provo's bicycle plan will liberate us from the car monster. Provo introduces the White Bicycle, a piece of public property. . . .
>
> The white bicycle is never locked. The white bicycle is the first free communal transport. The white bicycle is a provocation against capitalist private property, for the white bicycle is anarchistic.
>
> The white bicycle can be used by anyone who needs it and then must be left for someone else. There will be more and more white bicycles until everyone can use white transport and the car peril is past. The white bicycle is a symbol of simplicity and cleanliness in contrast to the vanity and foulness of the authoritarian car. In other words:
>
> A BIKE IS SOMETHING, BUT ALMOST NOTHING![5]

Even though the White Bicycle Plan didn't actually become a functional transportation mode, the idea of the shared bikes became legend. Some versions of the story say that the bikes were all thrown into a canal or had to be shut down due to vandalism. But the Provo action was really just a demonstration of a provocative idea, one part of a plan that included government investment in tens of thousands of these bikes combined with the removal of private motor vehicles. The White Bicycles were a challenge to car culture.

Throughout the decades that followed, white bicycle and yellow bicycle projects were tried on university campuses and in cities across the world.[6] As discussed in chapter 5, Bike Works was originally planned as a yellow bike program, though the organizers changed direction before releasing any bikes to the public. Most white and yellow bike programs were successful as demonstrations of an idea rather than a reliable, useful, and sustainable transportation system. Bikes may be relatively cheap, but they aren't free. For the idea to actually work, public investment was needed.

In the early 2000s, a far less radical but seemingly sustainable bike share model came into focus. Starting in a handful of European cities and usually funded by local governments, the systems involved installing special docking stations all over the city and stocking them with bikes that could be unlocked only by paying a rental fee. A user could then ride to another docking station near their destination to end their rental. The concept was simple to understand and immediately successful, spreading across Europe and Asia throughout the 2000s. China became the undisputed leader of bike share, creating massive and very popular public bike share systems in many cities. The Hangzhou local government invested a reported 180 million yuan renminbi (about $26 million) into Hangzhou Public Bicycle in 2008, followed by another 270 million yuan renminbi (about $40 million) in discounted loans, and by 2011 had more than sixty thousand bicycles and 2,416 docking stations.[7] The government never intended for the system to return a profit or even break even. Instead, it was largely an effort to reduce the amount of driving in the city, which was increasing rapidly as the city's residents gained wealth in the economically booming region. The majority of the largest public bike share systems in the world are in China, and most of them started between 2008 and 2013.[8]

The concept behind this form of bike share was compelling and simple: Transit is very effective at moving people across large distances, but it's not great at the so-called last mile problem. Transit, especially express transit like trains and rapid bus lines, just cannot get people to the front door of wherever each individual is trying to go. But it can get them in the neighborhood. From there, people need to either walk or wait for slower and often less-frequent local buses to complete their trips, a process that can easily take as long as or longer than a trip across the city on an express route. This added time makes transit use less appealing, but it's also very difficult and expensive to solve using traditional methods like adding more local buses.[9] Bike share solves this problem, at least for people able and willing to ride a bike. A person can take an express transit trip, then hop on a bike share to go the rest of the way. Bike share augments transit by bringing more homes and destinations within reach of more transit options. If a city just invested millions or billions into a new light rail line, then the obvious next investment would be launching bike share to help more people use that new line.

The United States was slow to get into bike share. Capital Bikeshare in Washington, DC, was the highest-profile early US system and a great demonstration of the potential for bike share because leaders from all over the country regularly travel to the nation's capital and can try it for themselves. The city-owned system launched in 2010 with forty-nine stations and 400 bicycles, but it quickly grew to a hundred stations and 1,100 bikes by early 2011 and continued growing gradually throughout the decade.[10] At the same time, a nonprofit organization in Minneapolis launched that city's NiceRide bike share system, and both Denver and Des Moines, Iowa, launched systems created by bike manufacturer Trek called B-Cycle.

Then came Citi Bike. New York City launched the biggest bike share system in the United States in 2013, and it immediately became the symbol of bike share in America. The system started with 6,000 bikes and 332 stations, but it quickly expanded. By 2015, Citi Bike was carrying ten million trips per year, making it the envy of cities across the nation. And to make their envy worse, Citi Bike did not require public subsidy. The sponsorship from Citibank and user fees were enough to keep the system going. But what other cities, including Seattle, perhaps failed to consider was that New York City is the exception to the bike share rules in many ways. The city is far denser than any other US city, and that means it is easier to attract more rides per bike and serve more people per docking station than any other city can hope to achieve. Also, New York City is New York Freaking City, so it can bring in a lot more money from selling a system sponsorship than other cities could reasonably expect.

Who Killed Pronto Cycle Share? 2014-2017

Bike share systems had found that increasing the density of stations dramatically increased the use of all stations, and a system is most successful when users can feel confident that there will always be a station nearby. But Seattle was unfazed by these and other challenges, such as funding sources. Bike share was flourishing in DC and New York, so of course it was going to flourish here. Initially imagined as a King County project that would serve the region, Puget Sound Bike Share launched in 2012 as a nonprofit with representatives from Seattle, Kirkland, Redmond, King County, Puget Sound Regional Council, Sound Transit, Washington State, Seattle Children's, Cascade Bicycle Club, and Microsoft all serving on its board of directors. "Non-profit is a good model for us because it's a lot easier to apply for public sector grants and [private] sponsorships," board president Ref Lindmark told *Seattle Bike Blog* in 2012.[11] The nonprofit was following a business plan created by Alta Planning and Design, a firm that just so happened to have founded Alta Bike Share. Alta Bike Share sold and operated the DC, New York, and Minneapolis systems, among many others. So it was no surprise when Puget Sound Bike Share selected Alta Bike Share as the system vendor and operator.

The business plan for Puget Sound Bike Share wasn't amazing, it wasn't nation-leading, and it wasn't going to revolutionize transportation and biking in the city, but it was fine. It was written during the aftermath of the 2008 recession, so perhaps that's why it set its sights so low. It seemed to assume that ongoing public investment was not on the table. The plan figured the program needed less than $4 million to launch phase 1A, which was a skeleton system of fifty stations and five hundred bikes spread out mostly in the central part of the city like downtown, South Lake Union, Capitol Hill, and First Hill with a handful of stations in Eastlake and the University District as well. Another $4 million or so would be needed for phase 1B, to complete phase 1 by more than doubling the number of stations and bikes within the initial service area. This expansion was needed to achieve the density required to make the system financially successful, with a goal to have stations no more than three blocks away from each other. The nonprofit's business model forecasted that the program would lose about $500,000 each of the first two years as it built out the system, but then would bring in about $1 million in the third year. Phase 2 would have added some more area in Seattle, especially in Fremont, the Central District, and SoDo, then phase 3 would have added Eastside cities, including Kirkland, Bellevue, and Redmond. Microsoft was also interested in funding its own expansion to cover its Redmond campus.[12]

In spring 2014, Puget Sound Bike Share announced that the system would be called Pronto! Emerald City Cycle Share and that Alaska Airlines would sponsor the system by kicking in $2.5 million over five years. With a couple of grants on hand, that seemed to be barely enough to launch phase 1A. Mayor Murray had declared that the system would launch by the end of 2014, so that had become the goal. All seemed well for a moment.

The launch was very exciting, even if it was poor timing to begin operations at the start of the rainy season. *Seattle Bike Blog* hosted an event called I Look Good on a Pronto that encouraged riders to bike to as many stations as they could and take selfies at each one. (It was 2014, and the world was very into selfies.) The bikes were great and very reliable. The docks worked well too. The only problem was that there weren't enough of them. Only about 14 percent of Seattle residents lived within walking distance of a station.[13] But this was just phase 1A, and more docks were on the way. Right?

The system never grew beyond phase 1A, with only fifty stations and five hundred bikes.

Even if built to completion, the plan excluded all of West Seattle and many communities of color in central and south Seattle. It also excluded Ballard, Green Lake, and all points north of the University District. It was designed to be able to fund itself entirely through user fees and sponsorships. Serving less dense neighborhoods farther from the center of the system would cost money to build and would bring in less income per dock. Because the assumption was that no public subsidy would be available, the basic rules of business required the nonprofit to build a system that focused on only dense parts of the city that analysis suggested would bring the biggest return on investment. From day one, the system was designed to barely stay afloat. This is a major way that capitalism reinforces systemic racism, because decisions like this happen all the time, as Charles Mudede wrote in *The Stranger*:

> The problem is the Pronto Cycle Share will begin by providing service to predominantly white neighborhoods. Even the Central District, which has been gentrified, is excluded. The south and racially diverse parts of Seattle are completely out of the picture at present. Yet, the thinking behind the bike locations and the planned expansion is not at all racist. How could this happen? Why doesn't innocence reproduce innocence? The reason why the racial map of Seattle is reproduced by Pronto's seemingly non-racial logic is it's a program that's tied to the logic of the market, and the market automatically, unthinkingly reproduces such maps. One law of capitalism: Money follows money. . . . The only kind of planning that can break with the automatic effects of the market has to be entirely public. It has to be deaf to the tireless call of money. If Pronto was

fully funded by the public, it might have avoided reproducing the racial/economic map of our city.[14]

Within three months of the system's launch, SDOT Director Scott Kubly was already talking about the city buying it, throwing out the slow-growth plan and instead dramatically expanding Pronto to reach much more of the city using public funds.[15] Kubly had been the acting resident of Alta Bicycle Share briefly before taking the SDOT director role. Before that, he had worked for transportation departments in Washington, DC, and Chicago, including work on those cities' bike share systems. His experience with bike share was one of the reasons Mayor Murray picked him, since Seattle was getting ready to launch a system of its own. Though Kubly's prior work at Alta was public knowledge, he did not get the waivers required under city ethics laws in order to conduct city business with a prior employer. He admitted the lapse and was fined by the Seattle Ethics and Elections Commission.

Before taking the Alta job, Kubly had helped launch Divvy, the huge public bike share system in Chicago. Compared to Divvy's plan to grow to 400 stations within the first couple of years, Pronto was minuscule in its ambitions. If Seattle wanted to really do this right, the city had to think much bigger. By May 2015, just seven months after Pronto launched, SDOT met with Puget Sound Bike Share to talk about the city buying the system. Pronto's ridership during its first winter was lower than what PSBS was hoping for, but usage was picking up in the spring. They were trying to sell sponsorships and win grants to fund the phase 1B expansion. But SDOT was developing a plan to grow Pronto from 50 stations to 250, bringing 62 percent of residents within walking distance of a station. The city also wanted the program to grow from 500 bikes to 2,500, with all of them being electric-assist bikes. "Having a massive expansion of the bike share will make it really functional public transit," Kubly told Seattle Bike Blog.[16] Investing public funds would also allow the system to operate even in places where it might need to be subsidized.

But as promising as this vision was, leaders had stopped focusing on the fragility of Pronto's existing business. Believing that Seattle was going to buy the system, Puget Sound Bike Share's executive director, Holly Houser, started positioning the organization for a transfer to the city. Barely more than eight months after launch, the nonprofit largely stopped following its business plan. This meant that they stopped trying to sell sponsorships and win grants that they needed to keep the system going. Houser resigned as executive director in September 2015, noting in an e-mail to Pronto members that the city was taking over.[17] "Now, Pronto is poised for its next phase of growth that will expand access to more users and communities across the Puget Sound region," Houser wrote. "We've been working collaboratively with the City of Seattle to make steps toward our vision to weave bike share into the region's public transportation network, and we're pleased to have them take on a more prominent role in leading those efforts. This is a natural progression for our program, and one that we believe best positions Pronto for a bright and vibrant future."

But then summer turned into fall. Puget Sound Bike Share had no executive director and was running out of money, but the city still had not taken over the system. SDOT Director Kubly spoke to *Seattle Bike Blog* about the city's takeover plans in October, noting that the city was still working to take over Pronto.[18] SDOT had assigned its chief of active transportation, Nicole Freedman, to essentially help run Puget Sound Bike Share in the interim. Mayor Murray included $5 million in his proposed budget to acquire and expand Pronto, and the city was hopeful that a large federal grant would come through to fund the rest of their plan. But the city did not get the federal money, and SDOT's transit division leader, Paulo Nunes-Ueno, a central figure in the Pronto expansion effort, resigned in early November 2015. Few people knew that Puget Sound Bike Share was running on fumes. When fall turned to winter, bills came due at Puget Sound Bike Share, and Pronto was officially in financial crisis. If the city did not acquire the system by March 2016, Puget Sound Bike Share would go bankrupt.[19] The Pronto system still had not even completed phase 1 of its plan.

The collapse of Pronto was incredibly frustrating because it was just so avoidable. The city and Puget Sound Bike Share just needed to pick a direction: either sell to the city or keep working on the original business model. Either way could have worked, but instead they chose neither and it became a crisis and a huge political problem for Mayor Murray, SDOT Director Kubly, and the bicycling advocacy movement as a whole. There was a lot of blame to go around. SDOT was clearly the most culpable because the agency should not have told PSBS it was going to take over the system until it had secured the funding. PSBS bears some blame, too, because it should not have abandoned its original business plan until the buyout plan was secured. And bike advocates, including myself, should have more carefully watchdogged the whole process.

Seattle City Council held a series of meetings in the winter of 2016 in which SDOT desperately tried to get the council to release the funds so the city could buy the system before it collapsed. At one point SDOT presented figures to the council showing that the system would operate at a $130,000 profit once the city took it over. But these numbers were misleading, and the system appeared in the black only because SDOT was not fully accounting for its own staff time and the $240,000 it had already used to bail out the system. When these accounting omissions came to light, in part due to *Seattle Bike Blog* reporting, the city council lost even more faith in SDOT's bike share plans.[20] But the council was eventually convinced that bike share was still a great public service, and it approved the $1.4 million buyout on the condition that SDOT had to present its expansion plans to the council before investing more public funds.

The buyout was controversial, and it became only more so following the ethics violation by SDOT Director Kubly. Pronto, still with only its initial fifty stations, hobbled along for another year as SDOT tried to work out a new plan using the remaining $3.6 million budget. By the fall of 2016, there was not enough support left for the city's bike share plan to keep it going. SDOT never did bring its bike share plan to city council. Mayor Murray announced in January 2017 that the city would abandon its bike share plans and shut down Pronto.[21]

On Pronto's last day of operations in March 2017, I joined a group of people, including City Councilmember Mike O'Brien, for a final Pronto ride together. After the ride, people headed to a bar for drinks. I asked people who'd gathered there what they thought of a new bike share business model that was booming on mainland China at the time. Private companies were placing bikes all over the major cities and were charging a very small fee to use them. There were no docks. Instead, people just parked them wherever they could when they were finished. None of the dejected bike share lovers in that bar could have guessed that by the end of the year, there would be thousands of bikes spread out across Seattle that cost just a dollar to ride. In fact, while we were taking our farewell Pronto ride, thousands of these bikes had already been loaded into shipping containers and were headed our way across the Pacific Ocean.

Private Bike Share Mayhem, 2017-present

Bluegogo had 3,000 bikes in a shipping container outside San Francisco that they wanted to place in Seattle. That's what a company spokesperson told me in spring 2017 just weeks after Pronto shut down.[22] All a rider had to do was download their app, put in their credit card information, then scan a QR code on the bike. The lock holding the rear wheel in place would automatically disengage, and the rider could bike wherever they wanted for as long as they wanted. When they were done, they would just lock the rear wheel and walk away. The cost? Only a dollar for every thirty minutes. In comparison, Pronto's daily rate had started at eight dollars, and there were extra fees if you rode for more than thirty minutes at a time.

Bluegogo's program didn't seem real. How could this company possibly hope to make money selling thirty-minute rides for a dollar? Nothing costs a dollar anymore. But Bluegogo was in a hurry to launch because they knew more companies and more bikes were coming. A lot more bikes. Perhaps even an irresponsible number of bikes, which is a phrase I could not have previously imagined ever saying. The story of the venture-capital-fueled global private bike share boom of the late 2010s is absurd. Companies grew into giants and collapsed spectacularly. It was business-speculation mayhem with bicycles. Hundreds of millions of dollars were lost globally, but in the process billions of trips were made by bike.[23] And by completely screwing up Pronto, Seattle had accidentally positioned itself right in the middle of the action.

There was already one Bluegogo bike in town in the spring of 2017, and I was able to talk my way into taking it for a test ride. It was obviously made cheaply, but it worked. The tires were solid and airless, so there was no need to keep them inflated or worry about flat tires. The lights were cheap, but they turned on when the bike moved. Every possible corner was cut in the making of this thing while meeting the minimum safety requirements under Washington State law. But it was a bike, and it cost only one dollar to ride for thirty minutes. However, news of that shipping container of Bluegogo bikes sent a shockwave through the US bike share industry. Nobody seemed to expect these bikes to arrive so quickly, and the one-dollar price point was terrifying to bike share systems already in operation.[24] Pronto hadn't made ends meet charging many times that much. Meanwhile, cities also panicked at the thought of bikes that could be parked anywhere. The docks of existing bike share systems kept the bikes very organized and contained in planned locations. These new bike share bikes didn't even need to be locked to a bike rack or signpost.

The initial business plan for many private bike share companies seemed to be to put the bikes out, become popular, then work with cities on regulations later, the way ride-hailing service Uber had done previously. However, Seattle and most other cities were clear from the start that the bike share companies would not be allowed to operate without permits. But what would a bike share permit scheme even look like? And what city was going to volunteer to be the first to try it out?

Well, Seattle, of course! The city had just shuttered its public bike share system despite clear demand for bike share in the city. Since Seattle had no existing bike share system to worry about, it was the obvious place to try something new. "For a top-tier city in the US, it's really rare to not have some form of bike share," Spin CEO Derrick Ko told *Seattle Bike Blog* in April 2017.[25] Spin was based in the Bay Area, and its goal was to adapt the business model of companies finding success in China to North America. The company was in a serious hurry to get ahead of the wave it knew was coming. It also realized that for this concept to work in the United States, an official, legal process was needed. So Spin focused on Seattle, working with SDOT to quickly craft a set of regulations that met the city's goals and would allow the bike share companies to function.

SDOT, on the other hand, just happened to have some staff who had been working on the bike expansion plan before Mayor Murray shut down Pronto. SDOT staffer Kyle Rowe was an SDOT staffer for years before taking a major career risk by agreeing to lead the electric bike share expansion planning project. The controversial city buyout of Pronto was complete before he'd signed on, and though the project was clearly troubled, the expansion had the potential of saving the city's ambitions. Rowe knew the plug could be pulled on the project at any moment, but he wanted to try. I talked to him in 2016 when he decided to change roles, and I remember he took a deep breath and said, "I hope I'm not making a big mistake."

Rowe spent the better part of 2016 working to finalize the details of the bike share project when the mayor canceled it, leaving his work and his career in limbo. But then the bike share companies called and he got to work inventing a permit scheme that was unlike any other permit the city offered. He managed to pull it off in just a couple of months. "[Rowe] is literally writing the rules other cities are following from a blank Word doc," said Toby Sun, CEO of LimeBike during the company's launch in Westlake Park. LimeBike and Spin launched in July 2017 in accordance with the city's new regulations, kicking off Seattle's private bike share experiment.[26]

The rules were initially fairly simple.[27] Bikes would be allowed to be parked only in the landscape zone—the space between a street and the sidewalk's clear walkway, also known as the parking strip. This is the area used for bike racks, street signs, newspaper boxes, et cetera. Bikes couldn't be parked too close to a corner, curb ramp, or bus stop. Companies had to start with just a few hundred bikes before scaling up gradually over time and capping out at a couple of thousand.

Spin and LimeBike (later known as just Lime) launched with five hundred bikes each, and ridership immediately eclipsed Pronto.[28] Because people could ride them anywhere in the city, they were much more useful than Pronto with its very limited number of docking locations. In its first week of operations, Spin said it had five thousand rides on its five hundred bikes, which was significantly more than Pronto's best week ever, and that was only a taste. Within months, three companies were operating fleets of thousands of bikes each. Spin was still in town, but its efforts were being eclipsed by the better-funded LimeBike and the Beijing-based bike share giant ofo.

Even with rides priced at only a dollar, companies flooded users with coupons. Ofo rides were supposed to cost money, but the company's app seemed to keep giving people free rides. The bike share companies were clearly more focused on growing their numbers of users than making money from user fees. By that measure, they worked wonderfully. As of May 2018, people in Seattle were taking more than 200,000 bike share trips per month.[29] In comparison, Pronto carried a total of 278,143 trips in its two and a half years of operation.[30] Though there were plenty of complaints about bikes being in the way or thrown into lakes or even tossed into trees, an SDOT survey found that people liked the bike share programs by an almost three-to-one margin.[31] It was a good time to be a bike share user in Seattle, even if it was obvious that one-dollar bike shares could not possibly last.

But wait—what happened to Bluegogo and its shipping container of bikes? That company was among the first of many major bike share implosions in China, and it did so in spectacular fashion. The company was by some reports the third biggest bike share company in China after Mobike and ofo, but Bluegogo was already facing some financial troubles when it made an epic, legendary marketing mistake. It was trying to gamify its system by rewarding people who hunted down and rode certain special bikes. The company did this by changing the icon from a bicycle to a tank for the special reward bikes within its app, then launched this promotion on June 4, the anniversary of the Tiananmen Square massacre.[32] Yikes. Needless to say, customers hated this promotion. But worse for Bluegogo, the Chinese government really hated it, and investors fled. The company reportedly had seventy thousand bikes in operation and about $120 million in investments behind it when it collapsed. Bluegogo did not launch in Seattle, and its failure was a warning sign that China's bike share bubble was becoming fragile.

ofo launched in Seattle in late summer of 2017 with enormous ambitions. A company spokesperson told *Seattle Bike Blog* that their goal was "to unlock every corner of the world, and to make bicycles accessible to anyone, anytime, anywhere."[33] Seattle was ofo's first US stop in its $2 billion global expansion strategy. The company brought as many bikes as its permit would allow (and, as some competitors complained to me, possibly more). When it launched in Seattle, the company already had more than 8 million bicycles on the ground in China, and it claimed to carry 25 million rides every day. The ofo spokesperson told me that they figured it would take a few months to a year before people across North America would be using ofo bikes as part of their daily transportation needs.

With about ten thousand bikes across three companies at its peak, bike share in Seattle had changed the city's biking habits forever. The number of bike trips across the city's bike counters dramatically increased. But as almost everyone suspected, there was no way it made any business sense to rent bikes for a dollar per half hour. The number of trips needed to make that pencil out was way out of reach for a city of Seattle's size and lack of density. These bikes were also flimsy, so they often didn't last very long before falling into disrepair.

ofo did not take over transportation across North America. In fact, the company abruptly and without warning left Seattle and the rest of its North American cities in July 2018, less than a year after first arriving in Seattle. By the end of 2018, the company was in full collapse back in

China. Photos showing mountains of bike share bikes, sometimes filling sports stadiums, made headlines across the world for months as people gawked at the result of this bizarre economic bubble. A lot of the bikes in those mountains belonged to ofo. As word spread that ofo was having financial trouble, its millions of customers tried to get their deposits back: in China, it's common for users to place a deposit in order to open an account, whereas credit and debit card agreements serve this function in the United States. Angry people lined up in huge crowds outside the company's headquarters to demand their deposits back. But the company, which had burned through more than $2 billion in investments in just a couple of years, was broke.[34]

The global bike share business was not over, but the bubble had burst. After this, business operations came back down a little closer to earth. The bubble burst was far less intense in the United States than it was in China. Companies here seemed to be more wary of the bubble and were focused on electrified services that could get more rides per vehicle while also charging a premium. Spin pivoted to scooters instead of bikes and left town because Seattle initially did not permit shared scooters.[35] Lime got rid of all its pedal-only bikes and replaced them with electric-assist bikes in 2019. They were a very nice upgrade, but they also cost a lot more to use. Uber then brought its electric bike share service Jump to town, so for a while Seattle had no pedal-only bikes but did have two competing e-bike services.

When bubbles burst, consolidation is the obvious next step. Uber invested in Lime, then transferred Jump to its previous competitor. By 2020, Seattle was down to just one bike share company, with about two thousand quality but relatively pricey electric-assist bikes.[36] That count is similar in scale to the all-electric fifteen-hundred-bike system that SDOT was planning back in 2016 when Mayor Murray pulled the plug on Pronto. It was a strange way to get here, but we got here. The city did eventually approve a scooter-share permit in summer 2020, and scooters quickly overtook bikes as the most common shared micromobility device available.[37] But as of this writing, the bikes and scooters have been operating side by side. What happens next is anyone's guess.

Phyllis Porter leads a group of protesters across Rainier Avenue South in a crosswalk in Columbia City on May 20, 2015. Protesters repeatedly crossed the street, calling for the city to improve safety. Photo by Tom Fucoloro, *Seattle Bike Blog*.

CHAPTER 9

Building a Better Bike Lane

Looking only at streets under Seattle's control (excluding federal freeways like Interstate 5 and state highways like SR 520), Seattle's annual traffic death count during the 2010s was down to between 15 and 20, with about ten times that many serious injuries. Compared to other big cities in the United States, a Vision Zero Seattle was very much in sight. Nearby Portland, Oregon, for example, had 47 traffic deaths in 2017, more than double Seattle's toll. A stunning 165 traffic deaths were recorded that same year in Jacksonville, Florida, meaning Jacksonville had 23 percent more residents but 768 percent more traffic deaths than Seattle.[1]

City traffic engineer Dongho Chang is a true believer in Vision Zero, unlike many traffic engineers. He believes that through a mix of strategies, including safer traffic engineering, Seattle can eliminate traffic deaths and serious injuries. "We will be the first large city to get to zero," he told me during a lengthy phone call in June 2019. These were not the aspirational words of a politician hoping to get reelected. Chang said this as a detail-oriented and data-driven engineer. "We have such small numbers that we're dealing with, but a lot of it is vulnerable users, people who are walking and biking. Mostly it's people walking now."

Seattle's New Traffic Engineer Focuses on the People, Not the Cars, 2012-2021

When Dongho Chang spoke to me about his work in the Seattle Department of Transportation, he constantly used the word *service*. Considering that the national transportation news site *Streetsblog USA* once called him "the coolest traffic engineer in the world," he could rightfully carry himself as some kind of hotshot.[2] But he did the opposite. As Seattle's city traffic engineer, a position he held from 2012 until he took a job at the Washington State Department of Transportation in 2021, he spent a lot of time simply listening to people in the community and biking around the city observing how the streets were (or weren't) working.[3] He was an important engineer in a major city's department of transportation, and yet if someone asked him on Twitter about a safety concern they noticed, he would track down the problem, get the appropriate team to fix it, then tweet back a photo showing the solution and thanking the person for letting him know. This level of hands-on service is unheard of in the traffic engineering profession, especially at Chang's advanced level. While customer service work wasn't his job, maybe doing that kind of work made him better at his bigger job. His touch was personal, genuine, and thoughtful, and that's why people trusted him.

Chang's response to the Reasonably Polite Seattleites who had glued unauthorized plastic posts to the Cherry Street bike lane under Interstate 5 in 2013 (see the preface) wasn't an attempt to make a big statement or catch national attention. He honestly appreciated the message Ivan had demonstrated that night. "That took me by a big surprise," he said when I asked if he expected national attention from his e-mail. "I was not expecting anything out of it." While Ivan was sleeping off a long night of pylon installation, Chang was talking with his colleagues at SDOT about what to do about these new posts. In a way, they had come at the perfect time.

"We were just coming up with our Bicycle Master Plan update, and we had just gone through that whole process of engaging our residents and community about what they would like to see," Chang told me. "And what we heard very clear was exactly what they demonstrated. That we need to be a lot more thoughtful. . . . What we heard was, 'That was great that we have all these bicycle lanes everywhere, but that's not for me. I wouldn't use it' or 'A child wouldn't use it.' And that demonstration was, like, 'If that's a new installation, you could have done better.' It was like, 'Aw, we let people down.' It was a good reminder that there are some things that we can do that would be low-cost that could make things so much better for people. It also told me that someone cared, and they wanted to utilize their time and resources to demonstrate for us how we could do better, and that we as the people who are responsible to serve and put these facilities in need to be thoughtful about it and listen."

Chang also understands what is at stake when transportation departments wait too long to make a safety fix. "When we're talking about safety, we're talking about people," he said. "It's not an abstract thing. It's real people that are affected on an everyday basis." At this point in our conversation, he began to tear up. "One incident that really stands out for me," his voice tensed as he paused, "as you can tell it still affects me." People in most cities do not cry with their traffic engineers, but Chang is not like most traffic engineers.

He told me a story from his time working for the city of Everett, about twenty miles north of Seattle. "When I worked in Everett, there was a community that I wanted to really help. Kind of like Rainier [Avenue in Seattle], it had a population of people who wanted to do better for their kids. It was on Casino Road in part of the town that had been neglected for a while. I had been working hard to improve sidewalks, connectivity, bike lanes, improve transit service. In that community, one of the grandmothers was going shopping to Fred Meyer," a big-box store similar to Wal-Mart, "which was maybe a mile away from this apartment complex, so not very far. She went there, went shopping, got on the bus and came back, and she was crossing this road—a very normal road, right?—and a driver ran her down. She was killed in front of her family." We paused our conversation for a moment because we were both crying. I had never heard the story before, but I could feel how much it still hurt Chang to think about it. "I found out that they were Korean, and I'm Korean. And it was very hard for me to go, but I had to talk to them and say, 'I'm sorry that this happened.' You know? I mean, there were projects that I had already in the works that would have helped that situation, but they were too late."

When community members in Seattle's Rainier Valley started organizing for a safer Rainier Avenue in 2014, Chang was not going to miss the opportunity to take action. Rainier Avenue South was a state highway until 1992, when it was decommissioned and turned into a city street. It serves as the main business district for many neighborhoods along its length, all of which had grown significantly since 1992. As a historically redlined area (most of Rainier Valley was listed as "declining" in the 1936 redlining map), many people of color excluded from other parts of the city formed communities in the valley. Immigrant and refugee communities have also developed along the street over the years, making the street a bustling multicultural place. But the infrastructure of the street itself remained largely the same as it was when it was State Route 167. Traffic speeds were fast because the street was designed to prioritize car throughput above the safety or mobility of people living or working along the street.

Phyllis Porter was already the leader of Rainier Valley Greenways in 2014 when a scary moment galvanized her into a powerful force for the neighborhood and the city's safe streets movement. She was headed to lunch from her job at Bike Works, the community bicycle shop and youth empowerment nonprofit in Columbia City described in chapter 5, when she narrowly avoided tragedy. "As soon as I stepped on the curb, all I could see was an SUV coming at me," she told KUOW.[4] Luckily she was able to get out of the way, but the person driving had lost control of the vehicle and crashed into Carol Cobb Salon on the corner of Rainier Avenue South and South Ferdinand Street. The vehicle continued all the way through the hair salon and into the Grecian Delight restaurant next door. Customers eating in the restaurant, including a family with children, were pinned to a wall inside. Several people were injured. The building was so damaged that the storefronts sat vacant for a long time while the structure was repaired. Neither Carol Cobb Salon nor Grecian Delight returned to the corner.

Porter emerged from her near-miss with fire inside her. She'd had enough, and she was going to make sure Seattle stopped dragging its feet and finally did something to make Rainier Avenue safer. She went on a local media tour, telling everyone about how Rainier was the city's most dangerous street and how nothing was being done to stop the constant stream of injuries and deaths. She told the story of her near-miss and talked about how that collision was just one of seven incidents where people driving on Rainier crashed into buildings that year. If even buildings weren't safe, then people walking on the sidewalks, crossing the street, or riding bikes didn't stand a chance. In just three years, 630 people had been injured in traffic collisions on Rainier Avenue, making it by far the city's most dangerous street. It had far more collisions per mile than the next two worst streets—Aurora Avenue and Lake City Way—both of which are state highways carrying many more vehicles per day. "The things that are happening in Rainier Valley, Columbia City, Hillman City," she told KUOW, listing neighborhoods along Rainier Avenue, "these things are unacceptable. And something needs to be done now."[5]

About a week after the collision at Rainier and Ferdinand, neighbors organized a "crosswalk-in" protest, walking back and forth across Rainier Avenue in front of the destroyed salon and restaurant in Columbia City carrying a banner that said "Slow Down! Keep Everyone Safe." The poster advertising the protest said the goal was "to promote action from SDOT to slow traffic on Rainier and improve safety for all." Bike Works, located just down the block, also urged SDOT to take action, calling for "some kind of road diet and restricted speed zone through the heart of Columbia City."[6] The protest and ongoing pressure worked. SDOT started to develop a safety project for the corridor. Porter organized another protest seven months later to keep the pressure on the city to make the changes. She brought together business owners, traffic collision victims, the Rainier Chamber of Commerce, and City Councilmember Bruce Harrell, who had not been a safe streets champion on the council before this point. SDOT implemented the first section of safety changes a few months later.

"I think that was my project that I felt the most proud of," Chang said of Rainier in our phone conversation. "Understanding that there's all this pent-up frustration from the community for many, many years. That they've been telling us, telling the city and others, that there's something wrong with this street, and we need to do something about it. And then going through the process and being able to make a change and see the immediate reaction, which is that it made things so much better." An SDOT follow-up study found that the number of people speeding declined, but most importantly the number of people driving forty miles per hour or faster declined by 70–80 percent.[7] Speeding is directly correlated with the severity of collisions, so while the total number of collisions fell only a modest 15 percent after the first full year the safety changes were in place, serious injuries were eliminated. In the ten years prior, an average of nine people per year were seriously injured along the studied one-mile stretch of Rainier Avenue. In the first year after the changes were in place, zero serious injuries and deaths were reported. "And now there's a cry, which is great, that we need to do more, and quickly," said Chang. "And hopefully we can continue to do that. There are so many needs that have been ignored in our city. . . . The satisfaction from being able to help people and make things better and improve how people get around, it's immense. I just enjoy working and serving people that way."

A Protected Bike Lane through Downtown Ushers in a New Era for City Bicycling, 2014

Ten days after Sher Kung was killed while biking in the old painted bike lane on Second Avenue (described in chapter 7), SDOT crews got to work building the protected bike lane Mayor Ed Murray had promised five months earlier during the 2014 Cascade Bicycle Club Bike Month Breakfast. It was devastating that the project, sought for so many years, was just ten days away from potentially saving Kung's life.

Compared to other downtown streets, Second Avenue's descent from north to south is gradual. This is why the street has been a major bike route ever since biking in the city first became popular in the 1890s. Before 2014, the skinny paint-only bike lane on the left-hand side of the one-way southbound street was widely considered to be the worst bike lane in Seattle.[8] Squeezed between parked cars and heavy downtown traffic, the bike lane had little room for anyone to make a mistake. If someone opened their car door, they could hit someone biking in the bike lane and send them tumbling into traffic. People driving who were making left turns to access I-5 or other downtown destinations also were not accustomed to checking for someone biking to their left, since most cyclists ride on the right side of the street. The result was that injuries were constant on Second Avenue, and many people biking downtown found it easier to take other routes instead, like biking in the bus lane on the opposite side of the street or riding down the Third Avenue bus corridor. Or perhaps most commonly, people would choose not to bike downtown at all.

In September 2013, five months after Ivan's action on Cherry Street, Cascade Bicycle Club created a similar demonstration on a block of Second Avenue during the international creative street-use celebration Park(ing) Day. Cascade got a permit to disallow parking on one block of the street to create a temporary protected bike lane. Cascade staffers and volunteers put flowerpots along the edge of their new lane, creating a bike oasis in the middle of usually stressful downtown Seattle. It was very effective at giving people a chance to experience how the street could be better.

But it was Mayor Murray's deadline that finally got the project moving. By the mayor's giving SDOT clear direction and a deadline, many of the typical bureaucratic barriers that slow or stop bike projects vanished for the SDOT team working on the bike lane. They suddenly had access to a full-time project designer, and their calls to all the other teams within SDOT became priority calls. The mayor wanted this done in just five months, so every team at SDOT needed to work together to make it happen. "You need to have a director who gets it. You need a [city] council that gets it. You need a mayor that gets it," said Sam Woods, head of SDOT's Bicycle Program at the time, in an interview for this book. "Mayor Murray did more for biking in Seattle than any other mayor," she said.

When all those pieces line up, a lot of work can happen. For example, Woods was having a hard time figuring out if SDOT would be able to install bicycle traffic signals along with the new bike lane. Because the new bike lane would be separated from general traffic, it was important that people in cars trying to turn left would have a red light when the bike lane had a green light. But it wasn't clear whether the existing traffic signal system had the capacity to add a new set of signals. If it didn't, the project's costs would increase and its timeline would become more challenging. Woods's first couple of tries to get an answer from the signals team didn't result in a clear answer. But when SDOT Director Scott Kubly called with Woods on the line, the signals team said they could make it happen. "You have to have, at the director level, that kind of support," said Woods. "Because that person was willing to jump through hoops for him, but not for me." People in any organization are going to answer more quickly to their boss than to someone else. "When you get that direction from the top, people fall in line."

It's hard to fully explain what it's like to ride in this new bike lane that was so transformational to Seattle. In a shaky helmet-camera video I shot before Seattle built the new bike lane on Second Avenue, I encountered some kind of hazard on every block. I had to put on the brakes because someone pulled out of a parking spot without seeing me, then someone turned left in front of me, blocking the bike lane. The whole way down the street, parked cars sat uncomfortably close to my left and car traffic drove uncomfortably close to my right. But in a video I shot on the new bike lane's opening day in September 2014, the street looked like it was from a different universe. The wide two-way bike lane was against the curb, so there were no cars to my left anymore, and the bike lane was separated from traffic by a few feet of paint and plastic posts (planter boxes filled with flowers and greenery would come later). Nobody pulled in front of me at any point in the video, and nobody blocked the bike lane either. There was no conflict and very little danger. It was a boring five minutes thirty-seven seconds of video, and that boredom was glorious. Having a space that felt safe even in the middle of a busy downtown brought so much of the city within reach. Excitement should come from seeing a friend or taking in an amazing view, not from the fear of a traffic collision. The number of other people biking through downtown increased dramatically almost overnight, and riding a bike finally felt like a normal way to get around town.[9] Biking became a reasonable option for many more people who would never have even tried biking on Second Avenue the way it was before. A place to be avoided at all costs became a destination.

The bike lane that opened in 2014 is not exactly the same as the bike lane that's there today, and that was by design. By using mostly low-cost materials, like paint, plastic posts, and plastic planter boxes with some flowers and long grasses in them, Chang, Woods, and others on the SDOT team were able to observe how the new bike lane functioned, then make adjustments later to address any problems. Changing paint, updating signs, or moving plastic posts costs very little money. Using temporary materials for the initial design also proved key to easing people's concerns about the street changes. If something ended up working poorly, people knew the city was prepared to fix it. Making such a promise helped garner trust and dampened opposition. "So much of Second Avenue was done right," said Woods. "It was done so fast, and then later we did upgrades."

The week the lane opened, the city and Cascade Bicycle Club had mobilized a lot of staff and volunteers to talk to people about the changes, especially at intersections. People driving were not used to having to wait for a left-turn light, and people biking were not used to needing to stop when the rest of the street, including people in the new left-turn lane, had a green light. The goal of the effort was to get a substantial number of users to follow the new rules so that others would follow suit. It also doubled as a chance for a lot of staff and volunteers to observe how people were using the street, ask users what they noticed, and suggest some early fixes. For example, people driving were turning into a busy parking garage without looking for people on bikes first, so the city moved the nearby parked cars back from the garage entrance to improve visibility. People driving were also ignoring or missing the "Left

Turn on [green dot] Only" signs, so they were changed to "No Turn on [red arrow]," which resulted in immediate improvements.

But most people did not spend much time thinking about the paint or the plastic posts or the signs. Most people just noticed that biking suddenly seemed like a viable option, at least on this one section of this one street downtown. Seeing people ride comfortably in a protected bike lane looked easy, safe, and fun. And if a bike lane like that can work in the busy heart of downtown, it can work anywhere.

It All Comes Down to Election Night, 2015

The movement for safe streets and bicycling was building to a crescendo in 2015. Neighbors had organized local safe streets groups in nearly all corners of the city; larger safe streets organizations like Seattle Neighborhood Greenways and Cascade Bicycle Club were getting serious attention from city leaders; the public's demands for street safety projects far exceeded the city's budget for them. Mayor Murray had demonstrated bold action for building the bike network by completing the Second Avenue project, and the opposition to such changes was quiet compared to the celebrations. The year 2015 was positioned to be a watershed moment for Seattle's turn away from car culture and toward a purposeful and hopeful alternative that places safety, walking, biking, and transit at the top of the city's transportation priority list.

Every city council seat was up for election that year as Seattle transitioned to a district-based council election system. The Bridging the Gap levy that had been developed under Mayor Nickels was set to expire that year as well, so the city needed voters to approve a replacement. The electoral challenges facing safe streets advocates in 2015 were enormous. They had to convince the city to craft as bold a transportation levy as possible before sending it to voters. Then they had to get voters to pass that levy. At the same time, they needed to navigate the brand-new district-oriented Seattle City Council election landscape to make sure that at least a majority of winners were either champions for safe streets or allies to the cause. But the safe streets movement had a big head start because people had just spent five years organizing into neighborhood-based advocacy groups. So that meant every city council district had a group or several groups of people ready to press their candidates on local safe streets issues.

The August 2015 primary was huge. "Approximately half the city's population is running for City Council right now," I wrote in the *Seattle Bike Blog* voters' guide for that election.[10] Forty-seven people ran for the nine seats in Seattle's primary, but only the top two candidates in each race would advance to the general election. When the dust settled on the frantic election, the few overtly antibike candidates failed to get more than a small percentage of votes and either did not advance to the general election or were in such a distant second place that they had no chance. The primary demonstrated that being openly against bike lanes was terrible politics in Seattle. Candidates who spoke against bike lanes appeared out of touch, a signal to voters that they were also unlikely to stand up for progress on other tough issues.

The biggest test of Seattle's changing transportation culture, however, was the November general election. Transit, walking, and biking advocates had teamed up to push for a dramatically expanded transportation measure to replace the expiring Move Seattle levy. After a lot of pressure, Mayor Murray's administration proposed a nine-year $930 million replacement for the expiring $365 million levy. But it wasn't just the size of the measure that was groundbreaking; the priorities within it were too. At least $400 million was slated for safety improvements, including nearly $100 million for bike-specific investments. Even more was earmarked for transit. The bulk of road funding was for maintenance of existing infrastructure, like seismic upgrades for bridges and repaving streets. The only significant new roads project in the levy was the Lander Street bridge over a railroad in SoDo, long a priority for freight interests. The levy promised to build half of the new Bike Master Plan's citywide network, putting the core element of the twenty-year plan on track. The levy also promised rapid-bus projects and at least one Safe Routes to School project to every public school in the city.[11]

The proposal was bold and unprecedented. The prevailing wisdom had previously assumed that if a strong majority of households own cars, the best way to pass a levy was to put forward promises to make driving easier. Unfortunately, that had been the lesson from the 1968 and 1970 Forward Thrust votes. But the Move Seattle levy challenged that assumption. It did not even pretend that it would build new infrastructure to make car trips faster. Instead, it promised to maintain existing roads and bridges while investing the bulk of its funding for new infrastructure into transit, walking, and biking projects. It was a big risk, and polling ahead of the vote didn't look promising. The mood from city staff and high-up campaign officials in the final days of the campaign suggested that many of them thought they were going to lose. One person who worked for SDOT told me they were all but packing up their desk at work earlier that day, assuming they would be fired as soon as the measure failed.

Before the polls closed and the initial vote counts were announced, few elected officials were in attendance at the party for the Yes campaign. The mood among supporters gathered in the bar was nervous. Campaigners knew the polls did not look great, but there was also a lot of volunteer power and enthusiasm behind the measure. Labor unions and transit advocacy groups were able to motivate a lot of people to help promote the measure. Cascade Bicycle Club and other bike advocates played a major part in the get-out-the-vote effort. A lot of biking and safe streets supporters volunteered a lot of time and effort knocking on doors and making phone calls to encourage passage of the measure. Years of organizing had led to this moment, when the voters of Seattle would decide whether they bought into the vision of biking, walking, and transit as the future of transportation in the city.

There is an amazing photo by *Seattle Post-Intelligencer* photojournalist Genna Martin centered on Shefali Ranganathan, cochair of the levy campaign, with her hands in the air and her mouth wide open as she yelled out to the room.[12] Her phone is in her hand, and you can see the bar chart from the elections website showing a clear win for the levy. But if you study all the faces in the room, you can see another emotion in addition to elation: people were surprised. Campaign staff were hoping that it would at least be close, giving the measure a chance to hobble over the finish line as votes arrived by mail in the following days. Previous elections had shown that younger people in Seattle were more likely to vote late, and younger people were expected to lean in favor of the measure. The initial results on election night were likely to be as bad as they were going to get, and an apparent slight loss could still have been good news. But the first result was not a slight loss. It wasn't even a slight win. It was a huge, decisive win on election night, and the margin only grew as more votes were counted over the following days. In the end, Seattle passed the measure by a landslide 17 percentage points.

As soon as the results came through and it was clear the effort was going to pass, elected officials swarmed in the bar doors to make sure they appeared in all the happy photos and to give speeches. It felt like they were waiting nearby to see which way it would go. In that moment, as politicians swooped in to take the stage, Seattle's transportation culture had changed. Or, more accurately, the city's leaders finally realized that the culture had been changing faster than they'd thought.

The moment was also a message to safe streets, walking, biking, and transit advocates that all that hard work for all those years to influence city policy and win hearts and minds across the city was working.

A large group of people pedal into Cal Anderson Park at the end of the Ride for Justice on June 11, 2020. The park was part of the Capitol Hill Occupied Protest area established after Seattle Police abandoned the nearby East Precinct building following a days-long standoff with protesters in the weeks after the murder of George Floyd by an officer in Minnesota. Photo by Tom Fucoloro, *Seattle Bike Blog*.

Epilogue

I started *Seattle Bike Blog* five years before that crucial 2015 vote as a news site that advocates for more and safer cycling in Seattle, and the Move Seattle vote felt like a culmination of a lot of work. It was the result of a changing biking and safe streets movement that I had documented daily. But the next morning, I woke up late from a night of celebrating in a much more somber mood. I sat down at my laptop to write a happy post about the win and the party the night before, but that's not what came out. Instead, I was thinking about Mike Wang, Brian Fairbrother, Robert Townsend, Sher Kung, Caleb Shoop, the whole Schulte family, and the twenty or so people killed every year in Seattle traffic collisions. I titled the post "The True Cost of Move Seattle":

> People shouldn't die just for trying to get around our city. Whatever our society thinks we're getting in return for all these deaths isn't worth the horrible cost. Not only can we end traffic violence, we realized, we have to.
>
> That's why the day after initial returns show the Move Seattle levy passing with a solid margin, I'm sitting at my keyboard trying to type this story through a stream of tears. The path from July 2011 to passing a measure that will invest at least $400 million into an unprecedented effort to end traffic violence—the amazing bloom of genuinely grassroots Seattle Neighborhood Greenways groups in all corners of our city, the Road Safety Summit that crafted our city's first plan to end deaths and serious injuries [from traffic collisions], the remake of the Bike Master Plan that lays out the path to crafting safe streets for people of all ages and abilities—was paved by the lives of people who did not need to die.[1]

A Single Election Will Never Be Enough

The strong vote in favor of the Move Seattle levy was symbolic of much more than just funding. It showed that the people of Seattle had signed on to a different vision for transportation than what had been sold to the city for a century. But a single levy vote in 2015 didn't change everything. Seattle is very much still a car-dominated city, and many projects that significantly challenge car culture still face opposition. Much of the safe streets momentum from the middle of the decade came screeching to a halt in 2017, along with a lot of other important work in the city, thanks to a shocking revelation about Mayor Ed Murray. Five men accused Murray of sexual abuse when they were underage teenagers in the 1970s and 1980s, including one allegation from a cousin of his. After fighting the allegations for months, Murray resigned in disgrace in September 2017.[2]

In the election to replace Murray, Jenny Durkan defeated Cary Moon, the candidate endorsed by most safe streets organizations, including *Seattle Bike Blog*. Though Mayor Durkan said when campaigning that she supported the Bike Master Plan, when she took office in late 2017, she quietly froze bike projects across the city. She didn't announce that she was doing this or provide any explanation to the public. Most projects weren't outright canceled, they just didn't happen. The whole Bike Master Plan was thrown into purgatory. Timelines kept moving backward. By the end of 2018, Mayor Durkan had constructed less than 4 percent of the 10.4 miles of protected bike lanes planned for that year.[3] When discussing the Second Avenue bike lane in chapter 9, SDOT Bicycle Program Manager Sam Woods described how important it was to have clear direction from the top in order for work to move through the department effectively and build bold projects. Unfortunately, the reverse is also true. Even a project that is planned and funded will crawl to a halt if the mayor isn't clearly behind it.

The pace of building out the Bike Master Plan slowed to such a crawl that people protested at City Hall. Apu Mishra and Tamara Schmautz stood in front of Seattle City Council in April 2019 and shredded copies of Seattle's Bicycle, Vision Zero, and Climate Action Plans to demonstrate how Mayor Durkan had seemingly discarded all these policies that the council had previously approved.[4] A few months later, a wide coalition of safe streets, accessibility, and transit organizations held a rally in front of City Hall. Afterward, hundreds of people biked down Fourth Avenue to protest the mayor's bike plan cuts.[5]

To make big changes, a movement challenging a culture as dominant as the one based on cars needs support from the people pulling every lever of power, and all those people must be effective in their work. It's so much easier to stop something than it is to create something. Transit-supporting freeway fighters learned this lesson the hard way with their 1960s and '70s ballot losses (described in chapter 3). The twenty-first century has finally seen flourishes of success for Seattle's transit, biking, and walking vision. But every step still requires a lot of organizing work, and there's no guarantee of success. No single election or funding vote will change that. Public opinion can shift a lot more easily than the infrastructure. Seattle, like the rest of the United States and much of the world, had spent a century investing heavily in driving private automobiles. Industry, neighborhoods, and sprawling suburban communities had been constructed around driving a car. Even many people who understand the problems caused by a reliance on cars often resist moving away from owning and driving a car themselves. There are many unique reasons why a person's life might require (or be much easier with) a car. People are living their lives within a society that has long assumed they would always have one. Car-centric infrastructure is steel and concrete. It doesn't change shape just because public opinion would like it to.

It can easily become overwhelming to think about the sheer scale of the problem that sprawling development across the United States and many other parts of the world has left us. The solutions are not going to be easy, and some of them won't be popular. Post-WWII infrastructure is aging and crumbling, and that's bad because we sure did build a lot of it back then. But in some ways, it also presents us with big opportunities to reimagine how our communities and regions work. The good news is that the solutions also happen to be more fun, and they are getting easier to implement as more communities, including Seattle, document their experiences and develop best practices. "What used to take decades, now you can go and do that in five to ten years," Pete Lagerwey told me in an interview for this book. Lagerwey worked in bicycle planning through the 1980s and 1990s, when too little attention was paid to street safety projects, so he would know. Now planners have lots of examples from cities like Seattle that are included in improved federal design guidebooks, so any place that wants to make their community more bike-friendly can immediately start making improvements to their streets. They just need to decide they want to do it.

The Seattle Department of Transportation has also developed a project that, if properly funded, has the potential to bring the city's traffic death count into the single digits or even to zero. SDOT's Pedestrian and Bike Safety Assessment Tool works by analyzing the road conditions surrounding past collisions. Staff can then use it to scan the whole city street system to identify other streets with characteristics similar to the collision location. The idea is that SDOT staff can make safety improvements to streets before serious collisions happen.[6] This is the next level of traffic safety design and engineering: finding a way to get ahead of deaths and injuries rather than chasing them. It's the kind of thinking any city is going to need if it hopes to reduce traffic deaths and serious injuries to zero. The problem is that the number of streets with dangerous designs in need of fixing is enormous, and the cost to fix them all will be high. But then again, the cost of failure is even higher.

"It's Systemic. How Can You Not See This Now?"

Ed Ewing left Cascade Bicycle Club and the Major Taylor Project in 2016 to pursue work in some other nonprofits in the Puget Sound area. Then 2020 happened. First a pandemic broke out, and Ewing was among the many people who lost jobs during the initial shutdown. Then police murdered George Floyd back in Ewing's hometown. "What 2020 did was, it showed us where our homework is," he said in an interview for this book. "It's systemic. How can you not see this now?" Just days after Floyd was murdered, Ewing and his friend Doc Wilson organized the first Peace Peloton. It was a ride to "bring awareness to and bring about positive change for black, brown, marginalized, and disenfranchised populations in our city through Economic, Public Health/Healthcare, and Criminal Justice reforms," as the event notice said.[7] Forty-eight hours after Doc first had the idea, 350 people showed up for the ride. The large crowd stopped several times to listen to speakers addressing the issues at the core of the ride's mission. It was a bike ride, sure, but it wasn't about biking. It was about mobilizing for justice and reform.

The bike became a tool during the summer's protests in a way Seattle hadn't really seen before. Edwin Lindo, a critical race theory scholar and cofounder of the community bookstore Estelita's Library, organized a huge Ride for Justice just a few days after the first Peace Peloton.[8] The ride traveled around the Central District, stopping for speeches near King County's youth jail before ending in the middle of Cal Anderson Park with riders forming a large circle, where a space was created for Black and brown people to say what needed to be said. The park at that time was part of the Capitol Hill Occupied Protest that formed when police abandoned the nearby East Precinct following a week of strong protests and violent police crowd-control actions. It was one of the largest bike rides Seattle had seen in a long time, and it wasn't about bicycling either.

At the same time, another group was organizing to help protect protests by handling traffic control duties and forming barriers using their bikes. The Seattle Bike Brigade put their bodies and bikes on the line to protect protests, but they also tried their best to make sure the protests, not the bikes, were the focus of attention. They refused to give interviews, for example, and if they carried signs, they bore the messages of the protest. Their job was safety, and they were effective.[9] All these efforts used skills and tactics learned during the fight for more and safer cycling. For example, riders controlled intersections ahead of protestors by corking, a skill developed during Critical Mass rides. Ewing's work with the Major Taylor Project made him an excellent ride leader, but the project also taught ride-leading skills to many other people throughout the community. Bike Works had a mobile bike-repair van that they had been driving around to different parts of town for years as a way of expanding their services to more places, so they were ready to show up at the start of these major rides to help people get their bikes ready. It felt like Seattle's bike scene (all of these examples are described in more detail in chapter 5) had been practicing for this moment.

Through these protests, perhaps the future of Seattle bike advocacy revealed itself. Maybe it won't even be called "bike advocacy" anymore. That phrase no longer captures the full extent of it. Bicycling has never been an isolated issue floating in a vacuum fully insulated from the rest of society. Since the very beginning, bicycling in Seattle has intersected with many other social issues, including racial justice. The first bike paths literally led the way to some of the city's first racially restrictive housing covenants in Interlaken. But those early bike boosters tossed their wheels into Elliott Bay as soon as cars showed up. The modern bicycling movement developed for very different reasons, and each generation keeps redefining what the bicycle means and what it can do for society. The lesson for modern bike advocates may be that biking itself is not the end goal of bike advocacy. Biking is a means to build community, make communities safer, and directly challenge a destructive and unjust car culture. The end goal of bike advocacy is to care for the people we love and keep them safe.

Fiona Learns to Bike

Through the course of writing this book, I have been teaching Fiona how to ride her bike. When I typed the first words, she could stand over her pedal-free balance bike and wobble slowly down the sidewalk. She went so slowly that we rarely made it a full block before she would stop, ding her bell, then put the bike down so she could run around instead. But as I complete this manuscript, she is, as she calls it, "zooming." She sits on the seat and, with just a couple of big pushes of her feet, gets enough speed to coast with her feet off the ground for half a block or more (depending on the incline). I have to run to keep up. She is now working on pedaling her big-kid bike. Some day she will be old enough to move around Seattle without me hovering nearby.

I want our city and its transportation system to value every person's life as much as I value hers. That sounds like a lofty goal, but nothing is more important than the people we love.

Acknowledgments

This book would not have been possible without the assistance of an entire community of Seattle bike riders and advocates. More than a hundred people pitched in a few dollars every month to support my work on my blog and this book. Without the collective financial power of the *Seattle Bike Blog* supporters, I would not have had the time and freedom to write this book. You made this happen. I also want to thank all the wonderful people who have done wonderful things for biking but did not get mentioned by name in this book. Thank you also to the archivists at the Museum of History and Industry, University of Washington Special Collections, Seattle Municipal Archives, Seattle Public Utilities, and Seattle Public Library. But most of all, thank you to my spouse, Kelli. She's the person who convinced me to start biking in the first place. Writing this book while having a young child at home has been a major challenge. The amount of support and patience Kelli has provided for this book effort is immeasurable.

Notes

Preface

1. Tom Fucoloro, "The Westlake Bikeway Is Officially Open, and It Was Worth the Compromises," *Seattle Bike Blog*, September 19, 2016, www.seattlebikeblog .com/2016/09/19/the-westlake-bikeway-is-officially-open-and-it-was-worth -the-compromises/.
2. *Open Street Map* (Madison Street between Fourth and Fifth Avenues), 2022, www.openstreetmap.org.
3. Linda Lam, "Seattle's Rainy Reputation Is Well-Deserved," *Weather Channel* (blog), October 15, 2016, https://weather.com/science/weather-explainers/news /seattle-rainy-reputation.
4. Hutchinson, *Re: Cyclists;* Jungnickel, *Bikes and Bloomers*; Walker, *How Cycling Can Save the World.*
5. I am not a trained academic historian, so I also had to teach myself how to properly cite resources in notes like these. I also received many editorial notes about using too much "snarky" language for a book.
6. Thrush, *Native Seattle.*
7. Natalie Dupille, "Dear Mom, I've Joined a Guerilla Bike Collective," *Slog* (blog), *The Stranger*, September 2, 2020, https://www.thestranger.com/slog /2020/09/02/44398894/dear-mom-ive-joined-a-guerilla-bike-collective.
8. Fucoloro, "Day after Council Votes to Slightly Reduce Police Funding, Officer Rolls Bike over Person's Head and Neck," *Seattle Bike Blog*, September 24, 2020, www.seattlebikeblog.com/2020/09/24/day-after-council-votes-to-slightly -reduce-police-funding-officer-rolls-bike-over-persons-head-and-neck/.

Introduction

1. Berger, *Pugetopolis.*
2. This shushing person is often me.
3. Joel VanderHoek, "Ballard / Seattle Superbowl Celebration with No Jaywalking," February 3, 2014, video, 39 seconds, www.youtube.com/watch?v=2FP9I-CPfL4.
4. Tom Fucoloro, "Guerrilla Road Safety Group 'Politely' Installs Illegal Bike Lane Protectors on Cherry Street," *Seattle Bike Blog*, April 4, 2013, https://www

.seattlebikeblog.com/2013/04/04/guerrilla-road-safety-group-politely-installs
-illegal-bike-lane-protectors-on-cherry-street/.

5. Katie Pearce, "Guerrilla Crosswalk Painter Arrested by Vallejo Police, Cheered by Neighbors," *Streetsblog USA*, June 4, 2013, https://usa.streetsblog.org/2013/06/04 /guerrilla-crosswalk-painter-arrested-by-vallejo-police-cheered-by-neighbors/.

6. Kathleen Cooper, "Tacoma Crosswalk Vigilantes Tell All," *News Tribune*, June 30, 2015, www.thenewstribune.com/news/politics-government/article25861150.html.

7. Fucoloro, "Guerrilla Road Safety Group 'Politely' Installs Illegal Bike Lane Protectors on Cherry Street."

8. Michael Andersen, "America's 10 Best Protected Bike Lanes of 2013," *PeopleFor-Bikes* (blog), December 3, 2013, https://peopleforbikes.org/blog/the-10-best -protected-bike-lanes-of-2013/ (page discontinued).

9. Fucoloro, "In 1990, Seattle Topped Portland and Nearly Every Other US City in Bike Commuting," *Seattle Bike Blog*, June 25, 2013, www.seattlebikeblog .com/2013/06/25/in-1990-seattle-topped-portland-and-nearly-every-other-us -city-in-bike-commuting/.

1. A Bike Boom in a Boomtown

1. Smethurst, *The Bicycle—Towards a Global History*.
2. George F. Cotterill, "Wheeling in Seattle," *The Argus*, December 17, 1898.
3. Crowley and HistoryLink staff, *Seattle and King County Timeline*.
4. Ordinance 4460, An Ordinance Providing for the Licensing of Bicycles in the City of Seattle and Creating a Bicycle Road Fund and Designating the Use Thereof, Pub. L. No. Ordinance 4460, April 1, 1897, http://clerk.seattle.gov/search /ordinances/4460.
5. Smethurst, *The Bicycle—Towards a Global History*.
6. Cameron, *Bicycling in Seattle 1874–1904*.
7. H. A. Chadwick, Cycle News, *The Argus*, February 6, 1897.
8. Cameron, *Bicycling in Seattle 1874–1904*.
9. Chadwick, Cycle Notes, *The Argus*, August 25, 1894.
10. Rob Ketcherside, "Seattle's YMCA Park, 1895–1903," *Ba-kground* (blog), January 10, 2019, http://ba-kground.com/seattles-ymca-park-1895-1903/.
11. "Racing Among Women," *The Argus*, June 27, 1986.
12. Chadwick, Cycle News, *The Argus*, February 22, 1896.
13. Cameron, *Bicycling in Seattle 1874–1904*.
14. Cotterill, "Wheeling in Seattle," December 17, 1898.
15. "Chadwick of The Argus Dies on Vacation," *Seattle Daily Times*, June 12, 1934.
16. Chadwick, Cycle News, *The Argus*, March 28, 1896.
17. George F. Cotterill, "Queen City Good Roads Club—Minutes of the Meetings," March 8, 1897, Special Collections, Suzzallo Library, University of Washington, Seattle; Chadwick, Cycle News, *The Argus*, March 13, 1897.
18. "Ever a Popular Pastime," *Seattle Daily Times*, June 1, 1902.

19. There is little agreement in Seattle on how to capitalize SoDo, which is not an official Seattle neighborhood term even though the city uses it often. So I went in search of the original uses of the term and found a 1990 *Seattle Post-Intelligencer* story that referenced it as "SoDo," citing "some local wags" who were using the term. After joking about this on Twitter and conducting a poll, Marina Gordon reached out and said her friend Rose Pike was that wag. Pike coined the term in a *Seattle Weekly* article in the 1980s to refer to "South of the Kingdome" and used the CamelCase SoDo.

20. An Ordinance Providing for the Licensing of Bicycles in the City of Seattle and Creating a Bicycle Road Fund and Designating the Use Thereof, Pub. L. No. Ordinance 4460 (1897).

21. Lucile McDonald, "When Seattle's Boulevards Were Bicycle Paths," *Seattle Times Magazine*, July 12, 1953.

22. "Eldorado Hill" was an old name for Queen Anne Hill to the west of Lake Union. "A Day on Seattle's Bicycle Paths," *Seattle Post-Intelligencer*, June 1, 1902.

23. McDonald, "When Seattle's Boulevards Were Bicycle Paths."

24. "A Day on Seattle's Bicycle Paths," *Seattle P-I*, June 1, 1902.

25. Cameron, *Bicycling in Seattle 1874–1904*.

26. Lunch Room details come from a photo by an unknown photographer taken circa 1901; Seattle history lover Gordan Macdougall found the photos in an estate sale. Feliks Banel, "Mystery Photo Album Discovered at Seattle Estate Sale," *MyNorthwest.com*, March 24, 2021, https://mynorthwest.com/2712701 /mystery-photo-album-seattle-estate-sale/.

27. Olivia B. Waxman, "The Surprisingly Complex Link Between Prohibition and Women's Rights," *Time*, January 16, 2019, https://time.com/5501680 /prohibition-history-feminism-suffrage-metoo/.

28. Chadwick, "The Mayorality," *The Argus*, January 30, 1904.

29. David Wilma, "Cotterill, George Fletcher (1865–1958)," *HistoryLink*, October 2, 2000, https://www.historylink.org/File/2709.

30. "Bit of Switzerland in Midst of Seattle," *Seattle Daily Times*, June 13, 1908.

31. Tom Fucoloro, "Searching for the 125-Year-Old Interlaken Bike Path," *Seattle Bike Blog*, August 5, 2021, www.seattlebikeblog.com/2021/08/05/watch-searching -for-the-125-year-old-interlaken-bike-path/.

32. "To Condemn the Bicycle Path," *Seattle Daily Times*, October 10, 1904.

33. "For Sale—The Good Road Lunch Room," *Seattle Daily Times*, March 15, 1901.

34. James F. Dawson, "Washington Park/ Seattle, WA./ Topo Map [orig]/ Notes on Ground by Dawson [r]/; Scale 100' = 1" [orig]," August 2, 1904, item number 2699-14, Olmsted Archives, Frederick Law Olmsted National Historic Site, Brookline, MA.

35. Chadwick, Cycle News, *The Argus*, May 29, 1897.

36. "Bike Path Ready," *Seattle Daily Times*, May 9, 1900.

37. Chadwick, Cycle News, *The Argus*, March 3, 1897.

38. Chadwick, Cycle News, *The Argus*, February 12, 1898.

39. "A Day on Seattle's Bicycle Paths," *Seattle P-I*, June 1, 1902.

40. Thrush, *Native Seattle*.

41. Jennifer Ott, "Seattle Board of Trustees Passes Ordinance, Calling for Removal of Indians from the Town, on February 7, 1865," *HistoryLink*, December 7, 2014, www.historylink.org/File/10979.

42. David Wilma, "Seattle Pioneers Petition against a Reservation on the Black River for the Duwamish Tribe in 1866," *HistoryLink*, January 24, 2001, www.history link.org/File/2955.

43. Klingle, *Emerald City*.

44. Chadwick, Cycle Notes, *The Argus*, August 1, 1896.

45. George F. Cotterill, "An American Engineer in Europe," Second Annual Convention of the Pacific Northwest Society of Engineers, Seattle, Washington, July 1, 1904, Special Collections, Suzzallo Library, University of Washington, Seattle.

46. Cotterill, in *Climax of a World Quest*, quotes the title of a painting by Emanuel Leutze, *Westward the Course of Empire Takes Its Way*, 1862, stereochrome, 20' x 30', US Capitol Building, Washington, DC, www.aoc.gov/explore-capitol -campus/art/westward-course-empire-takes-its-way.

47. "Claims an Ideal District," *Seattle Sunday Times*, April 15, 1906.

48. "Study This Map Carefully" (advertisement), *Seattle P-I*, April 15, 1906.

49. "Wheeling Notes," *Seattle Mail and Herald*, November 16, 1901.

50. "Queen City Club," *Seattle Daily Times*, April 10, 1902.

51. Friends of Seattle's Olmsted Parks, "A Brief History," accessed December 12, 2020, https://seattleolmsted.org/history/.

2. After the Bike Bust

1. "News Notes From Spokane," *Seattle Daily Times*, September 20, 1899.

2. "This Is the New Automobile Coat," *Seattle Daily Times*, October 21, 1899.

3. "The Hills of Seattle's Streets," *Seattle Post-Intelligencer*, October 9, 1902.

4. "When Santa Claus Will Come in His Automobile" (advertisement), *Seattle P-I*, November 28, 1901.

5. *Seattle Daily Times*, October 26, 1901.

6. H. A. Chadwick, Cycle Notes, *The Argus*, August 2, 1902.

7. Knute Berger, "The Car That Broke the Back of Seattle's Bike Craze," *Crosscut* (blog), September 25, 2013, https://crosscut.com/2013/09/bike-paths-seattle -history.

8. Chadwick, Cycle Notes, *The Argus*, July 26, 1902.

9. Chadwick, Cycle Notes, *The Argus*, September 3, 1904.

10. "Chadwick of The Argus Dies on Vacation," *Seattle Daily Times*, June 12, 1934.

11. "Dr. Matthews Is Agitating the Issue of Bonds," *Seattle Mail and Herald*, December 23, 1905. This passage appears in the paper's recurring Vanity Fair column written under the pen name Becky Sharpe after the character in Thackeray's novel of the same name (although with a slightly different spelling). The quoted line at the end is from Alexander Pope's classic 1717 poem *Eloisa to Abelard*. The full

stanza reads, "How happy is the blameless vestal's lot! / The world forgetting, by the world forgot. / Eternal sunshine of the spotless mind! / Each pray'r accepted, and each wish resign'd." I have been thinking about this stanza a lot ever since I read that line in the *Mail and Herald* because it is very instructive for understanding the lasting impact of Seattle's early bike boom. It is tempting to look back at old photos of lost bike paths and think that things used to be better before the city grew or before cars arrived and the paths were widened into boulevards that kicked bicycles to the curb. But this is an idealized, nostalgic, and unrealistic image of the past. "Eternal sunshine of the spotless mind."

12. James R. Warren, "United Parcel Service (UPS)," *HistoryLink*, September 20, 1999, www.historylink.org/File/1679.

13. "Access World News—Historical and Current," NewsBank database, accessed December 4, 2022.

14. "Bicycle Coming Back into Favor," *Seattle Daily Times*, September 28, 1919.

15. "Yoo-Hoo Skin-Nay Bike Club Enjoys First Picnic of Season," *Seattle Daily Times*, May 19, 1919.

16. "Snappy Events at Seattle Bike Races," *MotorCycling and Bicycling*, September 24, 1919.

17. "William Calvert Struck by Auto," *Seattle P-I*, September 25, 1919.

18. "Boy Struck by Car; Skull Fractured," *Seattle P-I*, October 19, 1929.

19. "Truck Hits Bicyclist; Pedestrian Run Down," *Seattle Daily Times*, October 20, 1929.

20. Christopher A. Sweet, "Bicycle Messenger Boys and the Evolution of American Labor Laws," in *Cycle History 29: Proceedings of the 29th International Cycling History Conference* (San Francisco: Cycle Publishing, 2018), 122–29.

21. "Traffic Drive Pays Dividends; to Be Continued," *Seattle Daily Times*, December 31, 1939.

22. "War Council Planned by Traffic Body," *Seattle P-I*, October 27, 1939.

23. "Death Ends Fourth Safety Campaign," *Seattle Daily Times*, July 4, 1939.

24. James A. Wood, "Making a Bad Record," *Seattle Daily Times*, November 23, 1940.

25. *Traffic Fatalities on Seattle Streets (as of 12/31/2020)—Seattle Vision Zero Program*, Seattle Department of Transportation, December 31, 2020.

26. "Safety Campaign to Center on Untested, Nonstop Cars," *Seattle Daily Times*, November 1, 1939.

27. Campbell's letter was reproduced as part of the article "Pedestrians May Be Jailed as Reckless," *Seattle P-I*, June 23, 1939.

28. An Ordinance Relating to the Duties of Pedestrians with Respect to Traffic Conditions, and Amending Section 38 of the Traffic Code to Prohibit Pedestrians Entering Arterial Highways in Certain Cases, Ordinance 69451, Seattle Municipal Code § (1939). This ordinance updated Ordinance 68700, a major traffic-laws revision passed in 1938, which allowed people to cross the street outside a crosswalk so long as they yielded to vehicles first.

29. "Pedestrians May Be Jailed as Reckless," *Seattle P-I*, June 23, 1939.

30. "Police Clamp Down in Third Deathless Drive," *Seattle Daily Times*, June 24, 1939; "47 Arrested as Jaywalkers by Special Police Squads," *Seattle Daily Times*, July 7, 1939.
31. "Jay-Walking," *Seattle Daily Times*, April 11, 1912.
32. "Why Jaywalking Is Called Jaywalking," *Word History* (blog), *Merriam-Webster.com*, accessed December 14, 2020, www.merriam-webster.com/words-at-play/why-is-it-called-jaywalking.
33. "Jay-Walking," *Seattle Daily Times*, April 11, 1912.
34. "Taking a Walk with 'Pedestrian,'" *Word History* (blog), *Merriam-Webster.com*, accessed March 21, 2021, www.merriam-webster.com/words-at-play/pedestrian-word-history-usage-dull-commonplace.
35. "Walkers Need Not Honk, but They Must Tread Warily Downtown," *Seattle P-I*, July 6, 1917.
36. "Stringent Traffic Code Effective in Seattle," *Seattle Daily Times*, July 6, 1917.
37. "Jay-Walking," *Seattle Daily Times*, April 11, 1912.
38. "Traffic Death Rate Lowest for Seattle," *Seattle P-I*, October 20, 1939.
39. Carl L. Cooper, "Elevated Road to Speed Traffic," *Seattle P-I*, May 26, 1939.
40. "Motor Vehicle Traffic Fatalities and Fatality Rates, 1899–2020," National Highway Traffic Safety Administration, June 2022, https://cdan.nhtsa.gov/tsftables/Fatalities%20and%20Fatality%20Rates.pdf.
41. Smethurst, *The Bicycle—Towards a Global History*.
42. Neil Thomas, "The Rise, Fall, and Restoration of the Kingdom of Bicycles," *MacroPolo.org*, October 24, 2018, https://macropolo.org/analysis/the-rise-fall-and-restoration-of-the-kingdom-of-bicycles/.
43. Berto, *The Dancing Chain*.
44. Conor McMahon, "26 Bicycle Industry Statistics [2022]: Market Size, Share, Growth, and Trends," *Zippia.com*, April 30, 2022, www.zippia.com/advice/bicycle-industry-statistics/.
45. "Hill Climber Bicycle" (advertisement), *The Argus*, June 18, 1903.
46. Berto, *The Dancing Chain*.
47. Helene G. Ryan, "The Blowout," unpublished manuscript, 1990, Museum of History and Industry, Seattle.
48. Tom Griffith, "Want Fun? Get on Bike and Travel," *Seattle Daily Times*, May 18, 1940.
49. John J. Reddin, "Cycle Fans Go by Auto to Reminisce," *Seattle Daily Times*, March 24, 1961, sec. A.
50. Russell Langstaff, letter to the Pacific Northwest Cycling Association, September 17, 1945, Museum of History and Industry, Seattle.
51. The address of the *Atlanta* was 2919 Fairview Avenue East, near the current location of the Eastlake P-Patch and swimming dock.
52. Ronald W. Gallup, "'Ship Ahoy'—AYH," *American Bicyclist and Motorcyclist*, August 1949.
53. Ryan, "The Blowout."

54. Helene G. Ryan, "35 Years of Hosteling for Northwest Bicyclists," *Seattle Times Magazine*, September 14, 1975.
55. Byron Fish quoted from John B. Speer's letter in "Commenting on a News Item," *Seattle Daily Times*, February 16, 1961.
56. Reddin, "Cycle Fans Go by Auto to Reminisce."
57. Jean Libman Block, "Tragedy on Two Wheels," *American Weekly*, June 28, 1953.
58. "Third Annual Bicycle Rodeo Opens Here," *Seattle Daily Times*, April 13, 1953.
59. "Seattle Police to Hold Bicycle Safety Roundup at 27 Schools," *Seattle P-I*, May 11, 1955.
60. "Boy Badly Hurt as Bike, Car Collide," *Seattle P-I*, August 6, 1959.
61. Lamps and Other Equipment on Bicycles, 46.61.780 Revised Code of Washington § (n.d.).
62. United Nations, "Convention on Road Traffic, Vienna," November 8, 1968, United Nations Treaty Collection, https://treaties.un.org/doc/Treaties/1977/05/19770524%2000-13%20AM/Ch_XI_B_19.pdf.
63. Tom Fucoloro, "Starting Jan. 1, Drivers Must Change Lanes When Passing People Biking or Slow Down and Give 3 Feet + More," *Seattle Bike Blog*, December 20, 2019, www.seattlebikeblog.com/2019/12/20/starting-jan-1-drivers-must-change-lanes-when-passing-people-biking-or-slow-down-and-give-3-feet-more/.
64. Reddin, "Cycle Fans Go by Auto to Reminisce."

3. Freeway Fighting

1. Charles Dunsire, "Our Costly Freeway: Oozing Hills Skyrocket Bills," *Seattle Post-Intelligencer*, January 19, 1964.
2. Dunsire, "Our Costly Freeway: Cut Called Disastrous by Critics," *Seattle P-I*, January 20, 1964.
3. Dunsire, "Our Costly Freeway: Route Selected After Long Survey," *Seattle P-I*, January 21, 1964.
4. Dunsire, "Our Costly Freeway: Route Selected After Long Survey."
5. Daniel DeMay, "Seattle's Freeway Revolt: How Residents Fought a Concrete Jungle," *Seattle P-I*, February 28, 2018.
6. Paula Becker, "Dusanne, Zoe (1884–1972)," *HistoryLink*, February 16, 2003, www.historylink.org/File/5222.
7. Troy Heerwagen, "Denny and Stewart Is Seattle's Worst Intersection Again," *The Urbanist* (blog), June 28, 2019, www.theurbanist.org/2019/06/28/denny-stewart-is-seattles-worst-intersection-again/.
8. Shell Oil Company, *Shell Street Map of Seattle* (Houston: 1956).
9. T. H. Bowden, *Home Owners' Loan Corporation Security Map and Area Descriptions*, January 10, 1936, Map and Atlases Collection, object number spl_maps_nara_001, Special Collections Online, Seattle Public Library, https://cdm16118.contentdm.oclc.org/cdm/singleitem/collection/p16118coll2/id/379.
10. Washington State Department of Highways, *Origin—Destination Traffic Survey, Seattle Metropolitan Area, Conducted by the State of Washington Department of*

Highways in Cooperation with Seattle Governmental Units and the US Public Roads Administration, Seattle, 1947, https://cdm16977.contentdm.oclc.org/digital /collection/p16977coll2/id/38287.

11. Richard F. Weingroff, "Federal-Aid Highway Act of 1956: Creating the Interstate System," Public Roads, Federal Highway Administration, Summer 1996.

12. Priscilla Arsove, Anna Rudd, and Seattle ARCH (Activists Remembered, Celebrated and Honored), "Seattle's Freeway Revolt: A Directory of Historical Resources," October 2017, Seattle Sawdust—Bits and Pieces from the Seattle Collection, item number spl_saw_00003, Special Collections Online, Seattle Public Library, https://cdm16118.contentdm.oclc.org/digital/collection /p15015coll6/id/8732.

13. Arsove et al., "Seattle's Freeway Revolt."

14. Arsove et al., "Seattle's Freeway Revolt."

15. Robert A. Barr, "8-Lane Tunnel Would Link Bridge and Mainland," *Seattle Times*, November 22, 1966.

16. Mike Conant, "Concrete Curtain Rising?" *Seattle P-I*, February 26, 1967.

17. Arsove et al., "Seattle's Freeway Revolt."

18. Arsove et al., "Seattle's Freeway Revolt."

19. Shelby Scates, "20 Groups in Revolt Against Third Span," *Seattle P-I*, October 14, 1969.

20. Charles Russell, "'Save, Don't Pave,'" *Seattle P-I*, May 5, 1969.

21. Mary T. Henry, "Ware, Flo (1912–1981)," *HistoryLink*, May 18, 1999, www .historylink.org/File/1145.

22. "Mt. Baker Residents Plan to Fight Interstate 90," *Seattle Daily Times*, September 15, 1969.

23. Charles Aweeka, "Foes Find Target at I-90 Hearing," *Seattle Daily Times*, June 14, 1970.

24. "Halt to Freeway Planning Is Urged," *Seattle Daily Times*, October 16, 1968.

25. Peter Blecha, "Washington's State Environmental Policy Act (SEPA) Is Approved on May 10, 1971," *HistoryLink*, April 10, 2011, https://historylink.org/File/9737.

26. Conant, "Concrete Curtain Rising?"

27. Dick Hubbell, "Room for Concern on Highway Cuts," *Seattle Daily Times*, August 30, 1970.

28. Walter A. Evans, "Seattle Group Hits Highways," *Seattle P-I*, December 13, 1967.

29. Minda Martin, *Ramps to Nowhere*, 2019, documentary film, 65 min., www .mindamartin.com/rampstonowhere/2021/3/30/ytlr2klda3nx3ssnfjxfrirnf72yob.

30. Carlos Moreno, "Decades After the Tulsa Race Massacre, Urban 'Renewal' Sparked Black Wall Street's Second Destruction," *Smithsonian Magazine*, June 2, 2021, https://www.smithsonianmag.com/history/black-wall-streets-second -destruction-180977871/.

31. "Jackson Ward and Its Black Wall Street," National Park Service, US Department of the Interior, June 22, 2021, https://www.nps.gov/articles/000/jackson-ward -and-its-black-wall-street.htm.

32. "Jackson Ward: Displacement and Buried History—GDES Workshop," accessed December 7, 2022, https://drewsisk.com/workshop/jackson-ward-displacement-and-buried-history/.

33. Parker Diakite, "Did You Know? There Was Once a Black Wall Street in Durham Called Parrish Street," *Travel Noire*, January 5, 2022, https://travelnoire.com/parrish-street-black-owned-wall-street-in-durham.

34. Susan Schwartz, "The Rise and Fall of Japantown," *Seattle Times Magazine*, February 8, 1976.

35. Sally Kazama, "Testimony of Sally Kazama, Asian/Pacific Women's Caucus," September 11, 1981, Commission on Wartime Relocation and Internment of Civilians Collection, object number ddr-densho-67-227 (legacy UID denshopd-i67-00227), Densho Digital Repository, Seattle, Washington, courtesy of Cherry Kinoshita, https://ddr.densho.org/ddr-densho-67-227/.

36. Walt Crowley and Kit Oldham, "Seattle Voters Scrap Proposed Bay Freeway and R. H. Thomson Expressway on February 8, 1972," *HistoryLink*, March 19, 2001, www.historylink.org/File/3114.

37. Crowley and Oldham, "Seattle Voters Scrap Proposed Bay Freeway and R. H. Thomson Expressway on February 8, 1972."

38. Josh Cohen, "How Seattle Blew Its Chance at a Subway System," *Crosscut* (blog), October 13, 2016, https://crosscut.com/2016/10/seattle-forward-thrust-sound-transit (page discontinued).

39. Alan J. Stein, "Boeing Bust (1969–1971)," *HistoryLink*, December 16, 2019, https://historylink.org/File/20923.

4. Biking Is Reborn

1. Classic Cycle, "Shifting Times," history of bicycle derailleurs, Classic Cycle Bainbridge Island Kitsap County, accessed April 18, 2022, http://classiccycleus.com/home/shifting-times/.

2. John Haigh, "Is There a Bike in Your Future?" *Seattle Times Magazine*, June 30, 1968.

3. Harry L. Coe, letter to Sam Smith, Chair of the Public Safety Committee, May 22, 1968, Seattle Municipal Archives.

4. Anders Anderssen, letter from the Seattle Mountaineers to Edward Johnson, Superintendent of Seattle Parks, April 19, 1965, Seattle Municipal Archives.

5. Frederick Mann obituary, *Star Tribune*, April 23, 2002, www.legacy.com/amp/obituaries/startribune/304771.

6. Mia Mann, letter to J. Vernon Williams of the Seattle Park Board, October 2, 1967, Seattle Municipal Archives.

7. Mia Mann, "A Resolution: Concerning the Implementation and Operation by the Park Department of a Program to Be Called 'Bicycle Sunday,'" November 13, 1967, Seattle Municipal Archives.

8. Mrs. Frederick M. Mann, letter to Mrs. Harlan Edwards, November 13, 1967, Seattle Municipal Archives.

9. Board of Park Commissioners, letter to Mrs. Harlan H. Edwards, November 21, 1967, Seattle Municipal Archives.

10. Edward J. Johnson, Superintendent of Seattle Parks and Recreation, letter to the Board of Public Works, March 14, 1968, Seattle Municipal Archives.

11. Emmett Watson, "This, Our City—These Foolish Things," *Seattle Post-Intelligencer*, April 5, 1968.

12. Edward J. Johnson, letter to J. D. Braman Re: Bicycle Sunday, May 9, 1968, Seattle Municipal Archives.

13. "Bike Day on Mercer Island," *Seattle Daily Times*, May 9, 1971, sec. A.

14. Marcia Friedman, "I-5 Expressly for Bikes," *Seattle P-I*, July 29, 1974.

15. "Bicycle Week Opens Today with Races, I-5 Cycling," *Seattle Daily Times*, May 4, 1975, sec. D.

16. "Bicycle Week Spins Its Last Wheels Tomorrow," *Seattle Daily Times*, May 22, 1976.

17. "Bike Sunday Postponed till June 18," *Seattle Daily Times*, May 19, 1978.

18. Elizabeth Rhodes, "Hey, Kids! Once Again, This Day Belongs Just to You," *Seattle Daily Times*, April 22, 1989.

19. "Air War to Intensify—Commanders Gather to Discuss Timing of Land Phase," *Seattle P-I*, February 8, 1991.

20. "Family Bicycle Race to Aid Disabled," *Seattle Times*, April 17, 1995.

21. Haigh, "Is There a Bike in Your Future?"

22. Harry L. Coe, "Bicycle Sunday," *Seattle P-I*, May 25, 1968.

23. Andrew Brandon, "Columbia and Puget Sound Railroad," Pacific Coast Narrow Gauge, December 17, 2015, http://pacificng.com/template.php?page=roads/wa/cps/index.htm.

24. Brandon, "Columbia and Puget Sound Railroad."

25. Seattle Channel, *History of the Burke-Gilman Trail Park*, lecture to the University Probus Club of Seattle, January 3, 2018, video, 51 min., www.seattlechannel.org/misc-video?videoid=x87288.

26. *History of the Burke-Gilman Trail Park*.

27. *History of the Burke-Gilman Trail Park*.

28. Paul Andrews, "North End Trail—Opposing Groups Trying to Get on Right Track," *Seattle Daily Times*, September 13, 1971. The "Hell's Angles" sign is notable because it absurdly equated people riding bicycles with the notorious motorcycle gang hired as "security" for the deadly Altamont Speedway Free Festival disaster a couple of years prior. The trial of the accused (and acquitted) killer, a Hell's Angels member, was in the headlines when this sign was made.

29. Thomas Hornbein and Jon Krakauer, *Everest: The West Ridge*, anniversary ed. (Seattle: Mountaineers Books, 2013).

30. *History of the Burke-Gilman Trail Park*.

31. Seattle Channel, CityStream, *Looking Back on the Burke-Gilman Trail*, June 21, 2018, video, 6 min., www.seattlechannel.org/videos?videoid=x92901.

32. Seattle Channel, CityStream, CityStream, *Looking Back on the Burke-Gilman Trail*.

33. Rails-to-Trails Conservancy, "United States: Rail-Trail Stats," accessed February 4, 2021, www.railstotrails.org/our-work/united-states/.

34. *History of the Burke-Gilman Trail Park.*

35. Rita Cipalla, "The Original 12.1-Mile Stretch of the Burke-Gilman Trail, Seattle's Popular Cycling and Pedestrian Trail, Is Dedicated on August 19, 1978," *HistoryLink*, July 11, 2019, https://historylink.org/File/20809.

36. Seattle Department of Engineering, "Evaluation of the Burke-Gilman Trail's Effect on Property Values and Crime," May 1987, Seattle Municipal Archives.

37. I know there are some cargo bikers out there who would disagree.

38. Emmett Watson, "Friday Fragments," *Seattle P-I*, September 18, 1970.

39. Jack Jarvis, "A Middle-Aged Cyclist in Red Vest," *Seattle P-I*, September 21, 1968.

40. "Voice of the People: Bicycles Are Best for the Burke-Gilman Trail," *Seattle P-I*, April 21, 1973.

41. Ross Reynolds, "Meet the 73-Year-Old Man Who Won the First STP and Rode in All the Rest," KUOW archive, September 15, 2015, http://archive.kuow.org/post /meet-73-year-old-man-who-won-first-stp-and-rode-all-rest.

42. Richard Hardesty, "Bicycling Through the Courtroom," *Seattle P-I*, June 1, 1976, sec. A.

43. This letter is quoted in Wendy Marcus, "Bike Group Raising Funds to Defend Rights," *Seattle Daily Times*, July 14, 1976, sec. D.

44. Larry Brown, "Court Upholds Bicycle Conviction," *Seattle Daily Times*, November 10, 1976, sec. B.

45. Briana Orr, "Early Members Spotlight: Amy Carlson," *Cascade Bicycle Club* (blog), April 10, 2015, https://cascade.org/blog/2015/04/early-members-spotlight -amy-carlson.

46. Tom Fucoloro, "The Seattle Bike Expo Is Dead," *Seattle Bike Blog*, October 10, 2014, www.seattlebikeblog.com/2014/10/10/bike-news-notes-fund-set-up-for -kid-hit-on-mlk-seattle-hiring-active-transportation-manager-bike-expo-is -dead/.

47. Fucoloro, "Report: When It Comes to Bike/Walk Advocacy Groups, Seattle Is in a League of Its Own," *Seattle Bike Blog*, April 17, 2014, www.seattlebikeblog .com/2014/04/17/report-when-it-comes-to-bikewalk-advocacy-groups-seattle -is-in-a-league-of-its-own/.

5. Bike Culture Grows in the Shadow of Freeways

1. Peter G. Peterson Foundation, "It's Been 28 Years Since We Last Raised the Gas Tax, and Its Purchasing Power Has Eroded," March 6, 2021, https://www.pgpf .org/blog/2021/03/its-been-28-years-since-we-last-raised-the-gas-tax-and-its -purchasing-power-has-eroded.

2. US Environmental Protection Agency, "Sources of Greenhouse Gas Emissions and Removals," last updated August 5, 2022, www.epa.gov/ghgemissions /sources-greenhouse-gas-emissions.

3. Forester, *Effective Cycling*.

4. US Census Bureau, "A Look at the Nearly 1 Million Who Ride Their Bikes to Work in the US," *Random Samplings Blog*, May 19, 2016, www.census.gov/newsroom /blogs/random-samplings/2016/05/a-look-at-the-nearly-1-million-who-ride -their-bikes-to-work-in-the-u-s.html.

5. Alternative Fuels Data Center, "Maps and Data, Annual Vehicle Miles Traveled in the United States," US Department of Energy, last updated June 2022, https:// afdc.energy.gov/data/10315.

6. Cascade Bicycle Club, "Chuck Ayers Announces Resignation from Cascade Bicycle Club," March 14, 2013, https://cascade.org/2013/03/chuck-ayers-announces -resignation.

7. Gene Balk, FYI Guy, "Seattle Growing Faster than Suburbs, First Time in 100 Years," *Seattle Times*, February 24, 2014.

8. Erik Lacitis, "Hostages!—The Multimillionaire Has Our Bike Trail, and All We Get Are Lame Explanations," *Seattle Times*, February 9, 1988.

9. Joni Balter and Carlton Smith, "BN Tried to Cut City Out of Sale—Memo Details Intent to Foil Burke-Gilman Trail Extension," *Seattle Times*, July 29, 1988.

10. "The House That Sponges Built: Why UM Owns a Mansion (and Plenty of Other Property, Too)," *Montana Kaimin*, November 14, 2017, www.montanakaimin .com/features/the-house-that-sponges-built-why-um-owns-a-mansion-and -plenty-of-other-property/article_cb4491a6-c8d3-11e7-9acf-4f471a2ada26.html. With no good moorage leads, Dennis Washington sold the *Lark* in 1988 to the inventor of the Today Sponge contraceptive, who burned it down a few years later in a failed attempt to collect the insurance money.

11. Dick Lilly, "Burke-Gilman Heading West—Work Has Begun to Extend Trail," *Seattle Times*, May 25, 1989.

12. Tom Fucoloro, "After WA Won #1 for a Decade, Bike League Changes Its State- by-State Report Cards," *Seattle Bike Blog*, December 5, 2018, www .seattlebikeblog.com/2018/12/05/after-wa-won-1-for-a-decade-bike -league-changes-its-state-by-state-report-cards/.

13. Andrew Lynn, Elizabeth Press, and Chris Ryan, directors, *Still We Ride* (New York: In Tandem Productions, May 12, 2005), documentary color film, 37 min.

14. Lynn, Press, and Ryan, *Still We Ride*.

15. Lynn, Press, and Ryan, *Still We Ride*.

16. Jack Broom and Susan Byrnes, "Bicycle Activists Set Downtown Rally to Protest Arrests," *Seattle Times*, February 6, 1997.

17. Dee Norton, "Four Arrested in Assault on Officers—Cyclists' Protest Turns Violent," *Seattle Times*, February 1, 1997.

18. Vanessa Ho, "Bikers Slow Rush-Hour Traffic During 'Uneventful' Protest," *Seattle Post-Intelligencer*, February 8, 1997.

19. Broom and Byrnes, "Bicycle Activists Set Downtown Rally."

20. Lynn, Press, and Ryan, *Still We Ride*.

21. Jon Naito, Phuong Cat Le, and Mike Lewis, "One Last Bike Ride in Cyclist's Memory—Family and Friends Mourn Loss," *Seattle P-I*, September 30, 2006.

22. An Ordinance Relating to Seattle's Complete Streets Policy, Stating Guiding Principles and Practices so that Transportation Improvements Are Planned, Designed and Constructed to Encourage Walking, Bicycling and Transit Use while Promoting Safe Operations for All Users, Ordinance 122386, May 7, 2007, http://clerk.seattle.gov/search/ordinances/122386.
23. Levi Pulkkinen, "Critical Mass Cyclists Fault Police for Not Investigating Driver," *Seattle P-I*, July 31, 2008.
24. Fremont Arts Council, "Fremont Solstice Parade," accessed December 9, 2022, https://fremontartscouncil.org/parade.
25. Dan McComb, director, *Beyond Naked* (Seattle: Lisa Cooper, May 13, 2013), color film, 1 hour 32 min., https://vimeo.com/ondemand/beyondnaked.
26. Seattle.gov, "About Seattle—Population," Seattle Office of Planning & Community Development, accessed December 9, 2022, www.seattle.gov/opcd/population-and-demographics/about-seattle#population.
27. McComb, *Beyond Naked*.
28. McComb, *Beyond Naked*.
29. McComb, *Beyond Naked*.
30. World Naked Bike Ride, home page, last updated July 2, 2009, www.worldnakedbikeride.org.
31. Racial Restrictive Covenant project, *Segregated Seattle*, "Racial Restrictive Covenants: Neighborhood by Neighborhood Restrictions across King County," Seattle Civil Rights and Labor History Project, University of Washington, 2005–present, accessed March 1, 2021, https://depts.washington.edu/civilr/covenants.htm.
32. Racial Restrictive Covenant project.
33. James Gregory, *Segregated Seattle*, "Seattle's Race and Segregation Story in Maps 1920–2020," Seattle Civil Rights and Labor History Project, University of Washington, 2004–2020, accessed March 1, 2021, http://depts.washington.edu/civilr/segregation_maps.htm.
34. Catherine Silva, "Racial Restrictive Covenants: Enforcing Neighborhood Segregation in Seattle," Seattle Civil Rights and Labor History Project, University of Washington, Autumn 2008, https://depts.washington.edu/civilr/covenants_report.htm.
35. Seattle.gov, "The Seattle Open Housing Campaign, 1959–1968," Online Exhibits, Seattle Municipal Archives, accessed March 2, 2021, www.seattle.gov/cityarchives/exhibits-and-education/online-exhibits/seattle-open-housing-campaign.
36. Seattle Department of Transportation bicycle facilities document, June 1990, emailed to the author.
37. Amber Bronnum et al., "Crossing Rainier Avenue: Two Studies Exploring the Pedestrian Experience in the Rainier Valley," Seattle Neighborhood Greenways, March 12, 2013, www.seattlegreenways.org/wp-content/uploads/Crossing-Rainier_Pedestrian-Experience_March-12-2013_FINAL.pdf.

38. King County, "Facts about King County's BNSF Rail Line Acquisition," April 26, 2006, https://web.archive.org/web/20060520050747/http://dnr.metrokc.gov/dnrp/pa/bnsf/fact-sheet.htm.

39. Whitehouse.gov, "Ron Sims to Be Nominated as HUD's Deputy Secretary," February 2, 2009, https://obamawhitehouse.archives.gov/the-press-office/ron-sims-be-nominated-huds-deputy-secretary.

40. A "century" is a 100-mile bike ride. Centuries are a lot easier in places that use the metric system.

41. Cascade Bicycle Club, "Major Taylor Project," accessed December 9, 2022, https://cascade.org/learn/major-taylor-project.

42. Fucoloro, "After Nearly 10 Years, Deb Salls Steps down as Bike Works ED + Ed Ewing Takes the Helm," *Seattle Bike Blog*, December 4, 2020, www.seattlebikeblog.com/2020/12/04/after-nearly-10-years-deb-salls-steps-down-as-bike-works-ed-ed-ewing-takes-the-helm/.

43. Bike Works, "Report Card, 2019," *About Bike Works*, Annual Reports, https://bikeworks.org/wp-content/uploads/2020/04/BW-2019-Report.jpg.

44. King County Metro's bus policy of the same name—free-ride zone—lasted almost forty years, from 1973 to 2012, according to Mike Lindblom, "Warning: Seattle's free-ride zone coming to an end," *Seattle Times*, September 14, 2012, www.seattletimes.com/seattle-news/warning-seattles-free-ride-zone-coming-to-an-end/.

45. Joseph Rose, "Remembering Portland's Disastrous Yellow Bike Project," *The Oregonian*, January 21, 2016, sec. Oregon History.

46. US Department of Justice, "Owners of Northwest's Largest Electronics Recycling Firm Plead Guilty to Wire Fraud Conspiracy," US Attorney's Office, Western District of Washington, November 16, 2018, www.justice.gov/usao-wdwa/pr/owners-northwest-s-largest-electronics-recycling-firm-plead-guilty-wire-fraud#:~:text=The%20owners%20and%20Chief%20Executive,conspiracy%20to%20commit%20wire%20fraud.

47. Judi Hunt, "Future of Bike Swap May Ride on Success of This Year's Event," *Seattle P-I*, May 7, 1999, sec. C.

48. Fucoloro, "At a Bike Works Volunteer Party, Bikes for Kids Are Pieced Together with Heart," *Seattle Bike Blog*, July 13, 2010, www.seattlebikeblog.com/2010/07/13/at-a-bike-works-volunteer-party-bikes-for-kids-are-pieced-together-with-heart/.

49. Bike Works, *Frameworks: A Modular Guide to Youth Development and Bicycle Repair* (Seattle: 2015), https://bikeworks.org/about/resources/.

6. Biking Tries to Go Mainstream

1. With the help of SDOT staff, I compiled Seattle traffic death data from multiple sources, including official SDOT numbers going back to 1980 as well as totals reported in the news. This figure comes from "Traffic Drive Pays Dividends; to Be Continued," *Seattle Daily Times*, December 31, 1939.

2. Automobile Association, "Evolution of Car Safety Features: From Windscreen Wipers to Crash Tests and Pedestrian Protection," September 25, 2020, www.theaa.com/breakdown-cover/advice/evolution-of-car-safety-features.

3. National Highway Traffic Safety Administration, "Motor Vehicle Traffic Fatalities and Fatality Rates, 1899–2020," June 2022, https://cdan.nhtsa.gov/tsftables/Fatalities%20and%20Fatality%20Rates.pdf.

4. Steve Davis, "More Highways, More Driving, More Emissions: Explaining 'Induced Demand,'" Smart Growth America, October 20, 2021, https://smartgrowthamerica.org/induced-demand-calculator/.

5. Susan Gilmore, "City Wants to Put 4-Lane Stone Way on 'Road Diet,'" *Seattle Times*, October 12, 2006.

6. Russ Zabel, "Westlake Corridor Sprucing up Moves Forward; Improvements to Utilities and Streets Include Public Art," *City Living Seattle*, Newsbank database, April 3, 2002.

7. Al Gore, "The Future Is Green," *Vanity Fair*, May 2006, https://archive.vanityfair.com/article/2006/5/the-future-is-green.

8. Tom Fucoloro, "Census Data Confirms Steady Climb in Seattle Bike Commuting, Driving Alone Now below 50%," *Seattle Bike Blog*, September 19, 2013, www.seattlebikeblog.com/2013/09/19/census-data-confirms-steady-climb-in-seattle-bike-commuting-driving-alone-now-below-50/.

9. Gilmore, "City Wants to Put 4-Lane Stone Way on 'Road Diet.'"

10. Erica C. Barnett, "City Stone Way Bike Protest," *Slog* (blog), *The Stranger*, August 1, 2007, https://slog.thestranger.com/2007/08/stone_way_bike_protest.

11. Seattle.gov, *Stone Way N Rechannelization: Before and After Study—N 34th Street to N 50th Street*, Seattle Department of Transportation report, May 2010, www.seattle.gov/Documents/Departments/SDOT/About/DocumentLibrary/Reports/StoneWaybeforeafterFINAL.pdf.

12. Erica C. Barnett, "McGinn Issues Mallahan's Press Release," *Seattle Met* magazine, September 21, 2009, www.seattlemet.com/news-and-city-life/2009/09/mcginn-issues-mallahans-press-release.

13. Barnett, "McGinn Issues Mallahan's Press Release."

14. Laura Onstot, "'Regular Joe' Mallahan's Stuck in the Bike Lane," *Seattle Weekly*, July 29, 2009.

15. RVO, "McGinn's Win Is Seattle's Biggest Upset in Decades," *The SunBreak*, November 10, 2009, http://sunbreakmagazine.com/2009/11/10/mcginns-win-is-seattles-biggest-upset-in-decades/.

16. Eric de Place, "The 'War on Cars': A Brief History of a Rhetorical Device," *Grist* (blog), January 7, 2011, https://grist.org/article/2011-01-06-war-on-cars-a-history/.

17. KING staff and KING 5 News, "Investigators: Parking along Light Rail Difficult by Design," September 23, 2009, www.king5.com/article/news/local/investigators-parking-along-light-rail-difficult-by-design/281-409907555.

18. Dan Bertolet, who attended the forum, blogged about it in "Do You Support the War on Cars?" *Hugeasscity*, July 31, 2009, http://hugeasscity.com/2009/07/31/do-you-support-the-war-on-cars/.

19. Linda Byron and KING 5 News, "Is There a War on Cars in Seattle?" aired on KING 5, October 19, 2010.

20. Emily Heffter, "Politics, Friction Reshape Influential Cascade Bicycle Club," *Seattle Times*, October 28, 2010, sec. Local News, www.seattletimes.com/seattle-news/politics-friction-reshape-influential-cascade-bicycle-club/.

21. Fucoloro, "Cascade's Board Has the Power to Fix the Club's Woes," *Seattle Bike Blog*, December 1, 2010, www.seattlebikeblog.com/2010/12/01/cascades-board-has-the-power-to-fix-the-clubs-woes/.

22. Heffter, "Politics, Friction Reshape Influential Cascade Bicycle Club."

23. In many parts of the country, a "greenway" is what people in Seattle call a trail. So a "neighborhood greenway" is sort of like a trail through a neighborhood, or at least that's the etymology.

24. Fucoloro, "Neighborhood-Powered Streets Part 2: Beacon Hill and Wallingford Groups Lead the Way," *Seattle Bike Blog*, May 3, 2011, www.seattlebikeblog.com/2011/05/03/neighborhood-powered-streets-part-2-beacon-hill-and-wallingford-groups-lead-the-way/.

25. Alta Planning and Design, *Beacon Hill Family Bicycle and Pedestrian Circulation Plan*, prepared June 23, 2011, for Beacon BIKES, www.seattle.gov/documents/Departments/SDOT/TransportationPlanning/beacon_bikes_family_pedestrian_and_bicycle_circulation_plan2011.pdf.

26. Fucoloro, "Neighborhood-Powered Streets, Part 1: Greenways Find New Political Momentum in Seattle," *Seattle Bike Blog*, May 2, 2011, www.seattlebikeblog.com/2011/05/02/neighborhood-powered-streets-part-1-greenways-find-new-political-momentum-in-seattle/.

27. Fucoloro, "Neighborhood-Powered Streets, Part 1: Greenways Find New Political Momentum in Seattle."

28. Fucoloro, "Car Driving Is down 91% from Pre-Outbreak Levels on the City's New Stay Healthy Streets," *Seattle Bike Blog*, May 12, 2020, www.seattlebikeblog.com/2020/05/12/car-driving-is-down-91-from-pre-outbreak-levels-on-the-citys-new-stay-healthy-streets/.

29. Anne-Marije Rook, "The First Crop of Advocacy Leadership Institute Graduates Heads out to Connect Our Communities," *Cascade Bicycle Club* (blog), October 16, 2012, https://cascade.org/2012/10/first-ali-graduates.

30. "Bicycle Advisory Board OK'd," *Seattle Daily Times*, May 11, 1977.

31. Ron Judd, "Temperatures Drop, Snow Falls, Interest in Ski Conditions Rises, and Outdoors Expands Coverage," *Seattle Times*, December 3, 1992.

32. Jasmine Mahmoud, "Biking Seattle's Redlining: An Interview with Merlin Rainwater," *Urbanculturalstudies* (blog), May 27, 2018, https://urbanculturalstudies.wordpress.com/2018/05/27/biking-seattles-redlining-an-interview-with-merlin-rainwater/.

33. Ann Dornfeld, "Hey, White People. Racism Is Your History, Too. Take This Tour to Learn More," KUOW, March 16, 2018, www.kuow.org/stories/hey-white -people-racism-your-history-too-take-tour-learn-more/.

34. Mahmoud, "Biking Seattle's Redlining."

35. Dornfeld, "Hey, White People."

7. Too Many

1. Staff writers, "Okay, Fine, It's War," *The Stranger*, September 14, 2011, www .thestranger.com/seattle/okay-fine-its-war/Content?oid=9937449.

2. With the help of SDOT staff, I compiled Seattle traffic death data from multiple sources, including official SDOT numbers going back to 1980 as well as totals reported in the news. This figure comes from "Traffic Drive Pays Dividends; to Be Continued," *Seattle Daily Times*, December 31, 1939.

3. Tom Fucoloro, "Person Killed in Dexter Hit-and-Run Identified as Mike Wang," *Seattle Bike Blog*, July 29, 2011, www.seattlebikeblog.com/2011/07/29/person -killed-in-dexter-hit-and-run-identified-as-mike-wang/.

4. "Photographer Michael Wang Documents Life in Bolivia for PATH," *International Examiner* (blog), December 6, 2006, https://iexaminer.org/photographer -michael-wang-documents-life-in-bolivia-for-path/.

5. Claire Allen, letter to the sentencing judge, August 10, 2012, published with her permission on *Seattle Bike Blog*, www.seattlebikeblog.com/2012/08/10/driver -who-killed-mike-wang-gets-maximum-penalty-his-widow-claires-letter-to -the-judge/.

6. Fucoloro, "Nine Days after Bicycle Wreck, Espresso Vivace Manager Brian Fairbrother Dies," *Seattle Bike Blog*, September 9, 2011, www.seattlebikeblog .com/2011/09/09/after-bicycle-wreck-espresso-vivace-manager-brian -fairbrother-dies-from-his-injuries/.

7. Fucoloro, "Robert Townsend, Killed in U District, Was Fastest Delivery Person on Staff," *Seattle Bike Blog*, September 12, 2011, www.seattlebikeblog .com/2011/09/12/robert-townsend-killed-in-u-district-was-fastest-delivery -person-on-staff/.

8. Jeff Hodson and Aaron Spencer, "Seattle Launches Road Safety Summit," *Seattle Times*, October 24, 2011, sec. Local News, www.seattletimes.com/seattle-news /seattle-launches-road-safety-summit/.

9. Jim Curtin and Rebecca Deehr, with assistance from Kiersten Grove, *SDOT 2012 Road Safety Summit Action Plan*, Seattle Department of Transportation, 2012, www.seattle.gov/Documents/Departments/beSuperSafe/SDOT -SafetyActionPlanWEB.pdf.

10. "Tell Us! Show Us! Seattle's Bicycle Master Plan Is Getting Updated," *SDOT Blog*, May 1, 2012, https://sdotblog.seattle.gov/2012/05/01/tell-us-show-us-seattles -bicycle-master-plan-is-getting-updated/.

11. Editorial Board, "Seattle Is Playing Catch-up on Bike Safety," *Seattle Times*, August 7, 2013, www.seattletimes.com/opinion/editorial-seattle-is-playing -catch-up-on-bike-safety/.

12. Scott R. Loss, Tom Will, and Peter P. Marra, "The Impact of Free-Ranging Domestic Cats on Wildlife of the United States," *Nature Communications* 4, no. 1 (January 29, 2013): 1396, https://doi.org/10.1038/ncomms2380.

13. @seabikeblog, "Oh No. '@KING5Seattle: Response from @SeattleFire and @SeattlePD to Car/Bicycle Accident at Dexter/Harrison Http://T.Co/ OaTRytWidz,'" *Twitter*, July 25, 2013, https://twitter.com/seabikeblog/status /360544293242408962 (page discontinued).

14. Fucoloro, "Dexter Protected Bike Lane Plans Include Shared Turn Lanes, Bus Stops," *Seattle Bike Blog*, September 30, 2014, www.seattlebikeblog .com/2014/09/30/dexter-protected-bike-lane-plans-include-shared-turn -lanes-bus-stops/.

15. Brandon Blake, *It's Bonus Time!* Bonus Time Music, 2018, album, 10 songs, 34 min.

16. Jim Brunner, "Dead Cyclist Was New Mom, Well-Regarded Attorney," *Seattle Times*, August 30, 2014, www.seattletimes.com/seattle-news/dead-cyclist-was -new-mom-well-regarded-attorney/.

17. Witt, Cammermeyer, and Connor, *Tell*.

18. National Highway Traffic Safety Administration, "Motor Vehicle Traffic Fatali- ties and Fatality Rates, 1899–2020," June 2022, https://cdan.nhtsa.gov/tsftables /Fatalities%20and%20Fatality%20Rates.pdf.

8. Seattle's Bicycle Ambitions Grow

1. Tom Fucoloro, "City Council Will Vote on Bike Master Plan + Next Step: How to Realize Its Vision," *Seattle Bike Blog*, April 14, 2014, www.seattlebikeblog .com/2014/04/14/city-council-will-vote-on-bike-master-plan-next-step-how -to-realize-its-vision/.

2. Fucoloro, "Westlake Group Drops Bike Master Plan Lawsuit," *Seattle Bike Blog*, February 14, 2014, www.seattlebikeblog.com/2014/02/14/westlake-group -drops-bike-master-plan-lawsuit/.

3. Fucoloro, "Say Hello to Pronto! Emerald City Cycle Share," *Seattle Bike Blog*, May 5, 2014, www.seattlebikeblog.com/2014/05/05/say-hello-to-pronto-emerald -city-cycle-share/.

4. Furness, *One Less Car*.

5. Stansill, ed., *BAMN*.

6. Joseph Rose, "Remembering Portland's Disastrous Yellow Bike Project," *The Ore- gonian*, January 21, 2016, sec. Oregon History.

7. Susan A. Shaheen et al., "Hangzhou Public Bicycle: Understanding Early Adop- tion and Behavioral Response to Bikesharing in Hangzhou, China," *Transporta- tion Research Record*, no. 2247 (January 1, 2011): 34–41.

8. Yes, I am citing Wikipedia. But this is the most comprehensive list of public bike share systems and their reported statistics that I could locate: "List of Bicycle-Sharing Systems," *Wikipedia*, November 20, 2022, https://en.wikipedia.org/w/index.php?title=List_of_bicycle-sharing_systems&oldid=1122884321.

9. Transitwiki.org, "Last Mile Connections," last updated May 20, 2019, www.transitwiki.org/TransitWiki/index.php/Last_mile_connections.

10. Ashley Halsey III, "New Bikeshare Program Provides Wheels to Casual Cyclists in D.C., Arlington," *Washington Post*, September 21, 2010, www.washingtonpost.com/wp-dyn/content/article/2010/09/20/AR2010092003815.html.

11. Fucoloro, "The Plan for Puget Sound Bike Share," *Seattle Bike Blog*, August 9, 2012, www.seattlebikeblog.com/2012/08/09/the-plan-for-puget-sound-bike-share/.

12. Fucoloro, "The Plan for Puget Sound Bike Share."

13. Fucoloro, "City Proposes 'Massive' Pronto Cycle Share Expansion," *Seattle Bike Blog*, June 8, 2015, www.seattlebikeblog.com/2015/06/08/city-proposes-massive-pronto-cycle-share-expansion/.

14. Charles Mudede, "Pronto Cycle Share and How the Market Reproduces and Reinforces Seattle's Racial Map," *Slog* (blog), *The Stranger*, September 5, 2014, www.thestranger.com/blogs/2014/09/05/20515725/pronto-cycle-share-and-how-the-market-reproduces-and-reinforces-seattles-racial-map.

15. Fucoloro, "City Proposes 'Massive' Pronto Cycle Share Expansion."

16. Fucoloro, "City Proposes 'Massive' Pronto Cycle Share Expansion."

17. Holly Houser, "Letter from Pronto ED Holly Houser," August 27, 2015.

18. Fucoloro, "Seattle Begins Bike Share Takeover, Budgets for System Expansion," *Seattle Bike Blog*, October 2, 2015, www.seattlebikeblog.com/2015/10/02/seattle-begins-bike-share-takeover-budgets-for-system-expansion/.

19. Fucoloro, "Pronto Needs City Buyout before End of March, How Did We Get Here?" *Seattle Bike Blog*, February 4, 2016, www.seattlebikeblog.com/2016/02/04/pronto-needs-city-buyout-before-end-of-march-how-did-we-get-here/.

20. Fucoloro, "A Sober Look at Pronto's Finances Ahead of Council Meeting," *Seattle Bike Blog*, February 18, 2016, www.seattlebikeblog.com/2016/02/18/a-sober-look-at-prontos-finances-ahead-of-council-meeting/.

21. Fucoloro, "Mayor Murray Cancels Bike Share Expansion, Will Shut down Pronto March 31," *Seattle Bike Blog*, January 13, 2017, www.seattlebikeblog.com/2017/01/13/mayor-murray-cancels-bike-share-expansion-will-shut-down-pronto-march-31/.

22. Fucoloro, "By Killing Pronto, Seattle Could Become the Center of Private Bike Share Innovation," *Seattle Bike Blog*, April 28, 2017, www.seattlebikeblog.com/2017/04/28/by-killing-pronto-seattle-could-become-the-center-of-private-bike-share-innovation/.

23. Alissa Walker, "The Quiet Triumph of Bike Share: How Bike Sharing in the U.S. Became This Decade's Biggest Transporation Success Story," *Curbed* (blog), December 16, 2019, https://archive.curbed.com/2019/12/16/20864145/bike-share-citi-bike-jump-uber.

24. Fucoloro, "Test Riding a Bluegogo Stationless Bike Share Bike in Downtown Seattle," *Seattle Bike Blog*, May 3, 2017, www.seattlebikeblog.com/2017/05/03 /test-riding-a-bluegogo-stationless-bike-share-bike-in-downtown-seattle/.

25. Fucoloro, "By Killing Pronto, Seattle Could Become the Center of Private Bike Share Innovation."

26. Fucoloro, "How a 20-Something SDOT Staffer Took on a Dying Program & Changed the Bike Share World," *Seattle Bike Blog*, November 10, 2017, www .seattlebikeblog.com/2017/11/10/how-a-20-something-sdot-staffer-took-on-a -dying-program-changed-the-bike-share-world/.

27. Fucoloro, "City Releases Draft Bike Share Pilot Permit + List of Interested Companies Grows to Ten," *Seattle Bike Blog*, June 9, 2017, www.seattlebikeblog .com/2017/06/09/city-releases-draft-bike-share-pilot-permit-list-of-interested -companies-grows-to-ten/.

28. Fucoloro, "Spin Smashes Pronto Ridership in Week One, Announces Improved Bikes," *Seattle Bike Blog*, July 25, 2017, www.seattlebikeblog.com/2017/07/25 /spin-smashes-pronto-ridership-in-week-one-announces-improved-bikes/.

29. Fucoloro, "A Look at the City's Updated Permit Rules," *Seattle Bike Blog*, July 13, 2018, www.seattlebikeblog.com/2018/07/13/bike-share-carried-209k-trips-in -may-a-look-at-the-citys-updated-permit-rules/.

30. Fucoloro, "Bike Share Pilot's Daily Ridership Blows Past Pronto's Lifetime Totals, Rivals Both Streetcars Combined," *Seattle Bike Blog*, December 15, 2017, www .seattlebikeblog.com/2017/12/15/bike-share-pilots-daily-ridership-blows-past -prontos-lifetime-totals-rivals-both-streetcars-combined/.

31. Fucoloro, "Survey: Ahead of Bike Share Permit Update, Survey Says Seattle-ites Are Very Supportive," *Seattle Bike Blog*, June 6, 2018, www.seattlebikeblog .com/2018/06/06/survey-ahead-of-bike-share-permit-update-survey-says -seattleites-are-very-supportive/.

32. Kirsty Needham, "Share Bike Company Bluegogo's Woes Blamed on Tiananmen Square 'Prank,'" *Sydney Morning Herald*, November 17, 2017, sec. World, www .smh.com.au/world/share-bike-company-bluegogos-woes-blamed-on -tiananmen-square-prank-20171117-gznyop.html.

33. Fucoloro, "Ofo Launches in Seattle, but Their Goal Is 'Unlocking Every Cor-ner of the World,'" *Seattle Bike Blog*, August 24, 2017, www.seattlebikeblog .com/2017/08/24/ofo-launches-in-seattle-but-their-goal-is-unlocking-every -corner-of-the-world/.

34. Raymond Zhong and Carolyn Zhang, "Ofo, Pioneer of China's Bike-Sharing Boom, Is in a Crisis," *New York Times*, December 20, 2018, sec. Technology, www .nytimes.com/2018/12/20/technology/ofo-bicycle-share-china.html.

35. Fucoloro, "Seattle's next Bike Share Battle Could Be between Lime, Uber and Lyft + Let's Start a Scooter Pilot," *Seattle Bike Blog*, August 20, 2018, www .seattlebikeblog.com/2018/08/20/seattles-next-bike-share-battle-could-be -between-lime-uber-and-lyft-lets-start-a-scooter-pilot/.

36. Fucoloro, "Lime Takes over JUMP as Part of Big Uber Investment Deal," *Seattle Bike Blog*, May 7, 2020, www.seattlebikeblog.com/2020/05/07/lime-takes-over-jump-as-part-of-big-uber-investment-deal/.
37. Fucoloro, "City Announces New Scooter and Bike Share Permits: Spin and Wheels Are Out, Bird Is In," *Seattle Bike Blog*, May 13, 2022, www.seattlebikeblog.com/2022/05/13/city-announces-new-scooter-and-bike-share-permits-spin-and-wheels-are-out-bird-is-in/.

9. Building a Better Bike Lane

1. Dan Scanlan, "Traffic Deaths Outpace Reputation of Homicides," *Florida Times-Union*, August 11, 2018, https://www.jacksonville.com/story/news/crime/2018/08/11/traffic-deaths-outpace-jacksonvilles-reputation-of-having-100-plus-homicides/6496894007/.
2. Angie Schmitt, "Q&A With Dongho Chang, a Traffic Engineer Who Stresses Safety Over Speed," *Streetsblog USA*, February 14, 2017, https://usa.streetsblog.org/2017/02/14/qa-with-dongho-chang-a-traffic-engineer-who-stresses-safety-over-speed/.
3. Tom Fucoloro, "Dongho Chang Leaving SDOT to Be State Traffic Engineer at WSDOT," *Seattle Bike Blog*, July 26, 2021, www.seattlebikeblog.com/2021/07/26/dongho-chang-leaving-sdot-to-be-state-traffic-engineer-at-wsdot/.
4. Jamala Henderson, "Rainier Avenue Has a Speeding Problem," KUOW, November 17, 2014, https://kuow.org/stories/rainier-avenue-has-a-speeding-problem/.
5. Henderson, "Rainier Avenue Has a Speeding Problem."
6. Fucoloro, "Harrell at Rainier Ave Safety Protest: We're Gonna Take Our Street Back," *Seattle Bike Blog*, May 21, 2015, www.seattlebikeblog.com/2015/05/21/harrell-at-rainier-ave-safety-protest-were-gonna-take-our-street-back/.
7. Seattle Department of Transportation, *Rainier Avenue South Safety Corridor—Rainier Pilot Project Evaluation*, February 2017, www.seattle.gov/documents/Departments/SDOT/MaintenanceProgram/RainierAveS_BeforeAfter.pdf.
8. Erica C. Barnett, "The Worst Bike Lane in the City," *Seattle Met* magazine, August 6, 2010, www.seattlemet.com/articles/2010/8/6/the-worst-bike-lane-in-the-city.
9. Fucoloro, "Bike Traffic on 2nd Ave Triples after City Builds Protected Bike Lane," *Seattle Bike Blog*, September 16, 2014, www.seattlebikeblog.com/2014/09/16/bike-traffic-on-2nd-ave-increases-300-after-city-builds-protected-bike-lane/.
10. Fucoloro, "Primary Ballots Are in the Mail! Here's What Candidates Say about Safe Streets," *Seattle Bike Blog*, July 17, 2015, www.seattlebikeblog.com/2015/07/17/primary-ballots-are-in-the-mail-heres-what-candidates-say-about-safe-streets/.
11. Fucoloro, "What a 'No' Vote on Move Seattle Actually Means," *Seattle Bike Blog*, October 28, 2015, www.seattlebikeblog.com/2015/10/28/what-a-no-vote-on-move-seattle-actually-means/.

12. Genna Martin, "'Move Seattle' Victory Party on Election Night 2015," *Seattle Post-Intelligencer*, November 4, 2015, www.seattlepi.com/seattlenews/slideshow /Move-Seattle-victory-party-on-election-night-119871.php.

Epilogue

1. Tom Fucoloro, "The True Cost of Move Seattle," *Seattle Bike Blog*, November 4, 2015, www.seattlebikeblog.com/2015/11/04/the-true-cost-of-move-seattle/.
2. "Seattle Mayor Ed Murray Resigns after Fifth Child Sex-Abuse Allegation," *Seattle Times*, September 12, 2017, www.seattletimes.com/seattle-news/politics /seattle-mayor-ed-murray-resigns-after-fifth-child-sex-abuse-allegation/.
3. Fucoloro, "Under Mayor Durkan, Seattle Has Only Built about 4% of Its 2018 Bike Lane Goal," *Seattle Bike Blog*, December 4, 2018, www.seattlebikeblog .com/2018/12/04/under-mayor-durkan-seattle-has-only-built-about-4-of-its -2018-bike-lane-goal/.
4. Fucoloro, "Seattle's Bike Movement Reinvented Itself in 2019," *Seattle Bike Blog*, December 30, 2019, www.seattlebikeblog.com/2019/12/30/seattles-bike -movement-reinvented-itself-in-2019/.
5. Fucoloro, "Hundreds Rally and Ride Downtown to Protest Cuts to Safe Streets Projects," *Seattle Bike Blog*, June 18, 2019, www.seattlebikeblog.com/2019/06/18 /hundreds-rally-and-ride-downtown-to-protest-cuts-to-safe-streets-projects/.
6. Seattle Department of Transportation, *City of Seattle Bicycle and Pedestrian Safety Analysis Phase 2*, February 4, 2020.
7. Fucoloro, "Noon Saturday: Ride in the 'Peace Peloton' Starting in Alki," *Seattle Bike Blog*, June 5, 2020, www.seattlebikeblog.com/2020/06/05/noon-saturday -ride-in-the-peace-peloton-starting-in-alki/.
8. Fucoloro, "Noon Thursday: Ride For Justice with Estelita's Library," *Seattle Bike Blog*, June 10, 2020, www.seattlebikeblog.com/2020/06/10/noon-thursday-ride -for-justice-with-estelitas-library/.
9. Natalie Dupille, "Dear Mom, I've Joined a Guerilla Bike Collective," *Slog* (blog), *The Stranger*, September 2, 2020, www.thestranger.com/slog/2020/09/02 /44398894/dear-mom-ive-joined-a-guerilla-bike-collective.

Selected Bibliography

These are just some of the books I visited during the research phase of this book. Not all were cited directly in the text, but they helped form my basis of understanding about these topics.

Berger, Knute. *Pugetopolis: A Mossback Takes on Growth Addicts, Weather Wimps, and the Myth of Seattle Nice*. Seattle: Sasquatch Books, distributed by PGW/Perseus, 2009.

Berner, Richard C. *Seattle in the 20th Century*. Seattle: Charles Press, 1991.

Berner, Richard C., with Paul Dorpat. *Seattle 1900–1920: From Boomtown, through Urban Turbulence, to Restoration*. Rev. ed. Seattle in the 20th Century, vol. 1. Seattle: Charles Press, 2009.

Berto, Frank J. *The Dancing Chain: History and Development of the Derailleur Bicycle*. 2nd ed. San Francisco: Van der Plas/Cycle Publications, 2004.

Blue, Elly. *Bikenomics: How Bicycling Can Save the Economy*. Portland, OR: Microcosm Publishing, 2013.

Cameron, Frank B. *Bicycling in Seattle 1874–1904*. Seattle: Self-published, 1982.

Carlson, Madi. *Urban Cycling: How to Get to Work, Save Money, and Use Your Bike for City Living*. Seattle: Skipstone, imprint of Mountaineers Books, 2015.

Cotterill, George F. *The Climax of a World Quest: The Story of Puget Sound: The Modern Mediterranean of the Pacific*. Seattle: Olympic Publishing, 1927.

Crowley, Walt, and HistoryLink staff. *Seattle and King County Timeline: A Chronological Guide to Seattle and King County's First 150 Years*. Seattle: HistoryLink, with University of Washington Press, 2001.

Dorpat, Paul, and Jean Sherrard. *Seattle Now and Then*. Seattle: Documentary Media, 2018.

Dunham-Jones, Ellen, and June Williamson. *Retrofitting Suburbia: Urban Design Solutions for Redesigning Suburbs*. New York: Wiley, 2011.

Forester, John. *Effective Cycling*. 7th ed. Cambridge, MA: MIT Press, 2012.

Furness, Zack. *One Less Car: Bicycling and the Politics of Automobility*. Philadelphia: Temple University Press, 2010.

Hanford, C. H. *Seattle and Environs, 1852–1924*. Chicago: Pioneer Historical Publishing, 1924.

Hoffmann, Melody L. *Bike Lanes Are White Lanes: Bicycle Advocacy and Urban Planning*. Lincoln: University of Nebraska Press, 2016.

Hutchinson, Michael. *Re: Cyclists: 200 Years on Two Wheels*. London: Bloomsbury Sport, imprint of Bloomsbury Publishing, 2017.

Jungnickel, Kat. *Bikes and Bloomers: Victorian Women Inventors and Their Extraordinary Cycle Wear*. London: Goldsmiths Press, 2018.

Klingle, Matthew. *Emerald City: An Environmental History of Seattle*. Illustrated ed. New Haven: Yale University Press, 2009.

Longhurst, James. *Bike Battles: A History of Sharing the American Road*. Seattle: University of Washington Press, 2015.

Lugo, Adonia E. *Bicycle / Race: Transportation, Culture, and Resistance*. Portland, OR: Microcosm Publishing, 2018.

Norton, Peter D. *Fighting Traffic: The Dawn of the Motor Age in the American City*. Inside Technology series. Cambridge, MA: MIT Press, 2008.

Ott, Jennifer. *Olmsted in Seattle: Creating a Park System for a Modern City*. Seattle: HistoryLink and Documentary Media, 2019.

Pomper, Steve. *It Happened in Seattle: Remarkable Events That Shaped History*. It Happened In series. Guilford, CT: Globe Pequot Press, 2010.

Seo, Sarah A. *Policing the Open Road: How Cars Transformed American Freedom*. Cambridge, MA: Harvard University Press, 2019.

Smethurst, Paul. *The Bicycle—Towards a Global History*. London: Palgrave Macmillan UK, 2015.

Stansill, Peter, ed. *BAMN: By Any Means Necessary: Outlaw Manifestos and Ephemera 1965–70*. New York: Penguin, 1971.

Thorness, Bill. *Biking Puget Sound: 60 Rides from Olympia to the San Juans*. 2nd ed. Seattle: Mountaineers Books, 2014.

Thrush, Coll. *Native Seattle: Histories from the Crossing-Over Place*. Seattle: University of Washington Press, 2008.

Walker, Peter. *How Cycling Can Save the World*. New York: TarcherPerigee, 2017.

Williams, David B. *Too High and Too Steep: Reshaping Seattle's Topography*. Seattle: University of Washington Press, 2017.

Witt, Major Margaret. *Tell: Love, Defiance, and the Military Trial at the Tipping Point for Gay Rights*. With Tim Connor and with a foreword by Colonel Margarethe Cammermeyer. Lebanon, NH: ForeEdge, an imprint of University Press of New England, 2017.

Woods, Erin, and Bill Woods. *Bicycling the Backroads around Puget Sound*. 2nd ed. Seattle: Mountaineers Books, 1981.

Index

First Avenue South Bridge, 98
First Hill neighborhood, 169
Floyd, George, xiv, 194, 198
Forester, John, 96
Forward Thrust, 69, 190
Freedman, Nicole, 172
Free Ride Zone, 120–22
freeways: Bay Freeway, 58, 59, 63–64, 68; fight against plans for (1960–72), 57–63; impacts, 53–57; Interstate 90 (I-90), 59–61, 64, 67–68, 115; Interstate 605, 60; racism of culture of (1956–72), 63–68; rapid transit and, 69–70; State Route 520, 18, 59, 61, 87; State Route 522, 59, 82; street widening for ramp access, 128–29; suburban sprawl and, 94–95; Thomson Expressway, 58, 61, 64, 67–68, 128–29; traffic studies and route plans, 57–58. See also Interstate 5
Fremont, 169
Fremont Fair, 109–10

Gallup, Ronald W., 48
Garcia-Reyes, Erlin, 148–49
gas prices, 93
Gas Works Park, 75
gear technology, 45–46, 73
Genesee Park, 121
ghost bikes, 141fig., 149
Gibbs, Dan, 64–65
Gifford and Grant, 45–46
Gilman, Daniel, 80
gold rush, 12
Good Roads Lunch Room, 10fig., 19–23
Gordon, Marina, 205n19
Gorton, Slade, 77
Gossett, Larry, 66
Gould, Vick, 69
Green Lake Park, 31
greenways, neighborhood, 140–45, 218n23
Greenwood neighborhood, 136
Gregg's Cycle, 89–90

Growth Management Act (WA), 101
guerrilla bike lanes, 4
Guide to Mountain Bike Riding in Washington (R and E Cycles), 91

Hahn, Peter, 3
Haigh, John, 73, 78
Hanson, Robert, 89
Harrell, Bruce, 185
Heerwagen, Troy, 56
Heffter, Emily, 139
Hellman, Chris, 120
Hell's Angels, 212n28
Hepp-Buchanan, Max, 143–44
Hershey, Barbara, 88–89
hike-in (2018), 82
Hill, Tim, 77
Hill Climber bicycle, 45–46
Hille, Merrill, 81, 82
Hiller, David, 134
Hillman City neighborhood, 184
Horn, Joel, 121
Hornbein, Tom, 83
Houser, Holly, 171–72
housing discrimination. See racism
Howlett, Kathy, 65
Hubbell, Dick, 64

Indigenous people, 25–27
induced demand, 129
Interlaken Boulevard, 22, 28, 31
Interlaken housing development, 28–29, 112, 199
Interlaken Park, 19, 22–23
Interstate 5 (I-5), 52fig.; Bike Day on express lanes, 76–78; impacts of, 53–57, 64, 69; Lake Union Bike Path and, 18; opposition to, 61; racism and, 67
Interstate 90 (I-90), 59–61, 64, 67–68, 115
Interstate 605, 60
Interstate Commerce Commission (ICC), 84, 100

Mount Baker neighborhood, 113
Mount Baker Ridge, 60
Mount Baker Ridge trail tunnel, 68
Move Seattle levy, 190–92, 195–96
Mudede, Charles, 170–71
multigear bikes, 45–46, 73
Murray, Ed, 164, 169, 171–73, 177, 186–90, 196

naked bike rides, 109–12
neighborhood greenways, 140–45, 218n23
neighborhood plans, 101–2
Neil, James, 108
NiceRide (Minneapolis), 168
Nichols, Brian, 110
Nickels, Greg, 130–31, 134–39, 189
Nihonmachi (Japantown), 67
North Beacon Hill neighborhood, 113
Northern Pacific, 79–80
Nunes-Ueno, Paulo, 172
Nye, Bill, 144

O'Brien, Mike, 130, 139, 173
ofo, 176–78
Oil, Davey, 149
Olmsted Brothers, 23, 30–31
Ordinance No. 5 (1865), 26

Pacific Northwest Cycling Association (PNCA), 47–49, 51, 73
Padelford, Gordon, 143
Parks Department, Seattle, 30, 74–76, 97
Peace Peloton, 198
Pedestrian and Bike Safety Assessment Tool (SDOT), 198
pedestrians: deaths, 39, 41, 183; jaywalking, 39–42; neighborhood plans and, 101; shifting attitudes toward (1910s), 41–44; as term, 42; walkable neighborhoods, 93–94; walk signals, 3, 115–16
People for Bikes, 5
People's Waterfront Coalition, 136–37
Pike, Rose, 205n19

police: bicycle safety roundups, 50; bikes in public thoroughfares and, 89; Capitol Hill Occupied Protest area and, 194*fig.*, 199; Cherry Street bike lane pylons and, 2; Critical Mass rides and, 104–8; jaywalking stings, 39–41; protesters and, xiv, 61; Solstice naked bike ride and, 110–11
population growth, Seattle, 6–7
Porter, Phyllis, 180*fig.*, 184–85
Portland, OR: neighborhood greenways, 140, 142; traffic deaths, 181; Yellow Bike program, 120. *See also* Seattle-to-Portland ride
Prince, Joseph E., 39
Prohibition, 20–21
Pronto, 162*fig.*, 164, 169–76
Provo, 165–66
Puget Sound Bike Share, 168–73

Quam, Mike, 86
Quam, Rick, 86
Queen City Good Roads Club (formerly Queen City Cycle Club), 15–30

racing: in 1880s and 1890s, 13–14, 16; Beat the Heat fund-raiser bike race, 78; Black bike community and, 116; hills and, 34
racism: Beacon Hill, 56–57; bicycle clubs and, 16; bike share and, 170–71; "Black History" as segregation, 145; Central Area and Judkins Park, 65–68; Cotterill's *The Climax of a World Quest* and white colonialism, 27–28; Donation Land Claim Act of 1850 and, 26; Duwamish tribal land and, 25–29; of freeway culture, 63–68; inequitable distribution of bike infrastructure, 115; Interlaken Land Company, 28–29; internment of Japanese Americans, 67; legacy of housing practices, 114; Ordinance No. 5 (1865), 26; redlining, 56–57, 113–15, 145, 183; restrictive cov-

enants, 29, 57, 112–13, 199; "security map" (1936), 57; systemic, 118–19; walk signal timing and, 115–16; zoning laws and, 114

rail banking, 85

railroads, 11, 27, 79–81. *See also* Burlington Northern

railway corridors and rail-trails, 84–85, 97. *See also* Burke-Gilman Trail

Rainier Avenue South, 180*fig.*, 183–85

Rainier Valley Greenways, 184

Rainwater, Merlin, 144–45

Ramps to Nowhere (documentary), 64–65

R and E Cycles, 90–91

Ranganathan, Shefali, 191

rapid transit. *See* transit

Ravenna Boulevard, 31

Reasonably Polite Seattleites, 2–6, 182

Red Line Rides, 145

redlining, 56–57, 113–15, 145, 183

Redmond, 88, 168–69

Refer, Kelli, 144

regulations: on bicycles, 50–51; on bike messengers, 38; on bike share, 175–76; on pedestrians, 42

Renton Hill Wheel Club, 14

Rice, Norm, 101

Ride for Justice, 194*fig.*, 199

"right side of the roadway" law, 51

Road Safety Action Plan, 151–52

Road Safety Summit, 150–52, 195

Roberts, E. I., 61

Rockafellar, Mamie, 81

Rodriguez, Ángel, 90–91

Rowe, Kyle, 175–76

Royer, Charles, 100

Rudd, Lewis, 116

Ryan, Claude, 36, 49

Ryan, Helene G., 47, 51

Safe Streets Social, 149–50

Salls, Deb, 122

Sand Point neighborhood, 113

Save, Don't Pave rally, 60

Scaringi, Susanne, 107–8

Scates, Shelby, 60

Schell, Paul, 130

Schmautz, Tamara, 196

Schulte family, 195

SDOT. *See* Seattle Department of Transportation

Seattle, Chief (Si'ahl in Lushootseed), 26

Seattle Bicycle Advisory Board, 90, 144–45

Seattle Bicycle Club, 13–14

Seattle Bike Blog: beginnings of, x, xi, 138; bike share and, 170, 172–73, 175, 177; "I Look Good on a Pronto" event, 170; "Neighborhood-Powered Streets," 142; Reasonably Polite Seattleites letter, 2–4; traffic deaths and, 149; "The True Cost of Move Seattle," 195

Seattle Bike Brigade, 199

Seattle Bike Expo, 91

Seattle Cycle Track, 14

Seattle Department of Transportation (SDOT): Beacon Hill neighborhood plan and, 140–41; Bicycle Master Plan update, 163–64; Bicycle Program, 97–102, 131–32; bike share and, 171–73, 175–76; Chang at, 181–83; Pedestrian and Bike Safety Assessment Tool, 198; Rainier Avenue and, 185; Second Avenue and, 186–87; Stay Healthy Streets program, 143

Seattle Engineering Department, 57, 78, 85–86

Seattle Kids Bike Swap, 121

Seattle Liberation Front, 61

Seattle Neighborhood Greenways, 115, 142–43, 189, 195

Seattle Seven, 61

Seattle-to-Portland ride (STP), 87–88, 91, 117–18

Seattle Traffic and Safety Council, 32*fig.*, 38, 40

Seattle Transportation Department (SeaTran), 101–2. *See also* Seattle Department of Transportation

About the Author

The author, his wife, and their daughter on the Westlake Bikeway. Photo by Brock Howell.

Tom Fucoloro is the founder and editor of *Seattle Bike Blog*, where he has published four thousand posts (and counting) since 2010. An independent journalist originally from St. Louis, Missouri, Tom sold his car to pay for his move to Seattle. He quickly learned to love biking while getting around this beautiful town. He believes in the power of independent journalism and that more people biking more places safely is a good thing for our society.

Seattle Neighborhood Greenways named Tom their 2014 Greenways Champion as "the individual who has most advanced the cause of safe streets in Seattle." In 2015 *Seattle Met* named Tom one of "The 15 People Who Should Really Run Seattle." Cascade Bicycle Club named Tom the 2023 recipient of the Doug Walker Award for an individual who has shown "outstanding leadership in creating a better community through bicycling."